# JUDAISM CHRISTIANITY AND ISLAM

Y0-AJP-587

# RELIGION AND MAN

Under the General Editorship of
W. RICHARD COMSTOCK

# JUDAISM CHRISTIANITY AND ISLAM

JANET K. O'DEA
University of California at Santa Barbara

THOMAS F. O'DEA
University of California at Santa Barbara

CHARLES J. ADAMS
McGill University

Harper & Row, Publishers
New York, Evanston, San Francisco, London

Cover photo: Allen Hagood, National Park Service

RELIGION AND MAN: JUDAISM, CHRISTIANITY, AND ISLAM

Copyright © 1972 by Harper & Row, Publisher, Inc.

The material in this book comprises Part Four and Part Five of *Religion and Man: An Introduction,* W. Richard Comstock, General Editor.

Printed in the United States of America. All rights reserved. No part of this book may be used or reproduced in any manner whatsoever without written permission except in the case of brief quotations embodied in critical articles and reviews. For information address Harper & Row, Publishers, Inc., 49 East 33rd Street, New York, N. Y. 10016.

Standard Book Number: 06-044893-8

Library of Congress Catalog Card Number: 79-185897

# CONTENTS

Preface vii

PART ONE
BIBLICAL RELIGIOUS TRADITIONS: JUDAISM AND CHRISTIANITY
JANET K. AND THOMAS F. O'DEA

Judaism in Historical Perspective 3
Christianity in Historical Perspective 29
Second Exile:
Israel Reconstitutes Itself 71
Faith and the Theological Tradition 78
The Jewish Religious Tradition 95
Man's Relation to God 111
Ecclesia Semper Est Reformanda 126
Bibliography 152

PART TWO
THE ISLAMIC RELIGIOUS TRADITION
CHARLES J. ADAMS

The Background and the Life of the Prophet 159
The Rightly Guided Khalifahs and the Expansion of Islam 168
The Qur'an 171
Islamic Theology 177
The Islamic Law 183
Islamic Worship and Religious Practices 192
Mysticism 199
The Shi'ah and the Sunnis 208
Islam in Modern Times 214
Bibliography 221

GLOSSARY 225

INDEX 237

# PREFACE

Religion is a persistent and pervasive feature of the continuing history of mankind. To some it is a superstitious barrier to man's progress; to others it is his most constructive activity providing an ultimate meaning to the projects of his culture. What is beyond controversy is the importance of appreciating the force of religion as a major influence in the life of man.

The present volume provides an introduction to the scholarly study of some of the religious traditions involved in human history. It can be read alone or as part of a three-volume paperback series which is also available in a one-volume hardbound edition. The authors of these volumes have sought to provide accurate descriptions of the rituals, myths, symbolic devices, belief systems, and social organizations of the world's religions. They have also provided sensitive interpretations of the ethos and the spiritual directions to which these various symbolic forms have pointed. In doing so the authors show how a religious tradition can be studied in such a way that both data and interpretation, fact and meaning, detail and the patterns unifying the detail into a dynamic whole can be recognized and appreciated.

Alfred North Whitehead once wrote: "The death of religion comes with the repression of the high hope of adventure." This volume is an impressive illustration of the fact that in the field of the study of the religious traditions of mankind this spirit of adventure is far from dead.

W. Richard Comstock

# JUDAISM CHRISTIANITY AND ISLAM

# PART ONE

# BIBLICAL RELIGIOUS TRADITIONS: JUDAISM AND CHRISTIANITY

JANET K. & THOMAS F. O'DEA

# JUDAISM IN HISTORICAL PERSPECTIVE

## GOD'S CALL AND THE COVENANT WITH ISRAEL

Biblical religion is grounded upon the experience of God's presence, a presence which transcends and which transfigures the life of the individual and the group. The encounter of man with a reality beyond himself to which he is related and with which he communicates is the essence of biblical religiosity and the constituting foundation of Jewish peoplehood and the Christian church. For the Israelites of the biblical age and their descendants, the relationship with their God, Yahweh, determined the meaning, the order, and the goal of their existence. On this foundation all later Western religion rests.

The nature and course of Israel's relationship to Yahweh is disclosed in the Bible, which is itself a record and interpretation of historical events within the framework of religious faith. The Bible tells who Yahweh is, how he chose a group of tribes to receive his revelation, and how these tribes responded to him. Yahweh was the God who revealed himself to Moses in a burning bush as the God of the Hebrew patriarchs and as the future God of the entire Hebrew people. It was he, Yahweh, who would be present to lead the tribes out of their bondage in Egypt, who would guide them through the wilderness, and who would establish a permanent covenant with them. Yahweh disclosed his name to Moses, *eh'yeh asher eh'yeh,* "I am who I am," meaning he is the being who will be eternally present to his people, there whenever his people need and call upon him. Moses was commissioned by Yahweh to lead the suffering Israelites out of slavery and to carry the divine word to this people. With Moses as his representative, Yahweh promised to lead the Hebrews forth and to be with them eternally as a guide and protector in their course through history.

The Bible tells how Israel responded to Yahweh's call to recognize his sovereign lordship, to submit to his rule, and to receive his benevolent care. Moses proclaimed the word of Yahweh to the people:

> *You have seen what I did unto the Egyptians, and how I bore you out on eagles' wings, and brought you to myself. Now therefore, if you will obey my voice, and keep my covenant, you shall be my own possession among all peoples; for all the earth is mine, and you shall be to me a kingdom of priests and a holy nation.*
>
> (Exod. 19:4–7)

Yahweh has delivered Israel out of the hands of the oppressive Egyptians and has singled out this people to draw near unto him and to enter a special covenantal relationship with him. He has created the whole world and all is properly his. Yet he has selected one particular people to fulfill his demands, to benefit from his promises, and to be his instrument in history. Israel's response to Yahweh was immediate.

> *And all the people answered together and said: All that the Lord has spoken we will do.*
>
> (Exod. 19:8)

Having experienced Yahweh's presence, having witnessed his redeeming action in the Exodus, and having heard his words, the Hebrew tribes willingly accepted his demand. Israel and Yahweh bound themselves to a covenant, which would determine a total life relationship. The disparate tribes united to become a nation dedicated to the service of the Lord. They are to be a holy people in imitation of the holiness of their God and in obedience to his commands. The decision to enter into the covenantal relationship was the great decision of Israelite history, resulting in the emergence of a special religious consciousness. For the Jew, the Exodus from Egypt became the central event in religious history. In it God's saving power had been revealed to Israel and the people had responded with the promise of constant service to him.

> *And Israel saw the great work which the Lord did against the Egyptians, and the people feared the Lord; and they believed in the Lord, and in his servant Moses. . . . The Lord is my strength and my song; and he has become my salvation; this is my God and I will praise him.*
>
> (Exod. 14:31, 15:2)

Israel had perceived Yahweh's presence in history and had come to understand that his power was behind all events. According to the biblical vision, it was Yahweh who ruled, who alone was master of history, and unto whom the people submitted in trust.

The covenant is the central conception of the Bible. The content and implications of the covenant formed the framework in which Israel understood its social constitution and historical meaning. At Sinai the clear will of Yahweh had been revealed and the clear response of the people had been enunciated. They accepted the covenant as a gift of the Lord which would establish a permanent relationship between him and them. They also accepted the divine law of the covenant, committing themselves to follow God's commandments in all areas of national and private life. The Bible presented the nation as founded in a religious event, and its rule as always to be religious law. The loose tribes were transformed into a people united by shared loyalty to Yahweh, and ordered in the political and social realms by his religious code. The God of the Bible laid claim to the actions of man. Deeds, particular acts, whether ethical or ritualistic, were the form and expression of the relationship of God and man. It was in his deeds that man demonstrated his faithfulness to Yahweh or strayed from the Lord. Israel was commanded to actualize Yahweh's will in the world, to be his witnesses, and by imitating his holiness, to bear testimony to his presence. For this reason, Law became absolutely central in the religious life of Israel. The civil and moral ordinances believed to be revealed by Yahweh to Moses were the constitution of the people who had vowed to serve the Lord in the way prescribed. Yahweh was the author of a code which governed the entire range of human life. His majesty and holiness were embodied in the Law which he had issued. Israel, in fulfilling the Torah, this law which is the way of the Lord, actualized his word in history and fulfilled its covenant obligation. For in the covenant Israel had pledged to submit itself to the omnipotent will of Yahweh and to realize his rule in the concrete activities of national life. Obedience to the law was seen, therefore, as an expression of love for its author as well as an acknowledgment of his sovereignty, while ignorance of the law or disobedience was considered a sin. The Lord had spoken to Israel face-to-face at Sinai and had contracted a sacred covenant with the nation.

> *Not with our fathers did the Lord make this covenant, but with us, who are all of us here alive this day.*
>
> (Deut. 5:3)

Therefore it is incumbent upon every Israelite to hear the commandments, to learn them, and to perform them.

> *Hear O Israel: The Lord our God is one Lord; and you shall love the Lord your God with all your heart, and with all your soul, and with all your might. And these words which I command you this day shall be upon your heart; and you shall teach them diligently to your children . . .*
>
> (Deut. 6:4–7)

It is only because he loved them that Yahweh had chosen Israel to be his special treasure and to serve his special mission in the world. Israel must return his love in every generation by acting to fulfill the sacred obligations of the covenant. This is the clear imperative which issued from the covenant relationship.

> *For this commandment which I command you this day it is not too hard for you, neither is it far off.*
>
> (Deut. 30:11)

Every man of the nation is able to understand and participate in the covenant and thereby share in realizing the divine life.

> *See, I have set before you this day life and good, death and evil. If you obey the commandments of the Lord your God which I command you this day, by loving the Lord your God, by walking in his ways, and by keeping his commandments and his statutes and his ordinances, then you shall live and multiply, and the Lord your God will bless you in the land which you are entering to take possession of it.*
>
> (Deut. 30:15–16)

Israel thus understood its relationship to Yahweh and to the world within the covenant framework. Yahweh had revealed himself in history to his people and had determined their historical destiny. The Israelites interpreted events in their national history, such as the exodus from Egypt, the revelation at Sinai, the conquest of Canaan, as religious symbols and as part of a sacred history. They, as a people, were partners with Yahweh in carrying out his plan for mankind and the concrete events of their history were to be understood within the structure of the divinely ordered drama. Yahweh had intervened in history to guide the destiny of man.

The conception of a God who acted in history and who participated in an ongoing historical relationship with a community of men broke with prevailing notions of deity, of nature, and of man in the ancient Near East. Ancient Near Eastern man viewed the world of nature as being alive with divine forces, which were of the same substance and which experienced the same needs as he himself. The gods as well as man were born out of a primeval matter, were subject to natural processes, and were ultimately subordinate to the laws of nature or fate. It is because the gods and man were of the same substance and subject to the same laws that man could manipulate the gods through magic and could actually become a god or semigod.

In contrast to the mythological deity, Yahweh was conceived by Israel as the absolutely transcendent Lord of the universe whose being was beyond nature and completely other than man. He was the all-powerful God, who had not been created out of primeval matter but who had himself created the entire universe. He was totally independent of natural processes, could not be controlled by magic, and certainly did not need the gifts of man for his existence. Because his being was totally different from the world which was his creation, Yahweh could not be fully comprehended by man and could not be embodied in any concrete form. The existence of Yahweh was not in any way parallel to nor comparable with the existence of man.

And yet this all-powerful, totally other, infinite Lord had chosen to relate himself to man. Yahweh had entered into human history, had encountered his creature, and had made his will known to him. He had even invited man to enter into a covenant which made man a partner in realizing the divine design for the universe. To Israel it appeared that history was the sphere of its relationship to Yahweh and was filled with sacred moments of divine action. The past, present, and future all received meaning in relationship to the will and word of the Lord. If Israel fulfilled its side of the covenantal relationship, the progress of history towards its ultimate goal would be advanced. If Israel failed to uphold the covenant stipulations, the divine plan would be frustrated and God's instrument subject to chastisement and punishment. Biblical history is thus the record of successive fulfillments and defections, of faithfulness and waywardness, of social peace and social disorder.

## KINGS AND PROPHETS: DISAPPOINTMENT AND HOPE

The tribes of Israel, under the leadership of Joshua, settled in the promised land of Canaan, and there renewed the covenant pact. They pledged themselves once again to form a community dedicated to Yahweh, who alone was God and who alone would guide their national destiny.

> *Then Joshua said unto the people: You are witnesses against yourselves that you have chosen the Lord, to serve Him. And they said, We are witnesses. He said, Then put away the foreign gods which are among you, and incline your heart to the Lord, the God of Israel. And the people said to Joshua, The Lord our God we will serve, and his voice we will obey.*
>
> (Josh. 24:22–24)

The Israelite tribes formed a confederacy whose unity was based upon the common covenant agreement. They came together for national worship and in times of danger, when Yahweh would raise up a leader to lead in the defense of the confederacy. These charismatic leaders, the judges of the Old Testament, were believed to be graced with the spirit of Yahweh and in a holy war carried the tribes to victory. In the consciousness of Israel it was the might of God and not the power of men which was decisive, and the charismatic judge served merely as a temporary instrument of God's will. The ideal form of Israelite communal life was most closely realized during this period of the judges. The tribes were linked by common faith and worship, and believed themselves to be protected by the spirit of Yahweh and his representatives.

However, the tensions between the ideal and the real were everpresent, and resistance to God's demands was constant. Throughout this period a rhythm of faithfulness and rejection, of fulfillment and defection, was evident. Israel forgot the commandments of Yahweh, turned to false gods and false pursuits, and was then punished by the Lord. However, because he was patient and anxious to restore his people, Yahweh delivered them from the punishment and accepted their penitent return unto him. This is the recurring pattern not only of the Book of Judges but it is indeed the recurring pattern of Israelite history. The inherent tension between divine demand

and human desires was experienced constantly as the nation developed. Would Israel submit to Yahweh's rule and adhere to the covenant or would it turn to the ways of man and the pursuits of nations? Who is ultimately the ruler of Israel and who determines the national destiny? The strain between the divine and human order became most intense when the question of monarchy arose, for with the institution of monarchy a permanent human ruler was placed over the people of God and secular interests were asserted over the moral and religious ideals of the Yahwist order.

In the story of the selection of Saul as the first Israelite king the conflict between the people's will and Yahweh's command is vividly portrayed. The people declared:

> *But we will have a king over us, that we also may be like all the nations, and that our king may govern us and go out before us and fight our battles.*
>
> (1 Sam. 8:19–20)

No longer were the Israelites willing to rely on Yahweh to raise up charismatic leaders to lead them, and no longer did Israel want to be distinguished from all other peoples. For these reasons the institution of monarchy threatened the foundations of covenant society.

> *And the Lord said to Samuel, "Harken to the voice of the people in all that they say to you; for they have not rejected you, but they have rejected me from being king over them."*
>
> (1 Sam. 8:7)

Although kingship was gradually integrated into the covenant religious order, the basic tension between divine and human rule was never overcome. The history of Israel under the kings was plagued by continual crisis both internally and externally. Political maneuvering in the international arena brought military defeat and finally downfall to Northern Israel in 722 and to Judah in 586. Conflicts arising from the economic exploitation of the common people by the ruling classes caused great social dissension in these kingdoms. The freedom and equality which the small farmers and sheep raisers had enjoyed during the period of the confederacy disappeared as peasants lost their land and had to work on state projects and became hopelessly indebted to the aristocracy. The social-ethical ideals of the covenant were abandoned as were the religious values. Israel turned to the false gods of the nations.

At the moment when Yahwistic religion and covenant existence were in the most extreme peril, the Bible describes the emergence of powerful religious leaders who opposed the secularizing idolatrous tendencies of kingship and called upon Israel to return to the covenant and to its God. These were the prophets, Yahweh's representatives, sent into the breach to war for the soul of the straying people. In the name of the religious and socioeconomic ideals of the covenant they battled against syncretism with foreign religions, economic oppression, social injustice, and international political involvement. The prophets called for an inner change, for a revival of the covenant, and a regeneration of religious life. From the ninth to the fourth centuries B.C., these unique individuals confronted the people and its leaders with the word of the Lord. Again Yahweh intervened in the history of Israel, revealing his will to his elect through the agency of his messengers, the prophets. With the spirit of Yahweh driving them on, often in the face of difficult internal conflict and external opposition, the prophets fulfilled this divine task assigned to them. They issued a sweeping critique of the social and religious aberrations of the present and interpreted Yahweh's actions for the future.

Elijah, the semilegendary prophet of the ninth century, in his figure and in his task was prototypical of the great classical prophets who followed him. This militant and eerie man of God completely dominates the First Book of Kings. Elijah waged a war to win back the allegiance of Israel to Yahweh and to demonstrate that the ethical imperatives of the covenant law were supreme over all men. Appearing suddenly from out of the desert, the prophet confronted Ahab, King of Israel, who had been led to worship the baalim, idols of Canaan, by his foreign-born wife Jezebel, and who had in turn misled the people of Israel. Elijah alone rose to challenge the baalists, in one of the most dramatic scenes in the Old Testament, and tested the religion of the idol worshipers.

> *How long will you go limping with two different opinions? If the Lord is God, follow him; but if Baal, then follow him.*
>
> (1 Kings 18:21)

It is only after the miracle Yahweh performed that the Israelites reply to the prophet's taunt.

> *And when all the people saw it, they fell on their faces; and they said, "The Lord, he is God; the Lord, he is God."*
>
> (1 Kings 18:39)

Responding to the religious fervor of the ecstatic prophet and the saving work of Yahweh, the nation finally reaffirmed that Yahweh is king over Israel and rededicated itself to the covenant.

The battle of Elijah was carried into the ethical sphere in the tale of Navoth and his vineyard. When Ahab, coveting the vineyard of Navoth, had requested to buy it, the Israelite farmer refused to sell the sacred ancient possession of his family. Jezebel, again the agent of corruption, had Navoth killed and turned the vineyard over to her husband. For this sin of arbitrary power, Elijah announced that destruction would befall the entire household of Ahab. The king could not raise himself above the commoner, for covenant law and justice were equal to all Israelites. The demands of Yahweh were defended by Elijah in both the religious and the ethical spheres. He stood as the prototype of the messenger, coming to recall an erring people and king to the traditional covenant order. Moses had revealed the order of Israel's society and Elijah defended it. The prophetic voice announced boldly that Yahweh would countenance neither apostasy nor immorality. He would punish the ordinary man and the king alike. The nation which long ago encountered Yahweh and accepted his covenant, stood responsible before him. In recalling the Law, issuing a warning, proclaiming judgment, and then offering a promise of salvation, Elijah the prophet outlined the tasks which those who followed him believed themselves commissioned to perform over and over again. For Israel persisted in its defection, the decline in religious life was unabated, despite the mighty effort of the prophets to return Israel to itself and thus save the nation from disaster.

The moral corruption of Israel deepened as the drive for economic, political, and social power increased. It was the prophet Amos who condemned this moral degeneration most thoroughly, finding Israel guilty in all manner of unethical behavior. The rich trampled the poor, crushed the needy, perverted justice, and were immersed in debauchery, sexual license, and drunkenness. Amos cried out against the oppression found everywhere in the land. He considered false religion to be chief among the sins of Israel, for the performance of cultic duties by immoral men was a base act reviled by Yahweh. Ethical behavior must precede ritual and the cult was secondary to the moral code. Those who trusted in the cult to satisfy Yahweh deceived themselves. Sacrifices and rituals were not the way to Yahweh,

> *For I know how many are your transgressions, and how great are your sins—you who afflict the righteous, who take a bribe, and turn aside the needy in the gate.*
>
> (Amos 5:12)

The demand of Yahweh was for adherence to ethical norms, and only then was the cult pleasing to him.

> *I hate, I despise your feasts, and I take no delight in your solemn assemblies. Even though you offer me your burnt offerings and cereal offerings, I will not accept them, and the peace offerings of your fatted beasts I will not look upon. Take away from me the noise of your songs; to the melody of your harps I will not listen. But let justice roll down like waters, and righteousness like an ever-flowing stream.*
>
> (Amos 5:21–24)

Through the prophet, Yahweh demanded righteousness and justice. It was only because the nation refused to meet this demand for ethical righteousness, because it continued to disappoint Yahweh and reject him, that he condemned them to grave punishment. Many times the warning had been given and ignored. Therefore the prophet announced, "prepare to meet your God, O Israel" (Amos 4:12). The compassion and mercy of Yahweh were not unending, and punishment was due the nation obdurate in its faithlessness and sin.

Amos proclaimed that according to the religion of Yahweh ethics was more significant than cult and that moral behavior would determine the national fate of Israel. This same proclamation was issued by later prophets.

> *How the faithful city become a harlot, she that was full of justice! Righteousness lodged in her, but now murderers. Your silver is*

> *become dross, your wine mixed with water. Your princes are rebels and companions of thieves. Every one loves a bribe and runs after gifts. They do not defend the fatherless, and the widow's cause does not come to them.*
>
> (Isa. 1:21–23)

And when the holy city resembled Sodom and Gomorrah in its iniquity, the performance of the cult would only be an abomination to the Lord.

> *What to me is the multitude of your sacrifices? says the Lord. . . . Bring no more vain offerings; incense is an abomination to me. New moon and Sabbath and the calling of assemblies—I cannot endure iniquity and solemn assembly. . . . When you spread forth your hands, I will hide my eyes from you; even though you make many prayers, I will not listen; your hands are full of blood. Wash yourselves, make yourselves clean; remove the evil of your doings from before my eyes; cease to do evil, learn to do good; seek justice, correct oppression; defend the fatherless, plead for the widow.*
>
> (Isa. 1:11–17)

To Isaiah, the worst of Israel's sins was pride, the self-assertion and self-confidence of man which inevitably led to rebellion against God. This basic pride caused Israel's leaders to pursue expansionist military policies. The monarchy was filled with arrogance and illegitimate ambition. Rather than seeking to establish a just state and trusting in God's power for protection and guidance, the ruling class trusted in its own might and political prowess. According to the prophet, reliance upon the work of man's hands and the accomplishments of man's power was leading Israel into disaster. He proclaimed that history was controlled by Yahweh and that human force did not determine its order. Trust in self was idolatry, a sin which Israel committed constantly. And punishment for this sin would come,

> *for the Lord of hosts has a day against all that is proud and lofty . . . the haughtiness of men shall be humbled; the Lord alone will be exalted in that day.*
>
> (Isa. 2:12–17)

The idolatry of self-assertion was only one aspect of the general sin manifested in Israel: forgetting of Yahweh and his covenant. Men worshiped idols because they had forgotten the true Lord. They were unjust, impious, and unrighteous because they had lost sight of the covenant ideals. According to the prophets, knowledge of God and knowledge of the covenant were absolutely essential if Israel were to realize its true national destiny, and yet it was just this knowledge which had been lost.

> *Hear, O heavens, and give ear, O earth; for the Lord has spoken: "Sons have I reared and brought up, but they have rebelled against me. The ox knows its owner, and the ass its master's crib; but Israel does not know, my people does not understand."*
>
> (Isa. 1:2–5)

The great Northern prophet Hosea bemoaned the consequences which followed from Israel's sin of forgetting Yahweh.

> *Hear the word of the Lord, O people of Israel; for the Lord has a controversy with the inhabitants of the land. There is no faithfulness or kindness, and no knowledge of God in the land; there is swearing, lying, killing, stealing, and committing adultery; they break all bounds and murder follows murder.*
>
> (Hos. 4:1–2)

Life without God had led to life without righteousness, life without truth, and life without mercy. These basic moral attributes are what Yahweh has demanded of Israel. Lack of them must result in punishment and national calamity, as every prophet warned. Yahweh had revealed himself to Israel, had let himself be known intimately to the people, and had actually betrothed himself to them. Yet his intimacy had been rejected and the betrothal bonds broken. Israel had gone awhoring after false gods, after idols, military might, economic gain. Man had erected false ultimates, rather than remaining faithful to the only true ultimate, Yahweh. This was the great wickedness of Israel, that they put man in place of God. They relied upon the kings, who knew not the Lord, upon fortifications, and upon warriors. They believed that alliances with idolatrous Egypt and Assyria would bring great success. And, further, in forgetting God they had lost their own selves, sinking into drunkenness and license. To Hosea, loss of self implied loss of the relationship with Yahweh and it was this sin of which Israel was guilty.

> *Return, O Israel, to the Lord your God, for you have stumbled because of your iniquity. Take with you words and return to the* Lord.
>
> (Hos. 14:1–3)

Hosea knew how deep was the corruption of Israel. He also knew how deep was the longing of Yahweh that his people would repent of this corruption and return to him. The special relationship of Yahweh and Israel had to be reestablished, and the love between them renewed. Israel did not repent, did not hearken to the warning, and did not seek to avoid the punishment.

> *My people are destroyed for lack of knowledge; because you have rejected knowledge, I reject you from being a priest to me.*
>
> (Hos. 4:6)

The Northern Kingdom of Hebrew tribes was finally defeated and crushed in 722 B.C. by Assyria. Towns were destroyed, the land ruined, and large sections of the population exiled. Throughout that century and the next, Judah too was threatened with subjugation. Her kings, in continuing to maneuver and maintain independence from the international powers of Assyria and Babylonia, brought her closer to disaster at the hands of these powers. In the eyes of the prophets the wrath of Yahweh had indeed been visited upon his people. Only return to him in genuine repentance could avoid for Judah what had already overcome her sister, Israel. Trust in military power would not insure national security. The safety and prosperity of Israel depended upon the protection of Yahweh alone, and this was granted only when the moral conditions of the covenant had been fulfilled. Isaiah and Jeremiah, prophets speaking at the height of the national danger, called Judah to repent, to cleanse herself, and thus to avoid catastrophe. It was not Yahweh who failed to protect his people, but his people who failed to respond to his call, to actualize his rule in their lives, and who thus brought doom upon themselves. As defection continued and the moral crisis deepened, the prophets looked away from the present toward the future. Israel persisted in disappointing Yahweh, yet this did not mean that Yahweh's plan for history was permanently overthrown nor that his promises were void. There was complete disorder in Israelite society, darkness covered all, but the prophets perceived meaning in this condition and projected new hopes for a renewed covenant people.

From 617 to 586 Jeremiah stood as a solitary defender of the covenant tradition and relationship which the people had abandoned. He represented the order of Yahweh against its enemies from within, announcing the will of God, warning the king and the people of the doom to come, and then finally promising hope for the righteous few who would survive the holocaust. Jeremiah, believed to be chosen from the womb to perform this critical task, was the personal servant of Yahweh, suffering deeply in empathy with the suffering of both the nation which he loved and the chastising father with whom he identified. Of all the prophets, the fate of Jeremiah was the most tragic. He prayed for the people, interceded on their behalf, and tried to turn them from the road of destruction. However, his warnings were ignored by the nation and his prayers rejected by God. The terrible strain of the prophetic task is reflected in the moving autobiographical outcries of Jeremiah, in which the prophet sought rest, consolation, and hope.

> *Woe is me, my mother, that you bore me, a man of strife and contention to the whole land!*
>
> (Jer. 15:10)

> *For I am called by thy name, O Lord, God of hosts. I did not sit in the company of merrymakers, nor did I rejoice; I sat alone because thy hand was upon me, for thou hadst filled me with indignation. Why is my pain unceasing, my wound incurable . . . ?*
>
> (Jer. 15:16–18)

To such depths of despair did the prophet sink that in the midst of great spiritual agony he cursed the day of his birth. The darkness which overwhelmed Jeremiah was the darkness overwhelming the nation, and in his own suffering he foreshadowed the suffering of the people. In his own personal experience Jeremiah depicted the terrible problems of prophetic existence, of the one who alone faced both man and God with knowledge that though his message would not be heard, he must persist in his efforts in obedience to the word of the Lord.

Jeremiah predicted that defeat would come upon the erring nation, but not complete doom. There would be suffering but there would also be salvation. This hope for salvation was tied to the entire prophetic theodicy, which attempted to make sense of the religious crisis and give meaning to the severe difficulties which the covenant people was to undergo. Jeremiah knew that punishment was inevitable, for there was no other way to atone for the massive sins of the generations.

> *Because your guilt is great, because your sins are flagrant, I have done these things to you.*
>
> (Jer. 30:15)

## THE EXILE: ISRAEL'S ABIDING FAITH

And that punishment, the doom which Jeremiah and the prophets before him had foreseen, came upon Judah in 587–586 B.C. Continuing to trust in her military capabilities, Judah participated in a rebellion of minor powers against Babylonia, which was crushed in 598. Jehoiachin, the newly crowned king, along with government officials, a number of important citizens, and priests, was exiled to Babylonia. Zedekiah became king of Judah. Having learned little from the recent defeat, rather than remaining an obedient vassal he began plotting another rebellion. Warnings from Jeremiah could not deter the fierce patriotic drive for political independence. In 589 the rebellion broke out. Babylonian forces arrived and laid siege to Jerusalem in 588. They took the major fortified cities throughout Judah and in July, 587 broke through the walls of Jerusalem. Zedekiah was captured, tortured, and died in exile, the last king of Judah. Another major portion of the Judean population was sent to Babylonia, and Jerusalem, the eternal holy city, was razed to the ground by fire in August, 587. Thus the Judean kingdom fell in ruin, and the defeated nation was cast into despair.

The survival of Jewry and Judaism can only be explained in terms of the religious faith which the prophets had instilled in the people and which they continued to teach them in the moment of crisis. Jeremiah had spoken. He had foretold destruction and exile, but he had also promised forgiveness and reconciliation that would come after the terrible judgment.

> *Behold the days are coming, says the Lord, when I will make a new covenant with the house of Israel and the house of Judah, . . . for I will forgive their iniquity, and I will remember their sin no more.*
>
> (Jer. 31:31–34)

This is the vision of the new covenant which would herald salvation for Israel, which became the comfort and hope of the disillusioned people. Man who had not been able to fulfill the old covenant would be changed in his nature. God would plant in him a new heart, a heart of obedience. Man would come to affirm God spontaneously, there being now but one heart and one way for both God and man. Man had been unable to change himself, so that God had had to transform him inwardly.

The promise of a new age was reaffirmed by the exilic prophet Ezekiel, who sought to comfort and give understanding to the community of Jews exiled in Babylonia. With tremendous zeal, imagination, and power he called out to the captives to repent. He was a watchman over Israel, rebuking and comforting, teaching and curing. First, he taught that God's actions were just, for the sins of Israel had merited the wrath he visited upon them. Every man suffered for his own deeds and Jerusalem had been destroyed because of the sins committed by its citizens. But to the plaintful cry, "Our bones are dried up, and our hope is lost we are clean cut off" (Ezek. 37:11), the prophet answered that while God is just he is also merciful. The real yearning and searching of the people would be heard by the Lord, who would raise up his elect, redeeming Israel and his own name from disgrace and suffering.

> *I will make with them a covenant of peace and banish wild beasts from the land, so that they may dwell securely in the wilderness and sleep in the woods. . . . And they shall know that I, the Lord their God, am with them, and that they, the house of Israel, are my people, says the Lord God.*
>
> (Ezek. 34:25–30)

The dead bones of the exiled people would be revived and live in a new manner of existence. Like Jeremiah, Ezekiel promised that the people would return to Jerusalem and there fulfill the covenant perfectly. Ezekiel offered sustenance to a disillusioned people with his explanation of history and his trust in a forgiving God.

> *Let us test and examine our ways, and return to the Lord!*
>
> (Lam. 3:40)

In this verse the court poet expressed the understanding of destruction which the people adopted. God was just and therefore the sins of Israel had caused the national catastrophe. In severe pain and suffering the people acknowledged their guilt.

> *The Lord is in the right, for I have rebelled against his word; but hear, all you peoples, and behold my suffering.*
>
> (Lam. 1:18)

And the people would now turn to Yahweh for forgiveness.

> *The steadfast love of the Lord never ceases, his mercies never come to an end.*
>
> (Lam. 3:22)

This basic understanding of sin causing punishment, the need for repentance, and the mercy of God which would bring salvation assuaged the soul of a broken people. This theodicy, that is, the justification of God's ways, enabled the exiles to recover the inner strength required for the reconstruction of a community dedicated to Yahweh's service on foreign soil.

The most elevated expression of Israel's renewed faithfulness to Yahweh, in the face of political and social conditions which might lead to total apostasy, is to be found in the writings of the anonymous exilic prophet whose message is contained in the latter part of the Book of Isaiah. Defeat of the government, ruin of the land, destruction of the Temple, and exile to Babylonia—these were sufficient to cause a people to question the power and justice of its God. In the midst of the attractions of pagan culture, as a defeated community, the exiles could have easily accepted the gods of the conquerors and the verdict of might. Yet the Jewish captives would not abandon Yahweh and denied that he had failed. The Bible tells how they yearned to return to their ancient God and to reestablish their ancient relationship with him. To this people the second Isaiah came with a message of consolation from the Lord. His words are found in the latter part of the Book of Isaiah and are close in style and in spirit to the original Isaiah, whose prophecies fill the first thirty-nine chapters of that book.

> *Comfort, comfort my people, says your God.*
>
> (Isa. 40:1 ff.)

In magnificent passages, rich in splendid visions and language, he captured the hearts of the people and brought hope to the sufferers. Deutero-Isaiah spoke of the great power of the Lord of the universe, who had created the cosmos and who was above all creatures. It was this cosmic creator God who had promised salvation to Israel and surely his word endureth forever. Soon

> *the glory of the Lord shall be revealed, and all flesh shall see it together.*
>
> (Isa. 40:5)

He who created Israel would soon redeem Israel.

The closeness of Yahweh to Israel was revealed in the joyous warm promises he made to the people.

> *I bring near my deliverance, it is not far off, and my salvation will not tarry; I will put salvation in Zion, for Israel my glory.*
>
> (Isa. 46:13)

It is true that Israel has suffered, but it is a temporary condition.

> *For a brief moment I forsook you, but with great compassion I will gather you. In overflowing wrath for a moment I hid my face from you, but with everlasting love I will have compassion on you, says the Lord your Redeemer.*
>
> (Isa. 54:7–10)

Yahweh had a plan for universal redemption, and it involved the special participation of his chosen people. Israel must spread the message of redemption and must demonstrate God's saving power to the nations. The task would be difficult, entailing suffering and humiliation.

> *Behold my servant, whom I uphold, my chosen, in whom my soul delights; I have put my spirit upon him, he will bring forth justice*

*to the nations . . . I am the Lord, I have called you in righteousness, I have taken you by the hand and kept you; I have given you as a covenant to the people, a light to the nations.*

(Isa. 42:1–6)

Yahweh addressed his servant, an idealized figure, commissioned to perform the weighty labor. At present the servant is himself despised and considered abominable. No one would take notice of him and no one would hearken to his message. But in the future all would listen to him, kings and princes would recognize the truth. The servant must suffer, but his suffering has redemptive value. For the suffering of the servant would atone for the sins of mankind and would bring liberation to others.

*But he was wounded for our transgressions, he was bruised for our iniquities; upon him the chastisement that made us whole, and with his stripes we were healed.*

(Isa. 53:5–6)

Deutero-Isaiah's image of the servant became the model for Israel, which interpreted its suffering of the present as having redemptive value. The pain of exile was necessary not only for self-purification and atonement, but the pain was also necessary for the sake of the salvation of mankind. Israel must become the servant, bearing witness to Yahweh. The servant, like the prophet, performed a mission which demanded suffering for the sake of all men. Through his example of righteousness, others would become righteous and would be led back to their creator. First, Israel itself would return and be redeemed. Then all flesh would know God, acknowledge his saving work, and seek to become part of his covenant.

This elevated universal message of salvation is reminiscent of the earlier universal messages of the first Isaiah. This man had prophesied that when the idols had fallen, when human pride and self-confidence had been unmasked as false trust, all men would turn to Yahweh and follow his ways.

*It shall come to pass in the latter days that the mountain of the house of the Lord shall be established as the highest of the mountains, and shall be raised above the hills; and all the nations shall flow to it, and many peoples shall come and say: "Come let us go up to the mountain of the Lord, to the house of the God of Jacob; that he may teach us his ways and that we may walk in his paths."*

(Isa. 2:2–3)

This was the great messianic hope of Israel. At the end of time, when all nations acknowledged Yahweh as sovereign king and true God, then universal peace would reign. At that time the cosmos itself would be transformed. Righteousness and peace would prevail among all creatures. The prophet conceived Yahweh's plan to be the progressive revelation of himself to the nations through the special mission of Israel toward the end goal of universal knowledge and universal peace.

> *Give thanks to the Lord, call upon his name, make known his deeds among the nations, proclaim that his name is exalted. Sing praises to the Lord, for he has done gloriously; let this be known in all the earth. Shout and sing for joy, O inhabitant of Zion, for great in your midst is the Holy One of Israel.*
>
> (Isa. 12:4–6)

Israel, defeated and exiled, believed in its sacred historic task and understood the meaning of its punishment. As a nation, Israel possessed and bore the saving religious truth which would eventually be the possession of mankind. Until that great day, Israel was obligated to fulfill the commandment of Yahweh in its communal life, whether in the Holy Land or in exile. The paradoxical fact that in reality this weak and defeated nation could not well represent the power of Yahweh to the world did not seem to disturb the Jews' self-conception, for they denied that political destiny and external reality testified to truth. The Jewish community determined to live by the reality of internal spiritual truth, in which Yahweh's relationship to his people and his plan for history had been revealed. They understood their role in history according to this internal reality and dedicated themselves to fulfilling their task in the face of whatever exigencies external reality might present.

The destroyed national institutions of Jewish life were replaced in Babylonia by two key religious institutions, around which community life was ordered. These were the synagogue and the Torah. With the Temple in ruins, a substitute for the official cult had to be found. To the challenge of how the Lord could be worshiped on profane foreign soil, the response was given that he could indeed be worshiped with a new cult, a cult not located in the Temple and not dependent upon sacrifices. Prayer in sanctuaries consecrated by the people, fasts, and the Sabbath celebration formed the core of the new worship. Israel might be estranged but it was not totally cut off from Yahweh, and the institution of prayer, the expression of the heart of the community and the individual, preserved the living relationship of the faithful to the Lord.

*A fourteenth-century manuscript depicting Haggadah, service for the Eve of Passover, illustrating the bondage of the Children of Israel in Egypt. (Courtesy of the British Museum.)*

There were individuals who did assimilate to the culture of Babylonia. However, the Jews, as a community, resolved not to accept the gods of Babylonia and not to assimilate to its culture. Rather, they determined to exist as a distinct community, loyal to its national past, guarding its religious tradition, and anticipating a national-religious restoration. The religious and national unity of Israel had been gravely challenged by the destruction and exile, and the challenge was met by the resolution to remain loyal to Yahweh and the religious values of the covenant tradition. The cornerstone of the exilic community was the Word of God, recollected in the sacred literary traditions of the past. Yahweh had disclosed himself to Israel, had spoken through his messengers and through his own acts, and this self-disclosure would now serve as the source of his continuous presence to his people. The traditions telling of Yahweh's acts and his relationship to Israel were gradually gathered together in Babylonia by the priests. These men, on the basis of these traditions, compiled a history of the world from Creation, preserved in ordered form the words of the prophets, and formulated a priestly code of ritual laws grounded upon earlier cultic prescriptions. These literary traditions became the foundation of exilic life, being the record of Yahweh's words and acts and thus the source of his holiness. They served as a guide to the community in its daily life. Study of the traditions revealed what was demanded in the present. Acquiring knowledge of the past and fulfilling God's commandments became the most sacred activities in the religious life of the Jew. Having accepted the prophetic theodicy and having rededicated itself to Yahweh's service, Israel found in its history and law the means whereby it might remain a holy people, although uprooted from its natural environment.

The duty to remain a holy people dedicated to Yahweh was interpreted by Israel as a duty to remain separate and distinctive. The kingdom of priests and holy nation, in imitation of the holiness of the Lord, would have to be vigilant in avoiding profane contacts with the profane idolatrous environment. A later rabbinical statement found in a commentary to the Book of Leviticus says, "If ye are separated from the nations, ye belong to me; if not, ye belong to Nebuchadnezzar, the king of Babylonia and his companions" (Sifra, Lev. 20:26, 93d). The measure of exclusiveness, which was necessary in order to constitute and maintain the holy community under the conditions imposed by exile, could be attained through legal prohibitions. The prohibitions against mixed marriage and the elaborate dietary laws prevented intimate contact with non-Jews. In addition, the calendar of special religious observances separated Jews from non-Jews and symbolized the determined separate existence of Israel.

The inner will of the exiles succeeded in enabling them to establish an integrated community life within the framework of the religious self-understanding and rule set out in the compilation of ancient traditions and interpreted by the priests. While remaining loyal to this framework and united within this community, the exiles acculturated to a certain extent to the Babylonian environment, achieved success in material pursuits, and reached high positions in the political and economic system. However, this success did not extinguish the sense of exile nor snuff out the hope for eventual restoration to the homeland. The prophet of exile had predicted a speedy redemption, in which all Jews would return to Israel and all nations would come to recognize Yahweh. The rise of Cyrus and his victory over Babylonia seemed to many Jews to signal the world-historical change, which Isaiah had prophesied and which Yahweh had promised. Indeed, in the first year of his conquest of Babylonia, Cyrus issued a decree permitting Jews to return to their land and to reestablish the cult there. This was part of the general policy of moderation through which Persian rulers encouraged local cultural and political autonomy. Thus in 538, permission had been granted and a restoration to the homeland could take place.

RESTORATION

Historical knowledge of the period of the restoration is quite scanty. However, it is certain that the initial response of the Babylonian exiles to the opportunity to return was weak. Under Sheshbazzar and Zerubbabel some did make the trip and did resettle in the homeland. However, most Jews, comfortably established in Babylonia, preferred to support the few returnees morally and financially, but themselves remain in exile. The newly established Palestinian community struggled for its very survival economically, politically, and religiously. The ideal of a glorious material and spiritual renewal was far from realized, and the great disappointment of religious leaders reflected the real situation. True, the Temple was rebuilt in 515 B.C., but only after a twenty-year struggle to obtain funds and labor. It was only with the administrative and religious reform work of Nehemiah and Ezra that order was restored. Nehemiah, appointed by the Persian court, arrived in Palestine between 444 and 440 and proceeded to set up a strong and honest government. He fortified the walls around Jerusalem, thereby providing residents with security from external threat, and he attempted to introduce religious reforms in neglected cultic and ethical law. A thoroughgoing reform in these areas was not instituted until the arrival from Babylonia of another imperial appointee, Ezra the Scribe. Of a priestly family, Ezra brought with him to Palestine the code of the law of Moses, consisting either of the entire Pentateuch or large parts of it compiled by the priests in Babylonia, and this code he proclaimed as the law of the land in the name of the King of Persia. The Law of Moses would be enforced as if it were the law of the Persian monarch, and all those claiming membership in the Jewish people and loyal to Jerusalem would be obligated to observe it. Ezra introduced the Law dramatically by gathering the residents of Jerusalem around him and, while standing upon a platform elevated above the crowd, read aloud from the book of the Hebrew Law. The assembled Jews were apparently quite struck by the reading, and recognizing their sins of violations, repented, knelt down, and worshiped the Lord. The reading was explained to the listeners in Aramaic, the language of daily speech, by the Levites so that all could understand. Study of this law continued in the following days while the Feast of Tabernacles was celebrated. At a later time the people confessed their sins to Yahweh and made a solemn pledge "to observe and act in accordance with all the commands of Yahweh, Our Lord, with his judgments and statutes" (Neh. 9:1–37; 10:29).

During this period the Five Books of the Law were finally canonized. This "Torah" was disseminated among the people; it was taught by the priests throughout the land and became the possession of every Jew. The ideal of piety as devotion to the Torah was accepted and the righteous Jew was one whose "delight is in the Law of the Lord; and on his law he meditates day and night" (Ps. 1:2). Thus, through the combined efforts of Ezra and Nehemiah the small and poor Palestinian community was reconstituted around the Law and recommitted to the fulfillment of Yahwist demands. Zion was once again the dwelling place of God and Jerusalem the cultic center of Judaism. The community based upon the Law was not

*An elaborate eighteenth-century Persian silver case used to preserve the Torah in the synagogue. (Courtesy of the Jewish Museum, New York.)*

simply a national or ethnic unit, but essentially a religious one. The Jew, no matter where he lived, was to be defined as one loyal to the Law of Yahweh, one devoted to the ancient beliefs and traditions recorded in the Torah.

The following four centuries, from the conquest of Alexander through the first century A.D., were tumultuous and crucial years in the history of the Jews and the evolution of Judaism. It was the time of national hopes and national frustration for the community in the homeland. It was the time of great growth of communities outside Palestine. And it was during this time that the institutions and ideas which would be the foundation of Jewish life until modern times emerged in clear form. By the end of the first century A.D., Judaism had proven that it would survive the spiritual and physical conflicts of the age, and by the third century A.D. the framework had developed, giving meaning and order to the lives of the Jews for the following fifteen hundred years.

The Persian Empire fell to the advance of Alexander's armies in 333. Following the division of Alexander's conquests, Palestine was first ruled over by the Ptolemies, and then by the Seleucids, who defeated the Ptolemies at Banyas in 198. The Seleucid king, Antiochus III, guaranteed autonomy to the Jews and supported the leadership and cult of Jerusalem, in the hands of the High Priest and wealthy aristocracy. The incorporation of Palestine within these successive empires brought Greeks with their economic and political institutions and culture into the land, thus introducing a strain between traditional Judaism and the advanced foreign ideas and values. This strain became increasingly severe. The same tension existed in all diaspora communities where Jews lived within their own religious framework and maintained allegiance to their national homeland but were attracted to and absorbed in part by the hellenistic culture of the environment. This clash between a self-enclosed and self-perpetuating Judaism and the influence of foreign culture, seen in the hellenistic situation, was in fact repeated throughout Jewish history. Later, under Islam, Jews were open to the penetration of Greek culture in Arabic forms and responded by creating a rich Judeo-Arabic culture. The interest in poetry and philosophy, both secular and religious, aroused by the mixing of cultures produced beautiful and highly significant works within the Jewish world. On the other hand, Jewry in Poland and Russia from the sixteenth to the eighteenth centuries responded negatively to foreign influences and gradually shut itself off from creative interaction with them. The tension between the native and the foreign was constant and was experienced as particularly difficult by the exilic communities within the Christian world, which struggled for their very existence.

During the hellenistic period acculturation to Greek ways was quite widespread. Jews became "hellenes" through *paidea* (education), but did so without abandoning their own religious and national culture. The translation of the Torah into Greek, somewhere around 250 B.C., and the translation of other Jewish works attest to this acculturation. The Jews of Alexandria, where the Scriptures were translated, who numbered up to two-fifths of the city's population by the first century B.C., were especially influenced by hellenistic ways and responded to them by adopting much of Greek culture into their own patterns. Philo, the great Jewish thinker of Alexandria, produced a Jewish theology in response to the thought of Plato and earlier Greek philosophers.

While they absorbed much of the new and the foreign, Jews propagated their own religious culture with apparent success. Adherence to Judaism by non-Jews was certainly not a new phenomenon. Deutero-Isaiah described "those who joined themselves to Yahweh"

*"And thou shalt smite on the rocke, and water shall come out of it, that the people may drink," a color lithograph by Marc Chagall from* The Story of the Exodus, *published by Leon Amiel, Paris, 1966. (Courtesy of the Museum of Modern Art, New York. Gift of Lester Avnet.)*

(Isa. 56:3–7), and there were occasional converts from the Babylonian period on. However, large-scale religious conversion dates from the hellenistic period, especially during the second and first centuries B.C. Many residents of the Roman Empire were searching for significant religious experience and meaning because philosophical sophistication and urbanization had undermined traditional paganism but had not provided any replacement for the religious relationship. The faith of Yahweh and the community of the faithful Jews were quite attractive, and many accepted Judaism fully or in part. Jewish missionaries carried the message of Yahweh throughout the hellenized world, emphasizing its universal and ethical aspects. It has been estimated that by the first century A.D. the Jewish population of the empire reached eight million and that one out of ten members of the empire was Jewish, and in the Eastern Mediterranean area one out of five was a Jew. Yet as Jews converted gentiles, they were themselves hellenized to one extent or another.

The hellenization of the Jews was not limited to the diaspora. The penetration of the universal hellenistic civilization, the civilization of the conquerors, into Palestine was quite extensive. A coterie of hellenized Jerusalemites, centered around the Greek gymnasium built within the holy city, attempted to spread their newly adopted cultural patterns to the majority of the Jewish population. The hellenizers, drawn mainly from the upper class, abrogated Jewish law in order to come closer to the life-style and ways of the non-Jewish powers. Under the leadership of Jason and then Menelaus, appointed High Priests by Antiochus IV Epiphanes, a policy of national hellenization was instituted. A fortified Greek polis called the *acra* was erected opposite the Temple mount, constituting a pagan city within the holy city. Engaging in Greek sports, imitating Greek styles in dress and appearance, and worshiping Greek gods were open activities within the precincts of the polis. Further, Yahweh was transformed by the hellenizers into a Greek high god, being identified with Zeus Olympus and becoming part of the hellenic pantheon. The cult of the emperor was also accepted.

To the traditional Jews of Jerusalem and the countryside, the ways of the hellenizers were a scandal and an abomination. The loyal and pious, the *hasidim,* were uncompromising in their refusal to adopt the innovations. Such intransigence frustrated the efforts of the aristocracy and angered Antiochus IV, who was intent upon establishing cultural and political unity within the lands under his control. Opposition to hellenization on the part of the faithful resulted in the proclamation of the oppressive decrees of 168 B.C. by the king. These decrees, which were fully supported by the Jewish hellenizers, prohibited regular sacrifices in the Temple; forbade the observance of the Sabbath and Jewish festivals; did away with circumcision; ordered the introduction of the cult of Zeus Olympus into the Temple, the construction of pagan altars in the land, and the sacrifice of swine upon them (forbidden in Jewish law); and finally commanded the destruction of Torah scrolls. The intent was to extirpate Judaism completely, and the response of the loyal Jews could only be one of total resistance. As the measures were enforced, many who refused to comply with them were slaughtered. Finally, full rebellion broke out, led by the priest Mattathias and his five sons. When Mattathias died in 166, his son Judah, called the Maccabee (which probably means hammer), took command. Jews, mainly from the peasantry, who would not be coerced into pagan ways, joined the rebel band and engaged in guerilla warfare. They were highly successful in raiding and harassing the more organized and technically advanced but less mobile Seleucid army. In a major engagement in 165, Judah defeated a large Syrian force under Lysias, and Antiochus, fighting a war against the Parthians in the east, was obliged to sue for peace. The hellenizing decrees of 168 were rescinded, the religious persecution ended, and the attempt to suppress Judaism defeated. Judah marched triumphantly into Jerusalem, removed the statue of Zeus—"the abomination of desolation" (Dan. 9:27, 11:31)—from the Temple, and reestablished the Law of Moses in the holy city. In 164, after thorough purification, the Temple was reconsecrated in a feast of dedication, Hanukah, which was then proclaimed as a national-religious festival for all Jews.

The victory of the Maccabees and the independent government which their descendants, the Hasmoneans, maintained for about one hundred years represents a brief chapter in the total history of Judaism. But it represents the victory of both national and traditional religious forces, the resistance of the old Yahwist order to forced hellenization. The yoke of the heathen was indeed removed from Israel. Although the conflict with hellenism, with foreign physical and spiritual forces, went on, the victory of the Maccabees lies in their reversal of the policy of total submission and total assimilation pursued by the hellenizing elite. During the following centuries Jews did accommodate to and adopt foreign values and ideas, but they were able to do so without abandoning their national and religious traditions. Judaism could develop creatively, remaining true to its essential self and yet open to the influences of outside culture.

## THE EMERGENCE OF THE APOCALYPTIC SPIRIT

The political independence established under the Hasmoneans was short-lived. In 63 B.C. the armies of Pompey conquered Palestine and the Jews became subjects of the Roman Empire, the greatest and most powerful empire of the ancient world. This loss of political autonomy had serious consequences for Jewish consciousness. First, the Hasmoneans had disappointed the hopes of the people by failing to inaugurate anything resembling the just and prosperous state projected in the religious ideals of the nation. And now once again a foreign power had subjugated Israel, bringing pagan ways and pagan authority into the Holy Land. Israel had been a worldly people whose deep religious hopes rested in the establishment of a kingdom of God on this earth. However, successive disappointments led to the development of more radical eschatological ideas. In this period of conflict and turmoil the notion that only a supernatural catastrophe could change the world and that only a totally new world order could save corrupt mankind became part of the Jewish consciousness. The world was too evil and men too sinful for the traditional religious conceptions of repentance, atonement, and renewal to be any longer sufficient. Nothing less than a total transformation, begun on the initiative of God and carried out by his transcendent agent, would effect an end to the sufferings of this-worldly existence.

Between the third century B.C. and the first century A.D. a rich literature describing the future catastrophic events which would bring about the longed-for total transformation developed in Palestine and in the diaspora. This literature is called "apocalyptic"—meaning the revelation of secret things, referring to the secret events of the end of days—and is characterized by rich fantastic visions and descriptions. The apocalyptic writer allowed his imagination to sketch freely a historical sequence in which the powers of evil are to be crushed by the powers of good; death, sickness, and suffering are to end; and the just, so long persecuted, are to be redeemed. This next world-age will be a transcendental one, totally different from the hopelessly corrupt world of the present. History, as it is known in this world, will come to an end, and an unknown and unearthly time will be inaugurated. Apocalypticism posits an inherent dualism between good and evil, between this aeon and the future aeon, a dualism founded in continuous frustration and disappointment. The visions of the prophets seemed to recede, as the course of history progressed steadily away from the paths of Yahweh toward the paths of evil.

Already in the time of Antiochus Epiphanes the limit of suffering in this world was being reached and apocalyptic hopes began to emerge. How long would the captivity endure? How long would the chosen people bear persecution? The author of the Book of Daniel asked these questions and presented a developed apocalyptic answer to them. In the seventh chapter he depicted the four horrible beasts representing the four successive oppressive international powers, which come before the throne of the Ancient of Days, Yahweh, to be judged for their evil deeds. Daniel described the execution of the divine sentence upon the evil powers and the establishment of the longed-for kingdom of the saints. He also described the apocalyptic figure of the "son of man," God's representative, who comes surrounded by clouds to bring in the kingdom. He is the apocalyptic Messiah, a semidivine and semihuman figure, called forth to accomplish the miraculous events of the eschaton.

> *I saw in the night visions and behold, with the clouds of heaven, there came one like a son of man, and he came to the Ancient of Days and was presented before him. And to him was given dominion and glory and kingdom, that all peoples, nations, and languages should serve him; his dominion is an everlasting dominion which shall not pass away, and his kingdom one that shall not be destroyed.*
>
> (Daniel 7:13–14)

Daniel forsaw an end to national and religious adversity. God's victory over evil would soon come and man's victory over suffering and death would be accomplished. To Israel the apocalyptic message brought consolation and hope.

> *And at that time shall arise Michael, the great prince who has charge of your people. And there shall be a time of trouble, such as never has been since there was a nation till that time; but at that time your people shall be delivered . . .*
>
> (Daniel 12:1–3)

The people of Israel, still trusting in the covenant, still atoning for their sins and enduring suffering, were promised redemption in the near future. Yahweh's kingdom would be established and the world utterly changed.

Of course, Daniel's vision was not actualized, but his hopes were adopted and intensified as political conditions worsened. Books like Enoch, 4 Ezra, the Sibylline Oracles, Jubilees, and the Testaments of the Twelve Patriarchs, known as pseudoepigraphical works because of their erroneous ascriptions to authors, developed legendary portrayals of the great end of days, which was always seen as near at hand. Jews yearned for that age to come, and found consolation in the apocalyptics' depictions of it. One group of Jews, the Essenes, separated themselves from the people in order to prepare for the end of days. Living an ascetic communal life on the shores of the Dead Sea, they formed an army of the purified elect, who would aid in the great process of transformation. The Essenes cultivated apocalyptic literature, fully believing in the immediate reality of its promises. Other Jews, not as radically inclined, were still highly influenced by the apocalyptic movement. Within Pharisaic circles (the more moderate but progressive stream of Judaism) certain apocalyptic notions, such as the radical breakthrough of a new order and the resurrection of the dead, were accepted and indeed cherished.

During this same period another trend within Judaism developed, based upon the desire for total change found in apocalypticism. This new religious development was *merkavah* mysticism, whose literary productions date from the first century B.C. and continue until several centuries after the common era, and whose doctrines became highly significant for all later Jewish and Christian mystical movements. The first-century mystical tradition is related to both apocalypticism and gnosticism. Indeed, it is rooted in the apocalyptic and gnostic rejection of history and in their desire to find meaning and solace in some ahistorical visionary reality. The mystic turned away from this world to speculate on a prehistoric age, the age of Creation, or the future posthistoric age. The story of Genesis (*maaseh bereshit*) and the chariot vision of Ezekiel (*maaseh merkavah*) served as his texts and formed the constant basis of Jewish mystical speculation.

The earliest mysticism was confined to small groups of men, drawn from apocalyptics and from important rabbinic circles, who elaborated an esoteric tradition around the interpretation of Ezekiel's famous first chapter, the chariot (*merkavah*) vision. Desiring desperately to find an escape from the cruel fate history had visited upon their people, these men yearned to step outside of time. They believed that the soul was imprisoned in an earthly cage, and they sought a route for its escape and return to its true spiritual home. The *merkavah* mystics described the ascent of the soul through seven heavenly spheres toward the throne of God, an ascent marked by obstacles presented by demonic powers and constant danger. The mystic trained himself for this ascent through ascetic exercises and intense spiritual reflection. He armed himself with magical devices which offered protection against the evil demons.

And he patiently labored to rise up, to overcome all barriers, and to reach his ultimate goal—a vision of the true King upon his throne. The Jewish mystical quest ended in vision rather than union. The distinction between man and God, the gulf between the finite and the infinite, was not to be overcome. Therefore, the mystic did not seek to lose his self in a final union with the deity, but attained a vision of the divine majesty which would enable him to live on, to survive in the reality of earthly existence. In a great mystical tract of the first century, the *Greater Hekhalot,* the true goal of the mystic quest is stated explicitly: "When will he see heavenly majesty? When will he hear of the final time of redemption? When will he perceive what no eye has yet perceived?" The Jewish mystic hungered for release from the evils of this world and the knowledge which would bring release for all men. He believed that what he in his individual ascent might learn would eventually become the property of mankind, in the end of time when all men would be redeemed and would all witness God's glory.

Although the masses of Jews did not join in mystical speculation, they shared the longings and hopes of the mystics. Rooted in more traditional religious concepts, they saw themselves as members of a community which politically and spiritually opposed those who ruled over that community. They desired freedom from the oppressor and freedom from the sufferings of this-worldly existence. The Jewish community of the first century B.C. and first century A.D. waited for redemption, mixing prophetic eschatological hopes with newer apocalyptic visions, but always trusting in God's speedy intervention. It was in the midst of this atmosphere of expectancy and hope that Christianity arose.

# CHRISTIANITY IN HISTORICAL PERSPECTIVE

## THE BEGINNINGS OF CHRISTIANITY

Christianity came into existence within Judaism and within the Judaic world of the first century of our era. It was the product of Jewish messianic hopes and expectations and was considered by its adherents to be their fulfillment. It was at first one more tendency or point of view within Judaism, but it soon gained gentile converts and before long became a separate and predominantly gentile religion. Christianity arose within a Judaism which had been restored to Jerusalem and the surrounding country when the Persian intervention put an end to the Babylonian exile (537 B.C.). It was a Judaism resulting from the renewal of Jewish religious life and national existence under Ezra and Nehemiah and which had seen the partially successful attempt of Judas Maccabeus to restore national independence and rid Judaism of alien intrusions into its religious life (165–161). It was a time when apocalyptic expectations had come to play an important part in Jewish psychology and when hopes abounded for God's intervention into the history of the people to bring about its fulfillment. Many related such intervention to political rebellion against the Roman rule as in the revolt led by Judas the Galilean about the beginning of the Christian era as we now reckon it.

Judaism after the exile developed several tendencies of religious opinion, and the religious and national situation into which the central figure of the new religion, Jesus of Nazareth, was born was a complex one. Aside from smaller sects, at least four groups may be distinguished, each of which had some influence upon the career of Jesus and the development of the early church.

First and most important are the Pharisees, probably derived from the "pious ones" (*hasidim*), who supported and were involved in the Maccabean revolt against Greek paganism. Josephus, the Jewish writer of the first century and historian of the Jewish War against the Romans in A.D. 66–70, considered them to be the leading Jewish religious group and the most accurate interpreters of the law. The Pharisees placed great emphasis upon obedience to the law, but they also looked forward to a fulfillment of Israel's sacred destiny and believed in the resurrection of the dead. Before the defeat of the uprising of 66–70, which was a terrible disaster, they probably shared the widespread apocalyptic hopes and messianic expectations. They were not simply concerned with Israel as a group; their expectation of the resurrection indicates the importance they gave to individual as well as group religiosity, to individual as well as group hope for delivery and salvation.

The next important group was the priestly aristocracy, the Sadducees, who controlled the ritual sacrifice and worship of the Temple. This aspect of Jewish life had declined in importance at a time when a majority of Jews lived outside Palestine and when the synagogue in Palestine and abroad had come to be a new center for the study of the law and for nonsacrificial worship. Yet Jerusalem with its Temple was the center of Judaism and the symbolic heart of its national and religious existence. All Jewish groups shared in its forms of worship, and the earliest Christian literature depicts not only Jesus but the early Church members in Jerusalem participating in its life. The Sadducees held their position as priests by hereditary right and were often wealthy. They practiced a kind of cooperation and compromise with the Roman power. They accepted only the word of scripture, tried to minimize the application of the law to the details of daily life in opposition to the Pharisees, and did not believe in the resurrection of the dead.

The third group important in the Jewish world in which Christianity arose were the Essenes, who unlike the first two, are not mentioned in the New Testament. Josephus speaks of them as cultivating "peculiar sanctity," shunning pleasures, and regarding self-control as "a special virtue." The discovery of the Dead Sea Scrolls less than two decades ago and the study of their texts has shed considerable new light upon this group. The Qumran group who left the scrolls behind were in all probability Essenes. They withdrew from the common life of the Jewish people and set up monastic communities taking the radical view of rejecting the evil and darkness of ordinary existence. They looked forward to a coming triumph of good over evil which would be both a culmination of history and a fulfillment of Israel. They saw themselves fulfilling the call of Isaiah to prepare a highway in the desert for God's coming. They lived in the tension of eschatological or apocalyptic hope and expectation and saw themselves as helping to hasten the blessed day.

A fourth group, of which the New Testament indicates that at least one of Jesus' disciples had been a member, is that of the Zealots. They probably originated around the time of the revolt of Judas the Galilean against the census taken under the Roman procurator Quirinius. They were absolutely opposed to foreign domination and the payment of taxes to the foreign rulers. They were a dis-

*The rock fortress of Masada, overlooking the Dead Sea, the site of major drama in the first century A.D. when Jewish rebels committed mass suicide rather than submit to the Romans. (Courtesy of the Israel Government Tourist Office.)*

tinct minority and appear to have been regarded with disapproval by the majority of Jews. They practiced political violence and the Romans referred to them as *sicarii*, or "stabbers," because of their prowess with the dagger. They became important in 66 as the leading advocates of war against Rome and remained important enough to take part in another rebellion three generations later.

The relation of Christianity to these groups is a difficult and a complex one, and we have little historical evidence allowing us to see it in detail. The New Testament speaks critically of the Pharisees and accuses them of hypocricy, yet Jesus and his followers shared their belief in the resurrection of the dead and their emphasis upon the individual as well as the collective aspects of religious life. Jesus also appears to have generally followed the Pharisaic religious discipline. Paul, who was most influential in setting aside the details of the Jewish Law for the new Church, was himself a former Pharisee.

The similarities of the teachings of Jesus to those of the Teacher of Righteousness mentioned in the Dead Sea texts has engaged the attention of scholars. The followers of Jesus soon came to set themselves apart, somewhat like the Essenes, though they did not form monastic communities, and, like them, they saw the present age as corrupt and evil. The new Christian Church did not insist upon the detailed Hebraic law as did the Qumran group, although they shared with them the high significance attached to moral standards.

The influence of the Sadducees upon the early Church appears in any immediate sense to be that of opposition to Jesus and his followers. However, they may be said to have had a remote and indirect influence upon the development of Christian ideas of worship. This becomes visible later on, when the Church began to interpret its own worship as a transformed version of temple sacrifice.

The relation of Jesus and his followers to the Zealots has fascinated some. It has been suggested that Jesus could have been a Zealot and that he expected to bring about a rebellion against the Roman power which would initiate God's intervention and the beginning of the messianic age. To hold this point of view one must interpret the peaceful messianic message of the New Testament as a later reaction coming after the defeat of Jesus and his alleged revolutionary plans. The evidence for such a connection of Jesus with the Zealots is fragmentary and like so much such evidence is open to contrary interpretations. It can at best be evaluated only by scholars thoroughly familiar with the data and it has certainly not been given credence by the vast majority of them.

Despite the divisions which we have indicated in Jewish life, Jewish religion at the time possessed a deeper unity. A complex of apocalyptic and eschatological ideas was central to it in quite strategic respects. The idea of God as Lord of history about to intervene to bring about its redemption and apotheosis, the centrality of the Jews as a covenant people in this historical and cosmic drama, the emphasis upon a sharp division between good and evil, and the tendency to see the Jewish role as an increasingly universal one bringing the light of Yahweh to the nations—all constitute a significant core of Jewish religiosity at the time. Jewish history had been a history of frustration and defeat punctuated by brief periods of triumph or respite. The Jewish religious writers who interpreted the meaning of that history for the nation, providing what became the widely accepted interpretation, saw all this as the favor and disfavor of Yahweh. Israel's misfortunes, so many and so harsh, were God's judgments upon his chosen people for their transgressions. Yet faith was not lost. Indeed, misfortune seemed to strengthen the abiding hope that God would intervene, would send his anointed one, would redeem Israel and begin a new age of the world for all men.

Those converted to Christianity felt that it was the fulfillment of these hopes. It took over the major Jewish ideas and wove them into the fabric of its own teachings. It saw itself as the renewal and fulfillment of the covenant and its extension to all who would believe. It embraced as central to the religious life the Jewish emphasis upon morality—upon righteousness as a personal disposition and sin as an offense against God himself. It saw God as the Lord of history and itself as the new community based upon the renewed covenant resulting from his intervention through Jesus in the "fullness of times." It saw Jesus as the Messiah of Israel, the expected one anointed of Yahweh, and it looked forward to his return to earth to be followed by the end of the present world, the resurrection of the dead, and the final judgment of all men.

Though Jesus was an innovator because he spoke and embodied God's revelation in a new time and became the bearer of its message to later gentile generations, the Jewish character of his central moral teaching is clear. The oldest Gospel records that when he was challenged by an opponent, " 'Which commandment is the first of all?' he answered, 'Hear, O Israel: The Lord our God, the Lord is one; and you shall love the Lord your God with all your heart, and with all your soul, and with all your mind, and with all your strength!' The second is this, 'You shall love your neighbor as yourself. There is no other commandment greater than these' " (Mark 12:28–31). It is significant that here Jesus quotes from the sixth chapter of Deuteronomy and from the nineteenth chapter of Leviticus. Jesus quoted what is known as the *Shema,* recognized from time immemorial as the central Jewish confession of faith and standard of morals. It is this which the devout Jew recites three times daily as the fulfillment of divine command. In faith and morals Christianity took its stand on the basis of the Judaic revelation. Moreover, all three Synoptic Gospels (Matthew, Mark, and Luke) show Jesus leaving Galilee after a time of preaching and teaching in his native region and going to Jerusalem. They all three show him at this time telling his disciples that he was the Messiah, thus identifying himself with the deepest yearnings and aspirations of the Jewish people.

> *And Jesus went on with his disciples to the villages of Caesarea Philippi; and on the way he asked his disciples, "Who do men say that I am?" And they told him, "John the Baptist; and others say Elijah; and others one of the prophets." And he asked them, "But who do you say that I am?" Peter answered him, "You are the Christ [that is, the anointed one, the Messiah]." And he charged them to tell no one about him. And he began to teach them that the Son of man must suffer many things, and be rejected by the elders and the chief priests and the scribes, and be killed and after three days rise again. And he said this plainly.*
> (Mark 8:27–32; see also Matt. 16:13 ff. and Luke 9:18 ff.)

Thus was Christianity founded by a prophetic Jewish figure who took his stand within the Jewish religious tradition and in the consciousness of his messianic mission announced its imminent fulfillment.

JESUS OF NAZARETH

We shall not attempt here to essay the impossible task of presenting the preaching, teaching, healing, and suffering of Jesus of Nazareth apart from the memory of them, the commentary upon them, and the development of their meaning to be found in the New Testament. Nor shall we try to reconstruct the image of the figure of Jesus himself as the historical personage which lies behind his impact on the Gospel narratives. The New Testament itself is the product of the early Christian community, which before the end of the first century began to write down its earlier oral traditions and to collect letters and other written matter which had circulated among its various churches. By the end of the second century these writings had been subjected to the critical appraisal of the Church, some accepted and some rejected, and what is called the canon (Greek *kanon,* "rule" or "norm") established. Twenty of twenty-seven books making up the present New Testament were accepted as canonical in the Church by the year 200, and the differences that did exist were decidedly of a minor character. Thus what the New Testament presents to us are those characteristics of Jesus and those aspects of his career which were the foundation of the faith of the Church seen in the light of the development of that faith that had taken place within the community in the first three or four generations.

According to the Gospel narratives Jesus preached, taught, healed, died, and rose from the dead. He preached the imminence of the Kingdom of God and called for repentance. "The time is fulfilled, and the kingdom of God is at hand; repent, and believe in the gospel" (Mark 1:15; see also Mark 4:17). The kingdom which Jesus proclaimed was an inner condition and relationship to God and an outer expression of moral behavior and compassion with respect to one's fellow man and also a personal and ethical reality which moved toward an imminent eschatological fulfillment as may be seen from his parables as set forth in the synoptic gospels.

In these Gospels one also sees the high esteem in which his followers and the early Church held Jesus. In the nativity stories (Matt. 2; Luke 1–2) Jesus' birth, which probably took place between 4 and 2 B.C., is told as accompanied by the apparition of angels, the visitation of gentile religious leaders bearing gifts, the alarm and violence of Herod threatened by the event, and by prophetic witness from pious Jews, which proclaimed the child "a light for revelation to the Gentiles and for the glory to thy people Israel" (Luke 2:32). Indeed he is born of a virgin and of the Davidic line, signifying his relationship to God and his special mission. Mark's account of his baptism by John the Baptist states that "when he came up out of the water, immediately he saw the heavens opened and the Spirit descending upon him like a dove; and a voice came from heaven, 'Thou art my beloved Son; with thee I am well pleased' " (Mark 1:10–11), an event which later gospels present somewhat more as an external happening. In the story of the transfiguration the three apostles Peter, James, and John see Jesus transformed in appearance and standing with Moses and Elijah, the two great archetypal Jewish figures symbolizing the Law and the prophets. Jesus' central

*Rembrandt,* Christ Preaching. (*Courtesy of The Metropolitan Museum of Art. Bequest of Mrs. H. O. Havemeyer, 1929. The H. O. Havemeyer Collection.*)

position symbolizes the Christian belief that he is the final fulfillment of both the Law and the prophets, which he declared he had "come not to abolish but to fulfill" (Matt. 5:17). In the temptation narrative we see Jesus challenged by the powers of evil and offered this-worldly success and glory which he spurns, quoting Deuteronomy, "Man shall not live by bread alone but by every word that proceeds from the mouth of God" and "You shall worship the Lord your God and him only shall you serve" (Matt. 4:4 and 4:10; see also Luke 4:1–13).

Central to Jesus' teaching was love of God and one's fellow man. Jesus accepted and took his stand upon the Hebraic conviction of the immediacy of God and the centrality of ethics, and in typical Jewish fashion he saw them as inseparable parts of a single reality. Central to his preaching was a call for repentance, a demand for justice and righteousness from men, and an assurance of mercy from God. Jesus stressed the importance of love—of man's love for God and God's love for man—thus giving renewed emphasis to ideas found in Hosea, Jeremiah, and Isaiah. The biblical idea of love is not, however, a phenomenon of structureless sentimentality to which everything is indifferently permitted. While it is a deep emotional reality characterized by man's yearning and God's mercy and consolation, it involves the ethical demands of Old and New Testaments as central to its essential character, and while it envisages God as the forgiving father and the good shepherd, it also sees him as the stern judge of the unrighteous and unrepentant. Indeed the Gospel of Matthew presents Jesus himself acting as judge on the day of final judgment separating the righteous from the evil ones "as a shepherd separates the sheep from the goats" and calling the righteous to God saying, "Come, O blessed of my Father, inherit the kingdom prepared for you from the foundation of the world; for I was hungry and you gave me food, I was thirsty and you gave me drink, I was naked and you clothed me, I was sick and you visited me, I was imprisoned and you came to me . . . *[for]* as you did it to one of the least of these my brethren, you did it to me." But to the evil and the unrepentant he says, " 'Depart from me, you cursed, into the eternal fire prepared for the devil and his angels' . . . and they will go away into eternal punishment, but the righteous into eternal life" (Matt. 25:31–46).

Like the pious Jew that he was, Jesus emphasized the importance of prayer although he was critical of some current practices. He counseled his followers against long prayers in public and admonished them to pray briefly and in private. Before his death we find Jesus subduing his own interior turmoil through prayer. Jesus teaches men to pray with assurance that prayer is answered. The only formal prayer attributed to Jesus himself by the New Testament is found in the Gospels of Matthew and Luke, where Jesus says: "Pray then like this:

*Our Father who art in heaven,*
*Hallowed be thy name.*
*Thy kingdom come,*
*Thy will be done,*
  *On earth as it is in heaven.*
*Give us this day our daily bread;*
*And forgive us our debts,*
*As we forgive our debtors;*
*And lead us not into temptation,*
  *But deliver us from evil."*

(Matt. 6:9–13)

The Gospel narratives depict Jesus performing miracles or what the Greek text sees as expressions of power (*dynamis*), feeding the hungry, healing the sick, and curing the tormented whom the New Testament sees as possessed by demons. Matthew reports that it was said of him with astonishment, "He has done all things well; he even makes the deaf hear and the dumb speak" (Matt. 7:37). Peter in The Acts of the Apostles is reported as saying that "God anointed Jesus of Nazareth with the Holy Spirit and with power; . . . he went about doing good and healing all that were oppressed by the devil, for God was with him" (Acts 10:38). These miracles so bothersome to modern thought were seen by the early Church as the breakthrough of divine power into the life of men, as mighty works of God heralding the kingdom, the signs (*semeoin*) and portents (*teras*) of its imminence. They were also understood in the early Church as the evidence of Jesus' victory over the demons which the popular thought of that period conceived as ubiquitous powers of present evil.

Of central significance to the meaning of Christianity and to the teaching of the churches for centuries is the passion and death of Jesus. All three Synoptic Gospels show Jesus deliberately going to

Jerusalem for the celebration of the Passover feast, an event he appears to have anticipated as closely bound up with the manifestation of his own messianic mission. At Jerusalem he entered the city riding upon an ass and receiving the acclamation of the multitudes according to the synoptic accounts, an expression of messiahship reminiscent of the ass-riding princes of the early Israelite confederation as portrayed in the Song of Deborah and recalling the words of Zechariah,

*Rejoice greatly, O daughter of Zion!*
*Shout aloud, O daughter of Jerusalem!*
*Lo, your king comes to you;*
*triumphant and victorious is he,*
*humble and riding on an ass,*
*on a colt the foal of an ass.*

(Zech. 9:9)

These Gospels show him driving out "those who sold and those who bought in the temple" (Mark 11:15), another act displaying messianic claims. On Thursday evening of that week he ate a supper with his disciples which has become the archetype of the basic Christian act of worship ever since. The bread and wine of the traditional seder were interpreted by Jesus as his body and blood.

*And as they were eating, he took bread, and blessed, and broke it, and gave it to them, and said, "Take; this is my body." And he took a cup, and when he had given thanks he gave it to them, and they all drank of it. And he said to them, "This is my blood of the covenant, which is poured out for many."*

(Mark 14:22–24)

After appearing before the Jewish Council (Sanhedrin), where he affirmed his messianic mission and made reference to the messianic Book of Daniel, and before the Roman procurator, he was put to death. On the cross on which he died the Roman procurator nailed a sign stating that this man was king of the Jews. Thus in the eyes of this world and by its standards the life of Jesus ended in bitter defeat and utter failure. He died forsaken. One of his own chosen twelve had betrayed him to his enemies and their senior member had denied him. After his death the others apparently returned to Galilee, their native region, disillusioned and discouraged in the death of him who they had hoped "was the one to redeem Israel" (Luke 24:21).

A short time after these seemingly disastrous events the followers of Jesus, except for him who betrayed him, who, according to Matthew's Gospel, hung himself in remorse, are found back together in Jerusalem and are actively propagating the messiahship of Jesus. It was the conviction of these men and the belief of the early Church which resulted from their efforts that Jesus had risen from the dead and that his death and resurrection taken together represented the beginning of that messianic kingdom which Jesus had proclaimed in

*Marcello Muccini,* Crucifixion, *1947; a plate from the portfolio* 6 Acqueforti di Muccini, Urbinati Vespignai. (*Courtesy of the Museum of Modern Art, New York. Purchase.*)

his own earthly ministry. The resurrection became the keystone of the Christian faith, the guarantee that Jesus was of God and the sign of the general resurrection to come. In one of the earliest Christian writings (A.D. 51 or 52) we find the Apostle Paul saying:

> *Now if Christ is preached as raised from the dead, how can some of you say that there is no resurrection of the dead? But if there*

*is no resurrection of the dead, then Christ has not been raised; if Christ has not been raised, then our preaching is in vain and your faith is in vain. We are even found to be misrepresenting God, because we testified of God that he raised Christ, whom he did not raise if it is true that the dead are not raised. If Christ has not been raised, your faith is futile and you are still in your sins. Then those who have fallen asleep in Christ have perished. If for this life only we have hoped in Christ, we are of all men most to be pitied. But in fact Christ has been raised from the dead, the first fruits of those who have fallen asleep.*

(1 Cor. 15:12–20)

There are several New Testament sources in which we find versions of the tradition of Jesus' resurrection as it existed in the early Christian community. Chief among them are 1 Corinthians 15:3–8, Mark 16:1–8, Matthew 28:1–20, Luke 24:1–53, and John 20:1–21:25. They differ among themselves in considerable detail. In the Pauline account Jesus after his death appears first to Peter, although in the Synoptic Gospels there is no mention of an appearance to Peter. In the Gospels of Matthew and Mark only the women visit the tomb, but in Luke's, Peter follows by himself. Such differences could be listed at length. But the testimony of all traditions is that Jesus, whom the early followers had known in his earthly existence, had been put to death, was interred in a tomb, had been raised from the dead, and had appeared to numerous eyewitnesses. This Easter event was the foundation of the Christian faith. It was not only a beginning of the new age, not only a victory over death, but a victory over sin. "For we know that Christ being raised from the dead will never die again; death no longer has dominion over him. The death he died he died to sin, once for all, but the life he lives he lives to God. So you also must consider yourselves dead to sin and alive to God in Jesus Christ" (Rom. 6:9–11). In this death and resurrection the followers of Jesus have been "set free from sin," and as a result share in "sanctification and its end, eternal life" (Rom. 6:22). The new messianic age had commenced. Jesus had returned to the Father but he would come again. The earliest gospel has Jesus saying at his last supper, "Truly, I say to you, I shall not drink again of the fruit of the vine until that day when I drink it new in the kingdom of God" (Mark 14:25). The new communities which came together in response to the preaching (*Kerygma*) of Jesus' disciples repeated the communion of bread and wine in which they felt the hidden presence of their risen Lord and in which they proclaimed "the Lord's death until he comes" (1 Cor. 11:26). They lived in the expectation of the return of Jesus in glory, an event which they apparently felt would come in their own lifetimes.

## THE EARLY CHURCH

Following the four Gospels in the New Testament is found the Book called The Acts of the Apostles. It was written by Luke, the author of the third synoptic gospel, sometime during the last two decades of the first century. It has often been called the first Church history because it gives us a picture of the young Christian community in the Apostolic age. Though it is not a history in our modern sense of the word, since it is written as a kind of apologia and from a particular theological point of view, it does reflect the early Church and provides valuable insights into its life. It begins by raising the question asked of the risen Christ of when the new messianic age would achieve its full realization.

> *So when they had come together they asked him, "Lord, will you at this time restore the kingdom to Israel?" He said to them, "It is not for you to know times or seasons which the Father has fixed by his own authority. But you shall receive power when the Holy Spirit has come upon you; and you shall be my witnesses in Jerusalem and all Judea and Samaria and to the end of the earth."*
>
> (Acts 1:6–8)

Then is recounted what Christians call the ascension of Jesus: "he was lifted up, and a cloud took him out of sight" (Acts 1:9). The second chapter begins with an account of the Pentecost event in which Christians believe the close followers of Jesus "gathered together in one place" were "filled with the Holy Spirit" which sent them forth preaching the message of the new Church (Acts 2:1–13).

Thus does a document of the early Church present the fundamental conditions characteristic of the infant Christian community—the absence of Jesus now believed to be risen and returned to the Father, the expectation of his return and the lack of knowledge of the times and seasons fixed by God for its occurrence, and the orientation to proselytism. We next read the preaching of Peter, giving us an example of the early *Kerygma.* Following this the book is divided into two parts, the first showing us the progress of the Church within Palestine, the second the development of missionary work abroad and its triumphant expansion in the gentile world. In the preaching of Acts we see the presentation of Jesus' career and its meaning and the liberal use of Old Testament quotations to support the argument and show Jesus as the promised one, as may be seen in the sermon of Peter in the second chapter and that of Paul in the thirteenth. The book reflects the conviction of the author that the promises to Israel were being fulfilled in the new Church, which was the new Israel and heir to the old. Here we see the new Church defining itself as the authentic covenant community and oriented to the conversion of gentiles, although it appears still predominantly Jewish in its composition.

We see in Acts the confrontation by the early Christian group of the first basic decisive issue of Christian history—the one whose outcome would decide whether or not there would be any Christian history. Will the new group, believing in the messiahship of Jesus and awaiting his second coming, remain a sect within the confines of Judaism or will it become an independent religious community with its own essential character and destiny? Of course the question, like all significant historical questions, was neither grasped nor met in this abstract form, but rather in terms of concrete incidents in the historical experience of the group. In Acts we see the author's conviction that the Jewish nation will not as a whole accept the new proclamation of Jesus' disciples, although Luke obviously considered it to be the legitimate continuation and fulfillment of the entire Jewish past. Thus, in speaking to Cornelius and his friends, Luke has Peter at the beginning of the gentile mission declare that "God shows no partiality, but in every nation anyone who fears him and does what is right is acceptable to him" (Acts 10:34–35). And the Book of Acts ends with Paul preaching to the Jews of the diaspora living in Rome and "trying to convince them about Jesus both from the law of Moses and from the prophets. And some were convinced by what he said while others disbelieved" (Acts 28:23–24). To those who disbelieved Paul quoted Isaiah and declared that "this salvation of God has been sent to the Gentiles; they will listen." In the speech and death of Stephen we find another incident and one in which Paul was involved in quite another way. The charges against Stephen indicate that he and other members of the new community were questioning the temple worship and the law, and the speech which Luke attributes to him sets forth a developed theological position, accuses the Jewish authorities of Jesus' death, and questions the efficacy of temple worship. Here we see not only difficulties between the new group and the religious authorities of Judaism but also the internal conflict within the new Church with respect to its own Judaic character. Chapter 6 of Acts speaks of two groups of Christians, Hellenists and Hebrews, and speaks of the murmuring of the former against the latter. Stephen apparently represents an extreme hellenist position which the dominant leadership of the new group and the Christians in Jerusalem are not ready to accept. A third expression of this fundamental historic choice facing the new Church is to be seen. We learn that there is a disagreement concerning whether or not the male gentile converts must be circumcised. Jews in the diaspora would not accord such gentiles a full membership, but admitted them to a kind of half membership in the synagogue without circumcision, a painful and possibly dangerous experience for adults under the conditions of the times. What should be their status in the new Church? Conversion of gentiles raised a question concerning the Jewish dietary prescriptions, which though less elaborate than later must have seemed difficult to understand and onerous in practice to gentiles. Acts attempts to solve the second question by recounting a vision of Peter setting them aside. Chapter 11 of Acts gives us the impression that Jewish Christians challenged the conversion of gentiles to the Christian fellowship but came to accept it as right and proper seeing that they "received the Holy Spirit just as we have" (Acts 10:47). It raises the dietary problem and suggests a permissive answer. Chapter 15 raises the question of circumcision of the converts and shows us a council of the early Christian group discussing and apparently deciding the issue. "For it seemed good to the Holy Spirit and to us to lay upon you no greater burden than these necessary things: that you abstain from what has been sacrificed to idols and from blood and from what is strangled and from unchastity" (Acts 15:28–29). This question is discussed by Paul both in Galatians and Romans where he declares that Abraham himself was justified by his faith rather than by circumcision. The church which issued from the experience of Jewish followers with Jesus of Nazareth was coming to seek its own fulfillment in the gentile world.

The Book of Acts, as we have noted, is not a reliable history in the modern sense. The author is trying to present an idealized picture of the early Church. Actually the early Christian community at this time was divided among a number of trends both within Palestine and among the Christian gentile groups. Despite its statement that "the company of those who believed were of one heart and soul" (Acts 4:32), the book does reveal the existence of the severe inner conflict that divided the Church over the status of the law and the temple in nascent Christian life. In addition to what we have already discussed, Acts shows us the followers of Stephen driven out of Jerusalem, Peter after his escape from arrest departing and going "to another place" (Acts 12:17) leaving James totally in authority, and the conflict of Paul and Hebrew Christians and his arrest in Jerusalem. In his own writings Paul reveals the depth of feeling aroused in the conflict. He tells the Roman Christians that he is going to Jerusalem with the collection money raised from the gentile converts for the poor in the church there. This collection was a symbol of unity between the conflicting groups and between the Christians of Jewish and of gentile origin; a symbol of the debt owed to the Jewish Christians by the gentiles, "for if the Gentiles have come to share in their spiritual blessings, they ought also to be of service to them in material blessings" (Acts 15:27). It symbolized Christian unity, as Jewish unity was symbolized by the temple tax paid each year by the Jews of the diaspora. In this situation Paul asks the Roman Christians to pray to God that he may be "delivered from the unbelievers in Judea" and that the collection which he presents and his work of proselytism for which its stands "may be acceptable to the saints" in Jerusalem (Acts 15:31). When Paul arrives at the holy city, James and the other leaders tell him that Hebrew Christians "all zealous for the law" believe that he is telling the Jewish Christians of the diaspora to "forsake Moses" and to give up circumcision (Acts 21:21), and are aroused against him. There follows Paul's arrest which eventuates in his martyrdom which, however, the book does not relate.

## THE GENTILE WORLD

Since the Babylonian exile Jews had started to settle in places outside Palestine—in Egypt and elsewhere—and, as we have seen, there arose groups of Jews living abroad known as the dispersion communities or the diaspora. Diaspora Jews were removed from Palestine and the close relationship of religion, temple, nationality, and land characteristic of the Holy Land was loosening in their minds. They were under these circumstances beginning to feel more like members of a religious group rather than a nation, although they did maintain an ethnic identity and a kind of social separateness. New forms of worship developed in the synagogue more like the later "church services" than like the temple. In short, a kind of growing universalism was becoming characteristic of diaspora Judaism and the kinds of questions about circumcision and proselytism plaguing the early Church were being raised there too.

At the time the early Church began its gentile mission in Antioch, where "the disciples were for the first time called Christians" (Acts 11:26), and Paul went "over to Macedonia" (Acts 16:9), most of the Jews of the diaspora spoke Greek. Alexander the Great (356–323 B.C.) in his conquests, which united southeastern Europe with much of western Asia, sought to spread Greek culture and the Greek language. This former student of Aristotle looked forward to a mixing of Greek and non-Greek cultural elements and the intermingling of biological stocks as well. He advocated the development of a unified culture based upon Greek throughout his empire. The world of the eastern Mediterranean and beyond, embraced in the Macedonian Empire, was a world which followed upon centuries of cultural development among Greeks, Persians, Egyptians, and others. It was a sophisticated world and to a considerable extent a highly urbanized one—in fact more urbanized than Europe would be again until after the Industrial Revolution. Moreover, Alexander made the cities of the region Greek cities and throughout the area hellenistic culture—the blend of Greek and indigenous elements Alexander had sought to bring about—flourished in the urban centers. Early in this hellenistic period of eastern Mediterranean culture, the Jewish Bible had been translated into Greek. This version, the so called Septuagint, was translated in Alexandria, in Egypt, sometime around 250 B.C. for the use of the sizable Jewish community resident there. Moreover, a form of common Greek speech and writing somewhat simpler than the Attic Greek spoken by Plato and Aristotle and known as the *koine* developed at this time. It became the *lingua franca* of the literate population. Although Alexander died prematurely and his empire did not hold together as one unit, his cultural efforts remained and the successor states maintained their hellenistic character. Thus a common language, somewhat of a common culture, and an available translation of the Hebrew Scriptures were part of the gentile world to which the early Church turned. The Church wrote its own scriptures in the common Greek of this world and soon became there a predominantly gentile religious phenomenon.

The gentile world into which the new religious movement came had been united into one political whole by Rome, and the Palestine in which Christianity originated had been incorporated into a Roman province with the dissolution of the Seleucid kingdom which had been one of the successor states of Alexander's empire. The Roman Empire, at the height of its expansion in the period when the New Testament was written, occupied the Mediterranean world from Syria and Palestine in the east to the Iberian Peninsula and the island we know as Great Britain in the west. It did not extend as far east as the empire of Alexander, which penetrated what is now India, but this was more than compensated for by its bringing together the regions of Britain, Gaul, and Spain with Italy and North Africa into one political unit with the Greek- and Semitic-speaking lands of the East. The Roman genius for order and administration and the power of Roman arms gave the world of the empire political stability and peace, which, though at times interrupted, exhibited a marked continuity and dependability. This was the period of the *pax romana,* the peace organized and enforced by Rome which lasted for two and a half centuries at the beginning of the Christian Era. Rome not only provided a condition of order and developed an advanced legal system, it also developed the most advanced system of roads on land and of sea transportation on the Mediterranean that had been seen up to that time, making possible orderly and secure transportation throughout the large extent of the empire. Thus Christianity came into an urban society, a society sharing a common language and culture to a marked extent, a society where travel though difficult by modern standards was easier than ever before, and a society enjoying peace and order.

The ancient world had known at an earlier period profound and bitter social and political conflicts, but these were greatly diminished and generally may be said to have ended since the time of Alexander. With the return of order came a return of prosperity and a marked bettering of economic conditions. Moreover, Greece and Rome had earlier aspired to a kind of fulfillment of man's hopes in the life of the city-state, but with the empire of the Caesars such political life ended and with it such political aspirations. The *pax romana* meant a reduction of the slave markets and political order as the basis for economic recovery. Consequently there was a gradual improvement in the conditions of urban life. The world of the Roman Empire and the *pax romana* was one in which an orderly world was ruled more and more by a skilled bureaucracy under the centralized authority of the monarchy, although there was at the same time the persistence of older republican forms now devoid of their former substance. It was a world of moderate economic prosperity in which urban lower middle classes achieved in some measure the minimum material means of life. In this situation human aspirations and human mobility tended to turn inward and the latter part of the ancient period sees a marked development of religious sensitivity and of creative religious experience. Into this world Christianity brought its religious message. It made converts first probably among diaspora Jews and proselytes who had been admitted into half membership in the diaspora synagogue. It soon, as we have seen, admitted gentiles and before long these constituted the vast majority of its members and converts. It made converts in all social classes as time went on but for the first many decades its members in the majority belonged to the lower middle classes of the cities. After the reign of Marcus Aurelius (161–180), upper-class people more and more became active in the life of the Church. The Christian message issued a call which the historical and social developments of the empire had prepared many to hear and disposed many to respond favorably to.

The period when Christianity entered the world of pagan antiquity was one in which the older popular religion was in decline. The educated no longer believed literally in the gods of the Greco-Roman pantheon and allegorical explanations and philosophical meanings were suggested by those philosophically inclined. Yet naive popular piety did remain and the traditional public religion of the empire, which Augustus (the emperor when Jesus was born) attempted to preserve and promote. Moreover, from this time the emperor himself began to be regarded as divine and libations were offered to him. Since such offering was seen as a kind of test of political loyalty and since the Christians refused to offer libations on religious grounds, it became a cause of difficulty and finally of persecution for them. Yet the loss of national independence for those peoples who had been incorporated into the empire and the mixing of peoples which the urban life and improved travel conditions of the empire made possible helped undermine the old traditional religions while the advance of learning made them unsuitable to the educated.

## THE RELIGIOUS TEMPER OF LATER ANTIQUITY

This world which saw the decline of the traditional religions remained, however, a religious world. Indeed it witnessed a deepening of religious concern and a decided turn toward religious interests and the interior life. Mystery cults rose, appealing to the individual and promising him some kind of renewal or regeneration. Most of them appear to have derived from older fertility rites, but to have become highly individualistic. They emphasized the individual and his needs and survival of the individual soul after death. They all had certain structural elements in common. They all secretly engaged in esoteric rituals which the adherents were sworn not to reveal. As a consequence, we do not have extant explicit descriptions of what went on and what we do know is reconstructed from fragmentary evidence—such as the paintings of the initiation rites of the mysteries of Dionysius found on the walls of Pompeii. The rites all appear to involve as their central element the ritual reenactment of archetypal events of the particular myth which was the cult's basic statement of meaning. The Eleusinian mysteries, for example, which originated in Greece, near Athens, were made part of the general state religion in the classical period. They were based on the myth of the rape and carrying off of Proserpine, daughter of Demeter, the goddess of earth and crops, by Pluto, god of the underworld, and of her mother's recovery of her annually for half the year. The myth and the rites reenacted represent the cycle of vegetation and the yearly death and rebirth of life. Through the rite the individual is integrated into this cycle and derives special strength from his relation to it. The mystery of Adonis which originated at Byblos in Phoenicia presented in a similar manner the dying and rising of the god of vegetation. This was a typical pattern—the death and rising of a fertility god. Frequently, the regeneration and renewal of life also involved survival after death; the older fertility and regeneration elements being given an interpretation in relation to the life and death of man. The Orphic mysteries, whose origins are lost in the obscurity of antiquity, possessed a developed cosmogony and theogony and explained the origin of man and his ultimate destiny, including a doctrine of the transmigration of souls. Orphism was one of the more profound of these groups and its ideas influenced Plato, the Pythagoreans, and others. The Isis and Osiris mysteries brought the Egyptian concerns with immortality to large numbers in the cities of the empire. The mystery of Mithra which originated in Persia was based upon a solar myth. It was extremely popular among the Roman soldiers and Mithraic archeological remains have been found as far west as Great Britain. It was probably the chief rival to Christianity among the mysteries in the late second and third centuries. The rites were the reenactment of these myths, a reenactment which was understood as a re-presentation, for the mythic events are understood as eternally present, making possible a participation of the individual adherent in them and his gaining of strength and immortality through them. They all seem to have involved an initiation rite, a ritual progress through various graduated stages of purification and a final achievement of perfection, such perfection involving the final insights arrived at in the ritual enactment. Human sexuality was often seen as closely related to this final insight and sexual elements were often important in the rites.

Not only have these cults embraced and dramatized the cycles of nature but they have extended them to cosmic rhythms which lead man beyond this earth to a future life. The similarities among these cults do not seem to be based upon borrowing but rather upon certain perennial religious needs which though originally concerned with man's relation to the earth and its mysterious powers of life and death came to be seen as centered upon individual life and individual psychological needs. In fact, the mystery cults would seem to express certain archetypal characteristics of religious thought and behavior—the need for some kind of strength from ultimate sources outside oneself and the longing for some kind of regeneration and transformation. They represent specifically religious groups organized around a complex of ritual and myth. They are typical of urban settings where people have been uprooted from the traditional relationship to the soil and the older kinship structures of human relations so closely connected with it. As such, it is not difficult to see why they flourished in the cities of the hellenistic and Roman periods. They were not state religions but private associations and they were not just widely believed as the older paganism but required voluntary adherence and admission by initiation. Yet they were not exclusivist in their demands. A person could be a member of the mysteries and also take part in the traditional or state religion. He could worship Mithra and Jupiter and together with the worship of both of them offer libation to the divine emperor. The early Christians considered most of these groups to be immoral and under the influence of demons and to be engaged in immoral rites. While this impression is probably exaggerated, the fact is that only Mithraism, which was based upon the ethical and ontological dualism of Zoroastrianism, saw existence as a struggle between right and wrong and took a serious ethical position. As the traditional religion declined, these groups increased in popularity and by the beginning of the third century Christians concentrated their polemics against them as chief rivals rather than the older paganism.

It was at one time a scholarly hypothesis that as Christianity developed its own ritual of worship and its own theology it was influenced by the mysteries against which it had long contended. Indeed Christianity has made use of and integrated into its thought and liturgy certain rites and concepts which antedate it. However, the hypothesis of significant Christian dependence upon the mysteries has generally been given up and the archetypal elements of Christian rites appear to be structural archetypes of religious thought and ritual behavior rather than the product of obscure cultural diffusion. Indeed many of them appear to be taken over from Judaic prototypes.

While these new groups were voluntary, specifically religious organizations, they did not represent new communities and new religions demanding the exclusive commitment of the individual. These cults involved parts of a man; they required his partial involvement, not all his heart, all his soul, all his mind, and all his strength as did the commands of Deuteronomy and Leviticus quoted by Jesus. Perhaps Orphism is an exception here, for there was talk of an Orphic way of life which involved an ascetic discipline. Orphism seemed addressed to suffering souls and to involve some real idea of conversion and salvation. Such profundity was not general. Even Mithraism with its moral elements was not something that demanded the whole man. This stands in sharp contrast to both Judaism and Christianity which demanded a genuine conversion—a profound interior turning around of the whole person—of those who joined their ranks. Moreover, in the mysteries one does not find the belief that their sacramental rituals in any way help men to lead a moral life here and now. Such profound conversion demands as those made by Judaism and Christianity appear elsewhere in the ancient world only in philosophy.

Greek philosophy exhibited two interests: one speculative or scientific and concerned with understanding the world in which men find themselves, the other concentrating upon the significance of human existence and seeking a basis for right conduct. The former interest began in the sixth century B.C. in Ionia, where human thought gradually emancipated itself from the mythic imagination and took its stand in the abstract conceptual formulation of man's experience. The latter interest may be said to have begun in Athens in the fifth century, when Socrates turned his attention to the examination of human life. Socrates set ancient men on the quest for understanding what man ought to do to live well and properly. His idea of knowledge was not simply intellectual; it involved an interior motion of the inner man to embrace truth when he found it, a motion that changed him in a profound manner. Pythagoras had given rise to a movement that was philosophical and highly concerned with mathematics but which was also of a marked religious cast. It was a philosophy, a way of life, and a community of believers as well. Plato, Socrates' outstanding disciple, developed the insights of his master and created the first rational theology making the transcendent good the measure of all things and urging the reformation of human life in its light. Early in his career Plato hoped to bring about general political change; he was without success and consequently turned his attention to the inner world and the perfection of inner man.

Following the end of the city-state and the rise of the Hellenistic Empire, further philosophical developments are to be seen in answer to the spiritual and psychological problems of men in the new kind of society which developed. Men were more alone, more individuated, less a part of stable groups with temporal continuity. They lived in a larger and more complex world. Already at the end of the classical period we see souls in need of cure and men becoming identified with philosophical movements. This need now greatly increased, and there arose to meet it two significant philosophical schools—Stoicism and Epicureanism. The latter was a materialist doctrine which saw the world outside of man as offering no guide and sanction to human life. The Epicureans did not deny the existence of gods but saw them as having no relation to men. Death is the dissolution of the human being and is final. Man must therefore find within himself a guide to a satisfactory life. The modern use of the term "Epicurean" is a caricature of its original meaning, for it was not a life of pleasure. Men were to seek freedom from pain, and in so doing they were to avoid involvement in pleasure or any other activity which might upset the steady unruffled way of life which was advocated, a life characterized by *ataraxy*.

The Stoics gave a quite different response to ancient man's new situation. They saw an ordered universe which was the expression of reason. Indeed, reason was seen as the soul of the universe, the god which is also referred to as nature. Man was made up of a spark of this reason as well as of lesser material elements. His true happiness was to be found in cultivating the former and leading a life in harmony with nature. The usual ways of the world were seen as errors and man must avoid them and find the true way beneath them. Thus will man recognize folly and find wisdom. He will lead a life of justice and restraint; he will not give himself to vanities. Like Epicureanism, the Stoic philosophy offered man freedom, but it offered it through identification with and cultivation of the divine element within himself and within nature as a whole. Stoicism too, like Plato, had intended to revolutionize political life and in fact did have some effect upon it, especially under the first emperor Augustus, who attempted far-reaching reforms of the political and social structure. The spirit of Stoicism had an effect upon the conception and spread of Roman citizenship in the empire and upon the development of Roman law. Its ideas influenced the later revival of Platonism and the development of Christian thought. St. Augustine tells how at the age of eighteen he was deeply affected and prepared for his later conversion to Christianity by reading Cicero's *Hortensius*. The Cynics (this word also is not being given its modern meaning but signifies a disregard for established customs and manners), too, developed a notion of a basic reality behind particular cultures and customs in relation to which men found or sought to find detachment and freedom.

The rise of philosophy was accompanied by the development of what we might characterize as a prototype of higher education. In the imperial period educated people learned grammar, then rhetoric, and then some went on to philosophy. Moreover, among the Romans the study of law was important. There were famous centers where men went to study philosophy such as the Platonic Academy in Athens, but most men learned philosophy from private teachers who were located throughout the empire. This study of philosophy with private teachers was at its height in the first century when Christianity came into the gentile world. Not only could one study philosophy in one's youth, but public lectures made it possible for older people to become involved as well. Philosophical literature received a wide circulation and exercised considerable influence. Moreover, a large number of elementary philosophic introductions and summaries were found. When Christianity came to face the challenge of ancient philosophy, its concepts were widely diffused among the literate classes.

These philosophical schools in the first century were less concerned with pure philosophical speculation and more involved in preaching the need for and way to a good life. They demanded something closely akin to religious conversion. They offered meaning and direction to men who could no longer find it in the older religious culture of paganism and whose needs had been deepened and made conscious by the intellectual and social developments of the preceding centuries. They made the universe intelligible and offered a way of life, an intellectually planned and justified mode of living. They offered an ascetic discipline for the taming of human passions based upon the understanding of man's nature and place in the universe. Stoicism later emphasized doing good and performing the duty of one's station in life. Its doctrine of moral progress gave the individual a path to self-development and improvement. In short these philosophical schools and movements offered intelligible explanations of the world and man's place within it and at the same time a life based upon an intelligent design or plan, a disciplined and intelligible mode of existence. They also offered a kind of brotherhood, and even held up heroic and ideal human examples before their followers, examples which would affect later Christian hagiography. For the deeper student, philosophy offered the joy and satisfaction of mystic and scientific contemplation, both of which involved an intellectual relationship with the deeper ground of existence. Ancient philosophy saw the life of contemplation as a higher expression of the human potential than the active life, a fact that reflected the inward turning characteristic of the ancient world after the classical period.

Such philosophy was a kind of religion. It was more profoundly religious in the sense in which that word can be applied to Judaism and Christianity than the older popular religion or even than the mysteries, since it demanded genuine inner change. Its literature urged repentance, conversion, deliverance, etc. In Seneca's words, it involved not only improvement but transformation. And it related men to what it saw as the basic ground of their existence and all existence.

Some time after the appearance of the mystery cults, the philosophical and religious phenomenon known as Gnosticism appears in the Greco-Roman world. It expresses severe disillusion with life in this world, as may be seen in various conflicting dualisms—spirit versus flesh, soul versus body, light versus darkness, life versus death, good versus evil, and God versus the world. In it we witness the effort to break out of the here and now to find salvation carried to exaggerated lengths. Where Gnosticism originated is not clear. It has been called Greek, Near Eastern, and Egyptian and its syncretic character shows elements of all these kinds. There was a Jewish Gnosticism which was considered heretical just as later there was a Christian Gnosticism which was considered heretical and combated vigorously as a dangerous heresy.

Gnosticism held the world in which man found himself, the world of matter and our daily existence, to be radically evil and man, or at least the spiritual element in him, to be imprisoned in it and in the body composed from its substance. Man is an alien here and is lost and out of touch with his original home, which was in the presence of a radically other-worldly God outside and beyond the world. He can find delivery from this predicament through a kind of secret knowledge (*gnosis*). This involves a knowledge of God and the divine realm, the nature of the transcendent world and the pathway leading to it. The reception of this saving knowledge is by means of learning esoteric doctrine and is often accompanied by a transforming experience of inner illumination. Thus is the spiritual element in man related to the hidden God and emancipated from its material and worldly prison. Moreover, the more intellectual forms of Gnosticism developed these doctrines in theoretical form, setting forth ideas concerning the nature of God, the universe, man's condition, and the way to salvation. Man's condition is one of radical and thorough alienation of his spirit from the world. His salvation is rescuing that spirit, promoting its escape, and allowing its return to the radically other-worldly God. Some Gnostic doctrines involved the notion of a divine agent sent to help man, an idea probably developed in imitation of Christianity. Christian Gnosticism saw Jesus in this role. The Christian Church was highly involved with and thoroughly challenged by the intrusion of Gnostic ideas and the Gnostic heresy came to comprise a dire threat to Christianity in the second century. Such Gnostic doctrines see the God of the Old Testament as an evil God related to or creator of this world, in opposition to the good God who is beyond this world. Saturninus of Antioch, for example, declared that Christ came to destroy the God of the Jews. Evidence of the conflict with Gnosticism can be found in such Christian writings as the New Testament books attributed to John, Colossians, and the Pastoral Epistles. There is also a large Christian literature of polemics against Gnostic ideas and practices, the most notable of which is *Against Heresies* by Irenaeus, a Church

Father of the late second century. We have also some Gnostic interpretations of Christianity, such as the Gospel of Thomas and the Gospel of Truth. This radical Gnostic dualism found two quite opposing interpretations of human behavior. Some Gnostics withdrew from the world and lived a disciplined life not indulging themselves in its pleasures or vices. For some, Gnosticism demanded asceticism. Others felt that since the flesh and the world were negative values, one could indulge oneself as much as one wished and it would not affect the spiritual reality of man's make-up. They felt sexual pleasure could be pursued without limit. Both groups, however, did not see the possibility of meaningful participation in the world's activities.

## THE UNDERSTANDING OF CHRIST: PAUL AND JOHN

The Christian Church that went out into this complex gentile world was one whose faith and hope were centered upon the figure of Jesus. A number of understandings and interpretations of Christ as the founding figure existed and eventually they were expressed in Christian writings—in the canonical New Testament and others. Paul presents us with what is probably the earliest extant statement of belief characteristic of that Church:

> *For I delivered to you as of first importance what I also received, that Christ died for our sins in accordance with the scriptures, that he was buried, that he was raised on the third day in accordance with the scriptures, and that he appeared to Cephas, then to the twelve. Then he appeared to more than five hundred brethren at one time, most of whom are still alive, though some have fallen asleep. Then he appeared to James, then to all the aspostles.*
>
> (1 Cor. 15:3–7)

Jesus was seen as the suffering servant of God who was "wounded for our transgressions" and "bruised for our iniquities" (Isa. 53:5). He had returned to the Father and was now "exalted at the right hand of God." He was the stone which the builders rejected that became the cornerstone (Acts 4:11; Ps. 118:22). Christian thinking would continue to ponder this figure, his meaning, and the implications of his career. He would be seen as

> *the image of the invisible God, the first-born of all creation; for in him all things were created, in heaven and on earth, visible and invisible, whether thrones or dominions, principalities or authorities—all things were created through him and for him. He is before all things, and in him all things hold together. He is the head of the body, the church; he is the beginning, the first-born from the dead, that in everything he might be preeminent. For in him all the fullness of God was pleased to dwell, and through him to reconcile to himself all things, whether on earth or in heaven, making peace by the blood of his cross.*
>
> (Col. 1:15–20)

We have seen that Christianity originated in Jewish apocalypticism and we know that the young Church expected an early return of

Jesus. But Jesus was seen to be more than was implied in the usual ideas of the Messiah. In him God had revealed himself in a special way to all men. The intellectual clarification of what the Church meant by Jesus as Christ and the character of his mission would be a cause of considerable conflict as time went on. The earliest contributions to this clarification (which is known as Christology) and the most basic are those found in the writings of Paul and the writings attributed to him and in the writings attributed to the apostle John.

Paul was a Jew who saw Jesus as the Messiah, but as more than the Messiah in the traditional sense. Paul was learned in Jewish thought and aware of the Judaic idea of the divine wisdom as present with God "at the first, before the beginning of the earth," as an entity which beside him "was there" when God "established the heavens" (Prov. 8:23, 27). He was also aware of Stoic ideas and the notion of God as divine reason. Paul, who is second to Jesus himself in his influence upon Christianity and its development, saw Jesus as a preexistent figure, "the power of God and the wisdom of God" (1 Cor. 2:24). Jesus was indeed the Davidic Messiah "according to the flesh," but he was "designated Son of God in power according to the Spirit of holiness by his resurrection from the dead" (Rom. 1:3 and 4). God is the creator of the universe; he is "our Father." Jesus, Paul calls "Lord" (*Kyrios*), the term Greek-speaking Jews had used for the Hebrew *Adonai* which was substituted for Yahweh in the reading of the Scriptures by Jews because pronunciation of the proper name of God had become taboo because of its sacred character. Jesus is a preexistent divine being who existed before the creation of the world, who had taken on human form and died for the sins of men, and who will return at the end of the world. Paul sees Jesus' death as a voluntary expiation of man's sins which reconciles God and man. The basis of man's relation to God and the condition of his reconciliation is faith. Paul also placed great emphasis upon man's justification—that man was "justified by God's grace as a gift, through the redemption which is in Christ Jesus, whom God put forward as an expiation by his blood to be received by faith" (Rom. 3:24–25). But he was no less insistent upon righteous conduct though salvation was not by works of the law. Paul concerns himself with the meaning of Jesus—his life, death, and resurrection—and approaches this meaning within the ideas of Judaism and its understanding of the relationship between man and God. For Paul the basic question is how man who is sinful and fallen can be reconciled with God and be counted as righteous in his eyes. In this context Paul deals with problems which will be central to Christian theology for centuries to come, problems of justification through good works versus justification by grace through Christ's death. In Christ, God gratuitously reconciled man to himself, not because man deserved it, but out of God's generosity. Man's way of acceptance was through faith. Man must believe in Jesus as the Christ—the Messiah and reconciler—and in the work of reconciliation which God has wrought through him. In this faith the believer begins to share in the new life which will be fulfilled after the Parousia, when Christ will come again. This enables him to walk in righteousness and to withstand suffering patiently. Yet in this context Paul makes much use of the imperative mode calling the Christians to live up to this new state.

Another important discussion of the meaning of Jesus for the Church is to be found in the Fourth Gospel. This book was written toward the end of the first or near the beginning of the second century. Here, as in the writing of Paul, Jesus is seen as a preexistent being closely associated with God's creativity. The Christian tradition long attributed this Gospel to the apostle John, the son of Zebedee and brother of James, who together with his brother and Peter are seen in the synoptics as specially close to Jesus. The Gospel contains references to "the disciple whom Jesus loved" (John 21:20) and identifies him as the author of the work. This was early thought to be the apostle John. Modern scholarship, however, considers such an authorship to be highly unlikely if not impossible.

In this work the words of Jesus are presented in discussions which are not like those of the Synoptic Gospels. The latter are collections of Jesus' sayings, the most famous being the Sermon on the Mount in Matthew's Gospel. In the Fourth Gospel a discourse develops each theme. Each discourse arises from some episode which symbolizes the theme presented in the discourse itself. The discourse has a kind of mystical character appealing to the religious intuition. Jesus moves through the Johannine Gospel as a sublime divine figure somewhat mysterious. We see this mode of presentation, for example, in the fourth chapter where Jesus asks the Samaritan woman for a drink of water. In the discussion that follows, Jesus makes statements that reveal his real identity and significance to the reader. "If you knew the gift of God, and who it is that is saying to you, 'Give me a drink,' you would have asked him and he would have given you living water" (John 4:10). In this Gospel Jesus' statements about himself are much different from those in the first three Gospels.

> *I have come in my Father's name.*
>
> (John 5:43)

> *My teaching is not mine but his who sent me; if any man's will is to do his will, he shall know whether the teaching is from God or whether I am speaking on my own authority.*
>
> (John 7:16–17)

> *I and the Father are one.*
>
> (John 10:30)

> *If any one serves me, he must follow me; and where I am, there shall my servant be also; if any one serves me, the Father will honor him.*
>
> (John 12:26)

> *I am the true vine, and my Father is the vinedresser. Every branch of mine that bears no fruit, he takes away, and every branch that does bear fruit he prunes, that it may bear more fruit.*
>
> (John 15:1 and 2)

*He who abides in me, and I in him, he it is that bears much fruit, for apart from me you can do nothing.*

(John 15:5)

*As the Father has loved me, so have I loved you; abide in my love. If you keep my commandments, you will abide in my love, just as I have kept my Father's commandments and abide in his love.*

(John 15:10)

*The Father himself loves you, because you have loved me and have believed that I came from the Father.*

(John 16:27)

*I glorified thee on earth, having accomplished the work which thou gavest me to do; and now, Father, glorify thou me in thine own presence with the glory which I had with thee before the world was made.*

(John 17:4–5)

Such are the sayings of Jesus in this Gospel. Jesus speaks of his union with God and of the mystical life man can have in union with him. He calls to a life which is not of "this world." "I chose you out of the world" (John 15:19). Moreover, in this Gospel Jesus is often spoken of as glorified or as manifesting his glory, a tendency found in far less striking manner in the synoptics. In fact here he is described as "making himself equal with God" (John 5:18).

The Fourth Gospel is a product of a later time in the history of the new Church. There had been somewhat of a waning of eschatological expectations and a consequent need to emphasize and develop a present relation to God in Christ. The Church at this time was also developing as an institution with its own needs, among which is an understanding of the meaning of Jesus under these new conditions. Moreover, the portrayal of the relationship between Jesus and the Jews reflects the later time the Gospel was written, a time in which, following the destruction of the Temple by the Romans, the Jewish Council at Jamnia, and continued separate Christian existence, increased hostility between Christians and Jews is evident.

Perhaps nowhere is the theology of the Fourth Gospel so succinctly stated and stated as a whole as in the opening or so-called prologue to the work. In it Jesus is called the "Word" (Greek, *Logos,* "Wisdom" or "Reason"). The term was a long-standing one in Greek philosophy going back to Heracleitus. Philo of Alexandria (20 B.C.–A.D. 50), a devout Jew learned in Greek thought, and Plato in particular, had used the term to designate the divine intermediary between God and the world, the divine reason which was the instrument of God's creativity. It is also found in Gnostic sources. But in the Johannine work the Divine Word or *Logos* takes on human nature and lives among men. Reminiscent of the opening of Genesis, the Fourth Gospel starts from the "beginning."

> *In the beginning was the Word, and the Word was with God, and the Word was God. He was in the beginning with God.*
>
> (John 1:1–2)

Thus is Jesus presented as the preexistent divine reason. He then is seen as the source of God's creative action:

> *All things were made through him, and without him was not anything made that was made.*
>
> (John 1:3)

The text now introduces those words so laden with religious meaning for the mystical tradition—life and light—both of which Jesus as *Logos* brings to men:

> *In him was life, and the life was the light of men. The light shines in the darkness, and the darkness has not overcome it . . . The true light that enlightens every man was coming into the world.*
>
> (John 1:5 and 9)

The Fourth Gospel sees the role of Jesus as enlightening men with the divine life which he communicates to men. It then summarizes his earthly career:

> *He was in the world, and the world was made through him, yet the world knew him not. He came to his own home and his own people received him not.*
>
> (John 1:10–11)

Both the other-worldliness of Jesus' followers and their separation from the Jews is now emphasized. But this is background for the enlightening and almost divinizing mission with which the prologue is concerned.

> *But to all who received him, who believed in his name, he gave power to become children of God; who were born, not of blood nor of the will of the flesh nor of the will of man, but of God.*
>
> (John 1:12–13)

Unlike Gnostic other-worldliness, however, the Fourth Gospel does not reject the flesh but rather sees Jesus' human condition as the medium through which is manifested his divine origin and character, and his gifts given to men.

> *And the Word became flesh and dwelt among us, full of grace and truth; and we beheld his glory, glory as of the only Son from the Father . . . And from his fulness have we all received grace upon grace. For the law was given through Moses; grace and truth came through Jesus Christ.*
>
> (John 1:14, 16–17)

The Fourth Gospel is concerned with Christology and in his discourses in this Gospel Jesus talks about Christology. We are given an explanation of the character and role of Jesus as Christ which Christians at the time could feel appropriate to their own feelings of his significance, glory, and power—and the relationship to him in which they were sustained by the spiritual food and drink he gave and by his light in which they walked. When in the fourth and fifth centuries the Church would be concerned with credal formulas, it would find important sources here.

## THE MAKING OF THE INSTITUTIONAL CHURCH

By the end of the first century the Christian Church had communities (or churches) in many places throughout the Mediterranean world. These groups did not enjoy full legality and Christianity was not granted the status of a licit religion under Roman law. Indeed this first century saw the churches persecuted. There was the violent turning against Christians in Rome under Nero in A.D. 64 which cost the lives of Peter and Paul, making that city the memorial city of the two great apostles. The persecution under Domitian followed in 95. The new religion, however, saw a rapid and wide expansion in the second century, following the trade routes of the empire. From Mesopotamia to the southern coast of Britain, on the Rhone and the Rhine, along the eastern shores of the Adriatic, and in North Africa into Egypt, Christian groups were to be found. At the same time the Church continued to grow in its older locations of Greece, Syria, Italy, and Asia Minor. This growth was basically an urban phenomenon, as the country districts remained traditionally pagan. In this century sporadic persecutions continued under the otherwise greatly admired Antonine emperors, Antoninus Pius and Marcus Aurelius, but it was not until Decius' reign in the third century (250–259) that systematic and thorough persecution got under way.

The second century was a most significant one in Christian history. It was the time when the Church put order into its beliefs and into its internal organization. Was Christianity to remain a Jewish sect or was it to become a universal religion addressing its message to the gentiles? We have seen that not without considerable conflict, the Church decided for the latter course. The second century presented four major issues of decision to the new religious movement which would eventually provide the basic direction of the Church in the entire later period of its history. Each of these fundamental challenges is a complex story in itself and many of the important details have been lost. We shall present here merely summary statements of the issues and their outcomes. It must also be remembered that human movements, religious or otherwise, do not face such questions in the abstract form in which we discuss them. Such movements are involved and embedded in specific historical circumstances and meet the problems as they arise concretely in different concrete settings, a process that is often gradual, confused, and even marked by contradictions.

The first of these major issues with which we shall deal is the failure of the Parousia, or second coming of the Risen Lord. We noted that Christianity began as a messianic and apocalyptic movement and that the first Christians expected the return of Jesus and the beginning of the new age of the world in their own lifetimes. In the writings of Paul and those attributed to him we note a movement from imminent expectation to an acceptance of postponement. At times the Synoptic Gospels give the impression that the Parousia is imminent, but like the Pauline writings they affirm that no man knows the time of the Lord's coming. The Fourth Gospel, which is the latest gospel, is hardly to be characterized as eschatological. In that work Jesus's glorification is already a fact and the believer is to share in it. The terms used, such as judgment, life, and and resurrection, do not carry the vivid apocalyptic connotations to be found in the Synoptics. In the Fourth Gospel we find the kind of present, here-and-now relationship to the Risen Christ which will more and more replace eschatological expectations as the core of the Christian religious relationship to God and the basic orientation of Christian devotion.

The post-Apostolic church contained a number of different ways of expressing the faith and hope of the Christians. Alongside the expectations of the Parousia there were also elements of an important present religious relationship. This is seen particularly in the Eucharistic worship in which a here-and-now relationship with the Risen Christ as well as an expression of the hope in his second coming was constitutive of the rite from the beginning. This meant for the earliest Church a close and intimate participation in the life of the Lord. In this rite Christ united himself with his followers. Also alongside the hope of an imminent second coming there were Christian hopes formulated in terms of the Greek ideas of the immortality of the soul, ideas which also quite possibly affected the Jews of the diaspora. Thus Christian fulfillment seemed to be expressible in two idioms—the Jewish one of Parousia and resurrection of the body, and the Greek one of immortality and life with Christ in another world after death. In fact we see both of these conceptions in the Pauline literature. Moreover, important as the expectations of the Parousia were in the early Church, they did not rule out vigorous missionary work in the present.

Thus in the Church of the first and early second century there appear to be temporal dynamic apocalyptic conceptions along with static ontological ideas of a present relationship to God through Christ. There appear to be ideas of a passing of the old world-age and the inauguration of the new one with Christ's appearance, and also ideas pointing to the significant division between life in this world and the life in the next, between the earthly and the heavenly life as most important. In the earlier period the Church as a whole seemed to give the dominant and presiding position to the dynamic eschatological ideas and orientations and to have fitted the others into their general context. In the later period the ontological ideas with their conception of a present relationship to the Risen Christ and a heavenly reward after death were given dominance and eschatology remained but was generally subsidiary to them. The change was one of enormous significance and the details of transformation are to be obtained only through the fragile and hypothetical reconstructions of scholarship.

When Christianity came into the gentile world in which the learned strata partook to one extent or another in Greek culture, it necessitated that the adherents of the new religion take this culture into account. The historic problem facing the new Church may be stated in this way: What of the wisdom of the gentiles? We have noted earlier that Philo, the Jewish philosopher, had sought to reconcile Plato and Moses. What would the Christian Church do?

The Church not only offered a sense of salvation to its converts, it also offered a definition of man and his world, and this definition of the meaning of man found itself in competition with the philosophy of the Greeks. Moreover, this competition existed in an atmosphere of official and unofficial hostility. In response to this situation there arose in the second century a group of Christian writers known as the Apologists. The term is used in its classical sense, to designate those who present and defend a doctrine or point of view. There were Apologies written by Aristides, Justin, Tatian, Athenagoras, Clement of Alexandria, Tertullian, and others. These men attempted to defend the faith and to show its superiority to Greek philosophy. In so doing they made use of Greek ideas and helped to introduce a Greek philosophical idiom into Christian theology. For example Justin Martyr, who was put to death in Rome in 165, speaks of the "Word" (*Logos*) as do other Apologists, and of "God who begat him" and sees the Word as "Teacher . . . the Son and Apostle of God the Father and Master of all, that is Jesus Christ, from whom we have received the name of Christians" (*Apology* 1.12). He sees this *Logos* always at work in the world teaching Greeks such as Socrates and Heracleitus and Jews such as Abraham and Elijah and so he finds all those that "lived by Reason" to be in some way Christians (*Apology* 1.46). The life of the historic Jesus is little stressed by Justin except as the great instance of the incarnation of the *Logos* and the occasion for the revelation of true philosophy. Writing to influence Greeks toward tolerance for the Church, Justin and the Apologists stressed similarities between Christianity and Greek thought and presented the former as a fuller version of what was present in less perfect form in the latter. Yet religion is not reduced to philosophy and Justin does speak of the passion and crucifixion of Christ which he suffered "cleansing by his blood those who believe on him" and also saying that "men of every nation will look forward to his coming again" (*Apology* 1.32).

The problem of how the new Church should react to Greek thought was however a matter of conflict. In Justin we see a positive approach to the question. "Whatever has been uttered aright by any men in any place belongs to us Christians; for, next to God, we worship and love the Word which is from the unbegotten and ineffable God; since on our account he has been made man, that, being made partaker of our sufferings, he may also bring us healing" (*Apology* 11.13). We find a similar attitude at the end of the century in the writings of Clement of Alexandria, who saw philosophy as "necessary to the Greeks for righteousness, until the coming of the Lord," and after that as assisting "toward true religion as a kind of preparatory training for those who arrive at faith by way of demonstration" (*Stromateis* 1.5.28). Yet this point of view met significant opposition as we see in the writings of no less a figure than Tertullian, who found his pagan analogies in Roman law rather than Greek philosophy. "What is there in common between Athens and Jerusalem? What between the Academy and the Church? What between heretics and Christians? . . . Away with all projects for a 'Stoic,' a 'Platonic' or a 'dialectic' Christianity" (*De praescriptione haereticorum* 7). The mode of relationship started by the Apologists persisted and the Church proceeded later to construct its theology on the basis of the Greek philosophical heritage and using the Greek philosophical language.

The historical process of bringing into contact philosophical ideas and the primitive Christian tradition was a chronic condition characteristic of the position of Christianity in the second century and reached an acute stage in the relations between Christianity and Gnosticism. Gnosticism appealed to many of the best minds in the early Church and at the height of its influence in the middle decades of the century threatened to infuse and change the beliefs of Christianity in a thoroughly substantial manner. At this time the Church was weakly organized; its beliefs were still largely undefined though they made up a common but differentiated tradition. We have already seen some of the resemblances between Christian and Gnostic ideas. These similarities made it easy for Gnostic meanings to penetrate the faith. Then Christ was seen as the emissary of the good but hidden God sent to rescue men of spiritual character by revealing secret knowledge. While Paul was certainly not a Gnostic, the Gnostics were able to use much in his teaching, as for example his idea of "a secret and hidden wisdom of God" (1 Cor. 2:7). The God who is the creator of the world was seen as an evil deity or at best an inferior demiurge. It was held in accordance with Gnostic dualism that Christ did not really become man, did not really assume human nature, but only maintained the appearance of so doing—a heresy designated as Docetism. Perhaps the most important figure here was Marcion, a man from Asia Minor converted to Christianity in Rome. Under the influence of a Roman Gnostic, Cerdo, Marcion began to develop a Gnostic Christianity. He was excommunicated from the Roman Church in 144. He then set up a separate church of his own, compiled a canon of Christian literature in which he accepted only the Gospel of Luke and ten Pauline epistles which he edited to meet his own Gnostic standards.

Much of ordinary Christian life in this century had become legalistic as people sought to work out practical everyday ways of living by their faith. From the Apologists and other Christian writings such as the *Didache* or *Teaching of the Twelve Apostles,* a church manual, the writings of Hermas, and the writings of early bishops known as the Apostolic Fathers, we get some idea of ordinary life in the Church. It was both ascetic and marked by a certain legalism. Wednesdays and Fridays were days of fasting. Prayer and almsgiving were held in high regard. Satisfaction as well as repentance was necessary for the forgiveness of sins. Marcion established his new church in part as a protest against the growing legalism in the Church.

Despite superficial similarities to Christianity, Gnosticism was

Christianity's most dangerous enemy and threatened to distort and transform the meaning of its faith from within. The result was a general Christian counterresponse in which the Christian intellectual leadership took up the fight to defend the faith from what was seen as a demonic subversion. The Church indeed responded in two spheres, in that of doctrine and that of organization. In response to Marcion the canon of the New Testament was established as we have already seen. Moreover, a formal credal statement was developed which became known as "The Apostles' Creed," an attempt to state in formal language the content and import of the Christian faith. The earliest confessions of faith which were used when converts were baptized were simple and consisted chiefly in declaring Jesus to be Lord. But now more detailed statements were developed, though not as detailed as they would become later. At the end of the second and the beginning of the third century the baptismal candidate in Rome was asked three questions.

> *Do you believe in God the Father Almighty?*
>
> *Do you believe in Jesus Christ the Son of God, who was born of the Holy Spirit and the Virgin Mary, who was crucified under Pontius Pilate and died, and rose the third day living from the dead, and ascended into heaven, and sat down at the right hand of the Father, and will come to judge the living and the dead?*
>
> *Do you believe in the Holy Spirit, and the Holy Church, and the resurrection of the flesh?*
>
> (Hippolytus, *Apostolic Tradition,* 21.12 ff.)

In the sphere of organization the response to Gnosticism was a development of the ecclesiastical institution. The Christian truth was seen to reside in the Church and the core of Church organization was the office of the bishop. Earlier the local churches were presided over by a council or group and this collegial leadership constituted what was later known as the clergy. This form of leadership began early to give way to a single ruling figure, the bishop, probably because collegial leadership is always unstable and tends to give rise to a one-man form. But this process was hastened considerably by the crisis in the inner life of the Church which Gnosticism had brought about. Christian faith came to be seen as entrusted to "those who, together with the succession of the episcopate, have received the certain gift of truth" (Irenaeus, *Against Heresies,* 4.26.2). The true faith was that of the apostles which is "preached to men, which has come down to us through the successions of bishops." Moreover, the Roman Church, indicative of much that was to come, was being accorded a certain strategic position in this transmission of the apostolic faith. It is that faith which is to be seen in "the tradition and creed of the greatest, the most ancient church, the church known to all men, which was founded and set up in Rome by the two most glorious apostles, Peter and Paul" (Irenaeus, *Against Heresies,* 3.1).

The second century and the struggle against Gnosticism saw the development in the Church of what we might call "Catholic consciousness" and "Catholic organization." What had emerged was an ecclesiastical structure and an institutional point of view. This was in part no doubt necessary and would have come about under any circumstance, for if Christianity did not define its basic ideas and achieve some kind of uniformity with respect to them it probably would not have survived, at least not as the significant cultural force that it became. In fact we see the beginnings of these developments before the Gnostic crisis. What was emerging was the "Catholic" Church. The word was first used in a letter from Ignatius to the church at Smyrna, written around the year 112, in which he also points to the significant position of the bishop (Ignatius, *Epistle to the Smyrnaeans,* 100.8). It is found again in another letter written around 156 by the church at Smyrna concerning the martyrdom of their bishop, Polycarp, which refers to "the whole Catholic Church throughout the world" (*Martyrium Polycarpi* 8). Between 160 and 190 the Church developed marked Catholic characteristics. The older situation of local churches was replaced by a greater degree of union, the older collegial leadership gave way to the monarchical episcopate, the older charismatic freedom was giving way to defined doctrine, the clergy were emerging as a leading and indeed an intellectual stratum in the Church, and the laity were entering a kind of status of religious tutelage. The Church based itself on what it called an apostolic succession of office and teaching. The Church repelled the Gnostic danger, but it changed itself considerably in the process. Yet it must be recognized that the necessity for objective intellectual and organizational points of reference for Christian life and thought—a requisite for Christian survival—would have demanded changes in the general direction in which they actually occurred. We may well suspect, however, that the depth and seriousness of the crisis gave these developments an exaggerated form. In this struggle we see the rise of a church characterized by explicitly defined doctrine, integrated organization, and law. The end of the second century saw one Catholic Church throughout the expanse of the empire and around it a number of sects calling themselves Christian as well but considered heretical and enemies of the faith by the Catholic Church itself. The beginning of the third century saw the emergence of the Church in the basic form which it maintained until the Reformation and which the Eastern Orthodox and Roman Catholic churches maintain to this day. Later developments were important but they were built upon the foundation already present by the year A.D. 200. In the following century these features were strengthened. The authority of the bishops was enhanced and the spontaneous character of church life—the "gifts of the spirit" characteristic of the first century—tended to become memory and a tradition, and such charismatic gifts became possessions endowed by clerical status. By the year 250 Cyprian of Carthage (who was martyred in 258) could say that the Church was based upon the unity of the bishops (Cyprian, *Letters,* 66–68.8). By now the word "clergy" (*kleros*), first found in a document of the year 95 (1 Clem. 93–97), designated a separate and superior order of men, while the word "laity" (*laikos*), used once in the New Testament in an un-

*Third-century synagogue on the shore of the Sea of Galilee at Capernaum. It marks the site of an older synagogue in which Jesus preached. (Courtesy of the Israel Government Tourist Office.)*

technical sense (1 Pet. 5:3) to designate those ministered unto, became the designation for the mass of the people. Many of these latter were by that time ignorant converts from paganism or "cradle Christians" born into the Church and lacking the enthusiasm of earlier generations, making for the coexistence within the Church of a kind of naiveté and a kind of worldliness. The bishops, who lead the services of worship and were increasingly seen as a priesthood, were the guardians of orthodoxy, and defined what was heresy. They were disciplinary officers as well. The lower clergy were their assistants. Hence in the last part of the third century the clergy had emerged into the status of teachers, rulers, and celebrants of worship possessing graces and gifts not available to the mass of believers. Admission to the clerical estate was, by ordination, a rite which went back to the earliest days of the Church as a mode of setting men aside for special duties, showing the early roots of these later developments. The election of bishops was still ratified by the total congregation, however, a practice that in time would disappear.

This tendency toward a loss of former spontaneity and the growing importance of structure led to protest within the Church. In fact the concept of protest is one of major significance in understanding the development of a religious movement. As such a movement becomes a stable institution, which it must do if it is to survive, there develops in response currents of antagonism and revolt against the loss of formerly prized characteristics of the group. And when the institutionalization process is advanced, completed, and even carried to excess and tends to stifle a living spontaneity, we see such protest asserting itself again. The great historical example of protest and of the protest of the latter type is to be seen in the Protestant Reformation of the sixteenth century. We have already noted that protest of the former kind increased the appeal of Gnosticism and strengthened that religious tendency. The second century saw another example of such protest rise up to challenge the Catholic Church and its ecclesiastical development. All such revolts come into existence in concrete historical circumstances and are affected by the ideas available in the tradition. They see the spirit tending to be smothered by form and they try to reassert what they see as its former vigor. Moreover, both in the second and the sixteenth centuries, revolt was at the same time a reaction to an increasing worldliness in the church.

We have seen that the early Church considered Christ divine and as such worshiped him with the Father. By the beginning of the second century, Christian thought had differentiated the Holy Spirit from Christ and had seen it as preexistent with Father and Son. This is seen in the Trinitarian baptismal formula to be found in Matthew's Gospel. There developed in the second century the idea that the Holy Spirit would come and bring a more abundant spiritual fulfillment. Thus the failure of the Parousia to come about and the fading of the earlier spontaneity in the Church which had been seen as the gift of the Holy Spirit gave rise to a hope in a new outpouring of the spirit. This would be the end of the old world-age and the beginning of a new one. This hope was expressed in Montanism. Around the year 156 Montanus announced himself to be the passive instrument through which the Holy Spirit was revealing himself. Thus the promise of Christ ("But when the Counselor comes, whom I shall send to you from the Father, even the Spirit of truth, who proceeds from the Father, he will bear witness to me" *[John 15:26]*) was being fulfilled, and the new age, the age of the Holy Spirit, was here. The end of the world was seen as imminent and the Montanists advocated that all should go to Phrygia, whence Montanus had come and where ecstatic religion was popular, for there the new age would soon commence in all its fullness. An arduous ascetic discipline was advocated including celibacy, fasting, and abstinence from meat. The movement achieved genuine popularity and the bishops of Asia Minor called the first synods of bishops in church history to combat it in the seventh decade of the second century. The Montanist doctrines were found in Rome around the year 170 and remained for some time a source of inner conflict in the Roman Church. Around the year 200 the great African apologist and Latin father, Tertullian, became a Montanist. Although the Church overcame this threat, Montanism was but the first example in the new Catholic Church of protest against formalism and worldliness assuming a radical apocalyptic stance combined with an ecstatic religious attitude and a highly puritanical moral orientation. In it we see a precursor of the more radical groups of the Reformation. Indeed, did not Tertullian anticipate at that time Luther's reassertion of the priesthood of believers—"Are not even we laics priests?"

## THE RISE OF MONASTICISM

If protest is a universal category of religious history, monasticism is one of its classic expressions. Monasticism involves the founding of separate and special ascetic communities, a phenomenon found not only in Christianity but in Judaism and in nonbiblical religions in many parts of the world as well. Monasticism is indeed a protest movement expressing withdrawal from or rejection of the world and of the Church which compromises with the world, with its sinfulness and halfheartedness. But monasticism is also more than protest. It represents the attempt to live in harmony with the highest and strictest ideals of a religious tradition, to assert those ideals, and to form an ideal community of believers. Already in the early Church before the beginning of monasticism there was considerable emphasis upon asceticism and avoidance of the temptations and dangers to the life of the spirit to be encountered in the world. In contrast to the developing worldliness and the consequent compromise of worldly Church members—conditions which were no doubt favored by the fading of apocalyptic hopes, the rejection of Montanism, and the increasing importance of form and structure—there were large numbers who sought to live according to a stricter interpretation of what they considered the counsels of the Gospels. "If you will be perfect, go, sell what you possess and give to the poor, and you will have treasure in heaven; and come, follow me" (Matt. 19:21). The same Gospel represents Jesus as saying, "there are eunuchs who have made themselves eunuchs for the sake of the kingdom of heaven" (Matt. 19:12). Moreover, superior pagan spirits also looked upon the world as morally questionable, advocated a restrained and austere life, and saw human fulfillment in contemplation rather than in action. This last idea was taken over by the Christians. The second century looked upon a life of voluntary poverty, celibacy, and contemplation as the Christian ideal and there were many who practiced it within the Church, without, however, separating themselves from the general community.

This situation gave rise to a kind of double standard. There were those who attempted to do the maximum in terms of the Christian ideal and there were others of whom this ideal could not be expected. A compromise with the world was inherent in the new existence of the Church as an established religious institution. As part of such a compromise, the Church evolved a higher and a lower morality. This expression of the more rigorous ideal led men into the desert as hermits where they led lives of extreme self-denial and even self-torture. The most important of these was Anthony (251?–356), an Egyptian who first took up the ascetic life in his native village but soon went into the wilderness. Many imitated him and the deserts were soon the scene of men alone or in small groups seeking extreme and zealous expression of their religious ideal. Much attention has been given to the demon-haunted life of Anthony and the inhuman austerities to which he subjected himself, but they were the gross expressions of an ideal of renunciation and of developing the power of the human will to follow an ideal. This hermit life was changed into a community, or cenobitic, form by Pachomius (292–346), who established the first Christian monastery at Tabenna on the Nile between 315 and 320 and a convent for women somewhat later. At one time he is said to have had seven thousand men and women living under his rule in a number of congregations. The rule he established called for a community of men or women involved in worship and work on a regular schedule, wearing similar dress, living in cells close together under the presiding governance of a paternal or maternal superior, an abbot or an abbess. Indeed a traveler to Egypt around the end of the fourth century felt there must be as many people in the desert as in the cities. Pachomius' monastic idea gained considerable following and it was reformed by Basil (330–379), who worked for its propagation from about the year 360 on. Basil's monastic rule is the basic constitution of monasticism in the Eastern Orthodox Churches to this day.

Monasticism was brought to the West by Athanasius, archbishop of Alexandria, and a friend of Anthony's. It was first looked upon with considerable suspicion although it met the approval of such great Latin Fathers as Ambrose, Augustine, and Jerome (a monk and the translator of the Bible into Latin). Western monasticism was disorganized until around 529 when Benedict of Nursia established the monastic rule since known as Benedictine and established his community at Monte Cassino, about halfway between Rome and Naples. Benedict built his way of life around worship and work. Worship took up four hours of each twenty-four-hour day. Work was both mental and manual, for it was concerned with intellectual as well as agricultural endeavors. Thus the Benedictines became important transmitters of culture. Moreover, their emphasis upon worship made their monasteries centers for the development of liturgy and for the development of the Christian culture of the early Middle Ages in which liturgy was a central element. Their concern for work made them pioneers in agricultural development and they made tremendous contributions to the progress of European agriculture in the early Middle Ages. But most significant was their missionary work, for Monte Cassino was a veritable schoolmaster of Europe and from it and its sister monasteries missionaries went to the North to bring Christianity to Teutonic and Celtic peoples. When the fall of the civilization of antiquity (from the late fifth century onward) brought retrogressive political and social conditions to the Empire, the disorder and misery of the age magnified the attractiveness of the monastic life and further exaggerated the contrast between the ordinary and higher morality which we have seen beginning in the second century. From the beginning, monasticism attracted the best people in the Church, and after the foundation of the famous Benedictine monastery at Cluny in eastern France in 910, and particularly in the eleventh and twelfth centuries, this was even more the case. Out of Cluny came a great reform movement to purify the Church which was bogged down and almost overcome by all the evils of that gross and violent age between the fall of the Empire and the rise of the civilization of the High Middle Ages. This movement known as the "cluniac reformation" fought simony, advocated clerical celibacy, and held before the world the monastic interpretation of the gospel ideal. It culminated in the election of the cluniac monk Hildebrand to the chair of the bishop of Rome, now long since the central, presiding, and ruling bishopric of the entire Church, but particularly of the West, since the East long contested Rome's claims. As Gregory VII (1073–1086), this reforming Pope became the outstanding figure of the time, journeying throughout much of Western Christendom, purifying the Church, and struggling against the political domination of the Church by the Christian emperor.

In contrast to Benedictine monasticism and its moderate ascetic ideal there arose in Ireland a recrudescence of the stricter Egyptian monasticism which flourished from the fifth to the seventh centuries in the Celtic British Isles. It combined ascetic rigor of an extreme sort with the most arduous missionary work in the British Isles themselves and on the continent. The Celtic Church was in fact organized around monasteries rather than the bishops, and their episcopal sees and Celtic monasticism adapted itself to the Celtic clan system so that monasteries were also clan organizations and abbots were hereditary offices. Irish monks played a strategic part in the conversion of Northern Europe, but in the later consolidation of the Church there the moderate and well-organized Benedictines proved superior. The practice of private confession had developed among the monks of both the East and West and the Irish missionaries of the sixth and seventh century introduced the practice to the laity as a whole, and with it a penitential literature which had flourished in Ireland. This practice replaced an earlier public confession of the community and became throughout the Middle Ages a long training school in introspection and self-examination for the individual Christian, a training school without which Martin Luther and his profound interior religious problems in the sixteenth century would hardly have been possible.

Monasticism gave an outlet to Christian ideals in the new ages into which the Church's existence was prolonged and offered a life of heroic piety and liturgical participation. It made possible some kind of realization of the ideal Christian community presented in the Book of Acts. As the gifts of the spirit were now attached to the charisma of office in the clerical order, so life according to the gospel ideal was now to be found in the institutionalized monastic form. The distinction between clergy and laity, a distinction of function, became a difference of religious worth and dignity. With monasticism there arose a new distinction—between people formally seen as "religious" and people living in the world. At first monasticism was a lay movement and indeed one with antiecclesiastical potentialities. But the rules of Basil and Benedict domesticated monasticism, so to speak, and brought it not only within the Church, but in the West especially put its huge religious energies at the Church's service. With the concentration on worship in Benedict's rule and the central position given to liturgy, monks soon became clerics or at least something closely akin to clerics. A third division had arisen in the church—between religious and nonreligious. When, in 1140 at Bologna where Roman law was again being studied, Gratianus, the great canonist and monk, collected his concordance of Church law and attempted to put order into it, he recorded a canon (which he says was authored by Jerome) which states that there are two genera of Christians—the first comprised of those dedicated to worship, the clergy, and those seeking the improvement of their lives

*Late twelfth-century enameled cross with five scenes from the Old Testament, attributed to Godefroid de Claire.* (*Courtesy of the British Museum.*)

according to Christian counsels, the monks; the second made up of lay people who live in the world and are compromised by it. And when Pope Honorius II in that same century confirmed the establishment of a new monastic order, the Premonstratentions, he declared, "From her beginning the Church has offered two kinds of life to her children: one to help the insufficiency of the weak, another to perfect the goodness of the strong." Hugh of St. Victor (d. 1141), a monk, a Christian Platonist, and by his own admission a man who loved all forms of learning sacred and profane, represented the

Church as two peoples—one following the pope made up of clerics and monks, the other following the emperor made up of princes, nobles, knights, and ordinary men and women, a representation that became more frequent in the fifteenth and sixteenth centuries.

## THE CHRISTIAN TRADITION

By the fourth and fifth centuries the traditions of Christianity had assumed the major forms which would characterize them for many centuries to come. First there were the scriptures of the Old and New Testaments, the basic sources of Christian thought and piety for all time. With the growing acceptance of revelation as finished and closed, the importance of these was enhanced. There was also (visible in the New Testament and in the formulation of creeds) the development of Trinitarian ideas which became the distinctive core of Christian theology. There were the efforts to relate Christian thinking and Christian life to the ideas and ideals of the higher secular culture, and to meet the intellectual challenge of sophisticated secular learning. Visible and central also were the ecclesiastical and institutional traditions, already expressed in the writings of the Apostolic Fathers and embodied in the Church seen as the safeguard and transmitter of the deposit of faith and the traditions of the fathers, a church speaking with the authority of the Holy Spirit, judging orthodoxy and proper morality, and disciplining its followers, at times to the point of excommunication. The Church of Rome, early the largest and most esteemed of the churches, rose to a position of leading influence, then to a primacy of honor, and finally to the Pope as a bishop of bishops and a ruler of the Western Church —a trend which despite opposition and reversals continued in Catholicism in the nineteenth century when the First Vatican Council defined the Pope as infallible when he speaks on matters of "faith or morals." Along with this development are the traditions of opposition to papal dominance, first in North Africa and later in the East, opposition which eventuates in a final rejection of papal claims by the Eastern Church and in rebellion against them by large numbers in the West at the time of the Reformation.

By the fourth and fifth centuries the Christian tradition of worship and prayer and the here-and-now relationship to God through Christ which flowers in later liturgical and mystical developments were well established. The cultivation of Christian feeling in connection with the Mass and the Divine Office, and the development of Christian mysticism, represents a profound deepening of the spirituality of Western man and his relation to God. Well established also was the tradition of asceticism—of self-denial, of an other-worldly orientation and a high estimation of virginity for men and women, of fasting and abstinence. Such ascetism is seen as part of the development of the Christian person, both as penance and reparation for past sins and as training in self-control in accordance with higher demands necessary for the achievement of "perfection." This emphasis often enough resulted in an extreme other-worldliness to the neglect of legitimate worldly demands and values, and a dark suspicion of sexuality which exaggerated and exacerbated the problems

*Mont-Saint-Michel, a town and abbey built on a huge rock off the coast of France. Crowned in prehistoric times by a Celtic temple, the island was fortified during the Hundred Years' War. Portions of the monastery date from the ninth century. (Photo by Engelhard, from Monkmeyer Press Photo Service.)*

of spirit and flesh throughout Christian history. Such extremes appear to have been conditioned by the lamentable moral and even physical conditions of sexuality in late antiquity and by the extremes of the reactions of the Gnostic groups as seen in their dualistic ideas and in both their asceticism and licentiousness. It was soon to be seen (with the early hermits and the first monks) to what extremes self-denial and asceticism could be carried. In the reaction of the institutionalized Church we see the beginnings of the tradition of official moderation and suspicion of extremes long characteristic of the Church in these matters.

Visible as well were the traditions of protest asserting freedom in the face of constraint and spontaneity in the face of form, as will be seen still alive in the medieval sects such as the Cathari and the Waldensians and later in the new churches of the Reformation. This tradition of protest was visible in two forms of expression—one in the groups which leave the great Church and pursue independently their own understanding of the Christian calling, and those who remain within as religious orders and are reconciled to the life of the great Church but find for themselves a special, separate, and often reforming status within. Noticeable also was the marked split between men of religion and men of the world which will long remain characteristic of the Western world and which even the best efforts of the Reformation will not overcome.

Finally we see the apocalyptic tradition out of which the Church came still rising to the surface. Men continued to expect a second advent or an age of the Holy Spirit and to find in the catastrophes of each age the propadeutic and initiating conditions of the coming of the New Jerusalem, a tradition ever driven underground and ever rising again. Chiliastic phenomena remained characteristic of Christian history from Montanist expectations in Phrygia in the second century to Millerite hopes in New York State in the nineteenth. So did the attempts to construct an ideal Christian community from Benedict's rule in 529 in Southern Italy to Joseph Smith's efforts in Kirtland, Ohio, in the 1830s. The expectation of an age of the Spirit was a real force in the Joachimite movement in the Middle Ages which saw it as an "age of monks" which was imminently expected. It remained important for the more radical groups in the Reformation. These traditions would be expanded, developed, and cast in novel forms of expression, but by fourth and fifth Christian centuries they were already present and already recognizable. From the religious life—the efforts, the sufferings, the hopes, and the disappointments—of these first centuries there had come into existence that religious and cultural phenomenon which we call Christianity.

# SECOND EXILE: ISRAEL RECONSTITUTES ITSELF

The bitter and harsh defeat of the Jewish rebellion in A.D. 70 left the population of Judea despoiled and depressed. Once again the nation had failed to achieve independence, the Temple lay in ashes, and the people of Yahweh were subjugated to the rule of a pagan power. Reminiscent of the destruction of 586 B.C., a crisis of order and meaning arose. And again reminiscent of the first destruction, this crisis, the situation of disillusionment and chaos, was overcome through a communal reaffirmation of religious faith and a reconstruction of the religious foundations of the community.

Jewish legend attributes the rescue of the community from total crisis to Rabbi Yohanan ben Zakkai. According to the legend, Yohanan, recognizing that defeat was inevitable, had himself smuggled out of Jerusalem in a coffin during the final stages of the battle. Carried to Vespasian, he pleaded and received permission from the Roman commander to found an academy at Jamnia. Whatever the historical accuracy of the legend, this academy of rabbis maintained stability and self-government after the defeat and exercised decisive leadership in reconstituting the Jewish people. The disastrous results of military efforts seemed to vindicate the more moderate nonactivist position of the Pharisaic party. That party now came to rule. Its leading rabbis, gathered at Jamnia, declared what was binding upon the community in all areas of activity. The Jewish people, with the experience of the first reconstruction behind them, accepted both the rule of the rabbis and the traditional explanation of this latest disaster which had come upon them. This is revealed in the following Apocryphal quotes:

> *Righteousness belongs to the Lord our God, but confusion of face to us and our fathers, as at this day. All these calamities with which the Lord threatened us have come upon us . . . for the Lord is righteous in all his works which he has commanded us to do.*
>
> (Bar. 2:6, 8)

> *Why is it Israel that you are in the lands of your enemies? . . . You have forsaken the fountain of wisdom. If you had walked in the way of God you would be dwelling in peace forever.*
>
> (Bar. 3:10, 13)

The ideas and institutions which emerged from the crisis of A.D. 70 reenforced the religious structure and religious self-understanding which already existed, and became the permanent foundation of Jewish religious and communal life until modern times.

It was most important, in the emergency situation following the fall of Jerusalem, that a legitimate authority emerge which would organize communal life. The rabbis who gathered at Jamnia derived their authority from their knowledge of Scripture (the Written Law) and their ability to interpret it. Their interpretations of the Law formed the Oral Law. These men were considered to be legitimate successors of the priests and scribes, empowered to interpret the word of the Lord. In the *Mishnah* of *Avot* it is written: "Moses received the Torah on Sinai, and handed it to Joshua; and Joshua to the elders, the elders to the prophets; and the prophets handed it down to the men of the Great Synagogue . . ." (*Avot* 1:1). The rabbis of the Pharisaic party claimed and were recognized as the next step in this continuous chain of tradition. Descendants of the great sage Hillel became heads of the Academy at Jamnia and held power from A.D. 85, under Gamaliel II, to 425, when permission to appoint a successor was denied by the Byzantine emperor. While the Patriarch of the house of Hillel held ultimate authority, decisions were generally made on the basis of a majority vote among the rabbis who constituted the academy. They debated issues brought to their attention and then passed a ruling. Local courts and schools ruled on local cases and referred problems to the central academy when difficult disputes arose. The Jamnia body produced the laws, judges, and teachers necessary for the governance of a community whose life was framed within the religious structure of the Torah. The rabbi, from this time forward, was the head of the Jewish community, rendering decisions in religious matters and wielding the authority which gave order to the life of that community.

Jews living in the diaspora were organized in the same way as those living in Palestine. They were governed by rabbis, who from their schools issued decisions in social and religious matters. In Babylonia, the largest diaspora community, civil administration was in the hands of the Jewish exilarch, who deferred to the rabbis of the leading academy in religious concerns. The schools of Babylonia grew rapidly and renowned rabbis emerged there who would eventually become the chief authority of Jewry when the Palestinian

*The Wailing Wall in Jerusalem, part of the western wall of the Temple, believed to be part of Solomon's Temple. Since the Middle Ages, Jews have come to this wall to lament the destruction of the Temple and to pray for the restoration of the Jewish people. Frequently prayers and requests are written on slips of paper and inserted in the crevices between the ancient stones. (Courtesy of the Israel Government Tourist Office.)*

schools had declined. In the first centuries A.D. all diaspora communities turned to Palestine for final guidance, used the Palestinian traditions as the basis of their own rulings, and regarded the Palestinian academy as the spiritual center of Jewry. This recognition of Palestinian leadership was crucial in evolving generally uniform patterns in religious order and communal organization.

The emergence of the rabbis as the effective authority in self-governing Jewish communities must be understood as a consequence of the function which the Torah fulfilled within Jewish life. This in turn must be understood within the Jewish concept of covenant and religious law. Within Judaism the religious experience of revelation, the disclosure of God to Israel, had been given specific definition and content within the structure of biblical law. The Law was considered to be a gift of Yahweh, which established a permanent relationship between him and his chosen, and which provided a constant source of his presence to his people. From its earliest stages, Judaism concentrated upon the sphere of action, emphasizing fulfillment of God's commandments as the essential activity of the religious life. One was a member of the covenant community upon obligating oneself to observing covenant law. Commitment to God's law was an expression of commitment to God himself, an acknowledgement of his revelation and a positive response to it. This is the context of meaning within which the elaboration and observance of specific commandments must be understood. Underlying the detailed structure of law is the concept that the love of God, a vital binding relationship to him, must be actualized in concrete deeds. Every aspect of behavior was seen as an opportunity in which the Jew asserted his commitment to the Lord by fulfilling the divine will.

It is this basic concentration on commandment, on the deed which fulfills the Word, which was responsible for the development within Judaism of the Oral Law and the neglect of intellectual definition in the form of theology. This is not to say that the Jew did not embrace specific beliefs, but rather that these basic beliefs were assumed, implicitly accepted, and generally not transmitted in objectified formulated creeds. The distinctive religious creation of Judaism is the *halakah,* the law. It is this law which has sustained the order and given the form to Jewish life, a life constantly threatened by the many disruptive and disintegrative forces inherent in the situation of exile. *Halakah* in its broadest sense is more than *nomos,* that is, law as statute. *Halakah* refers to a universal cosmic principle, which is contained in the Torah and its commentaries. It is really the way of the universe established by God for the governance of man. In rabbinic literature one reads that the Torah preexisted the world and that God fashioned his creation on the basis of the Torah. God himself is said to study this law, such activity being the highest value. Indeed, it is claimed that the whole universe is maintained for the sake of the Torah.

Study of the law and the interpretation of its meaning, both for the sake of practical behavior and for the attainment of answers to the questions of meaning, became the most valued activity in Jewish society. At Jamnia, the immediate need was for a codified body of law which would establish norms and give a degree of uniformity to Jewish life both in Palestine and in the diaspora. The rabbis set themselves to this task, and during the first and second centuries A.D., they gathered opinions on all issues, evaluated them, and ruled between conflicting views. Finally in A.D. 200, Rabbi Judah the Prince issued the *Mishnah,* a practical code of law which set definite standards in civil and religious matters. This work, the first and most important code, was accepted throughout the diaspora. As the rulings in the Mishnah are interpretations of biblical law in application to concrete life situations, so the decisions of the Mishnah were further interpreted within constantly changing circumstances. The process of interpretation has been continuous throughout Jewish history, and centers of learning have been established from Babylonia to Egypt, North Africa, France, Germany, Poland, and Russia. Following the decline of the Palestinian schools, the main decision-making institutions were the academies of Babylonia at Sura and Pumpedita. Learned rabbis from all over the diaspora consulted the Babylonian authorities. The compilation of the Babylonian interpretation, the Babylonian Talmud, became the authoritative code of Jewish law and the primary text of study for all later periods.

Commentaries upon commentaries have been elaborated to guide the community of the pious along what was considered to be the proper path of life, the path pleasing to God. While this heavy corpus grew, there remained the underlying notion that the total body of law could be reduced to the essential precept to love man and to love God. Hillel had said, "Be of the disciples of Aaron, loving peace, pursuing peace, loving men, and bringing them near to the Torah" (*Avot* 1:12). In bringing them near to the Torah one led them to God's precious gift, the source of his love and the source of righteousness. Rabbi Akiba, one of the greatest rabbis of Jewish tradition who lived in the first century A.D., stated, "Thou shalt love thy neighbor as thyself, that is the greatest principle of the Law" (*Sifra* 89b). All of the commandments and all of the commentaries could be leveled down to this essential moral precept, without which the entire elaborate structure was meaningless. Micah had stated the demand of God, "to do justice, and to love kindness, and to walk humbly with your God" (Mic. 6:8), and this ethical demand remained primary.

The rabbis did not consider mere external observance of the law, even in its most minute detail, to be proper or sufficient. Conformity to the law was to be based upon an inner intention. Certainly, the fixed objective structure was to be followed, but the interior subjective attitude was of decisive importance. The heart was to be directed toward heaven. Hillel is said to have said, "Let all thy deeds be for the sake of heaven." The law was indeed compared to a yoke which brought freedom and purification to man. This was its true goal—spiritual perfection.

This sense that the law brought freedom and that it was a source of benefit to man underlay submission to the "yoke." The traditional pious Jew assumed the regimen of the religious life because he trusted that the word of the Lord, as interpreted to him by his rabbis, was binding upon the chosen people and that he personally, as an elect member of that people, was responsible for realizing the word. Through his actions, carried out in conformity to the objective structure and with the proper intention of true service, he felt that he contributed to the perfection of himself and to the perfection of the world. It is not possible to understand the continuous devotion of the Jewish community and the determined will to survive in exile unless one understands this basic religious trust and positive faith. The law was a total way of life which segregated the Jew from the environment of the non-Jew. This rigorous segregation and the full structure of Jewish practice which maintained it could not have survived without the conviction that such a way of life was a sanctification which brought man near to God. "It is not an easy thing, but it is your life" (Deut. 32:47). Such was the lot of Israel, singled out to be God's special agent in history. The law was God's own gift to his people and a symbol of his love for his chosen son.

> *With everlasting love hast Thou loved the house of Israel. Thou hast revealed to us a Law and commandments, statutes and judgments. Therefore, O Lord our God, when we lie down and when we rise up we shall attend to thy statutes. Yea, we shall rejoice in the words of Thy Law and in Thy commandments forever and ever. They are our life and the measure of our days and we will meditate upon them day and night. Mayest thou never take away Thy love from Israel. Praised be Thou, O Lord, who lovest thy people Israel.*
>
> (Prayer from the Evening Service)

The development of the *halakah,* the legal literature, served to give structure and organization to Jewish life. At the same time there arose the *aggadah,* the literature concerned not with practical behavior but with the ideas and values which are the ground of that behavior. The rabbis speculated upon things divine and things human. They asked questions of why and wherefore, and sought to understand the basic questions of meaning inherent in human life. In traditional Jewish manner, they went to the Bible for clues to the answers to such questions and developed their own notions as exegesis upon the biblical text. Their folkloristic opinions of metaphysical and theological problems are contained in the various volumes of the *midrash,* written at the same time as the legal matter contained in the Mishnah. In addition to these separate works, one-third of the Babylonian Talmud, and one-half of the Palestinian Talmud, consists of aggadic material. The importance of such material in expressing the religious insights and deep sentiments of the Jewish soul has been enormous. Indeed, without the *aggadah,* Judaism would be a petrified legal system. The rabbis recognized this when they commented upon the blessing which Isaac gave Jacob, "God give thee the dew of heaven, the fat of the earth, and plenty of corn and wine. Dew of heaven is Scripture, the fat of the earth is mishnah, corn is halakah, wine is aggadah" (Genesis Rabbah 27:28).

*Aggadah* is thinking about man, his relation to God and his relation to his fellowman. It is insight into the mystery of the universe, and speculation upon God's presence in the universe, in history, and his relationship to man. The entire legal structure of Judaism rests upon these insights. *Halakah* and *aggadah* are mutually dependent. Judaism teaches that there must be both objective obedience and subjective understanding; there must be discipline but also freedom. The dialectic of the external act and the internal intention is constant. Both *halakah* and *aggadah* developed continuously wherever Jews engaged in the study of tradition.

Judaism accepted the notion that the Torah, revealed to Moses on Sinai, was eternally true and binding. This Torah was made relevant to everyday life by the constant process of interpretation on the level of both *halakah* and *aggadah.* In the area of *halakah,* general prescriptions and proscriptions, such as not cooking a calf in its mother's milk or not working on the Sabbath, had to be applied to concrete situations and elaborated fully. From such elemental negative commands, a complicated body of dietary laws and a full regimen for Sabbath observance emerged. In the area of *aggadah,* explanations for the acts of God and of man in concrete situations had to be sought. In order to apply Scripture, years of study were required. Indeed, study of the tradition was considered the highest religious duty, and education became an ideal value to all Jews. Had it not been commanded that "thou shalt meditate upon them day and night, that thou mayest observe to do all that is written therein" (Josh. 1:8)? Study, like prayer, was a religious act which must be directed heavenward. It was to be the occupation of a lifetime, beginning with the learning of Scripture at the age of five and continuing into advanced exegetical interpretive work of mature scholars. Rabbi ben Bag Bag had said, "Turn it over and over again, for everything is in it, and contemplate it, and wax gray over it, and stir not from it" (*Avot* 5:25). His suggestion became the ideal of the people of the book. The structure of belief and law evolved by the rabbis saved Judaism from destruction following the fall of the Jewish state in A.D. 70. From that time until the period of Emancipation in the eighteenth century, Jewish life became a spiritual reality, with the laws of God serving as its ordering constitution, its principle of national coherence, and its source of ultimate meaning.

# FAITH AND THE THEOLOGICAL TRADITION

WHO IS CHRIST?

Christianity confronted the intellectual culture of antiquity and related itself to it in a positive way. It is true that such a positive reaction was opposed in the spirit of Tertullian who declared that "after Christ Jesus we desire no subtle theories" (Tertullian, *De praescriptione haereticorum,* 8) and that the positive reaction itself was selective. Christian thinkers and writers were indeed inclined to take over and use those elements of the philosophy and ethics of late antiquity which exhibited an affinity for Christianity and expressed the inward-turning and growing other-worldly orientation of the period. It found its chief material in this respect in Platonism and in the Stoic ideas of a rational ethical natural law which it related to Hebraic ideas of morality. The history and the criticism of the secular culture were neglected, and in harmony with the general spirit of declining antiquity its empirical scientific elements were not taken up. Yet this adaptation of the intellectual heritage of the Greeks to serve Christian ends was a most significant one for the future. The struggle against Gnosticism had already given an intellectual cast to the clerical mentality. The acceptance of the Platonic and Stoic heritage would impart to the Christian tradition two characteristics which would remain constitutive of it throughout its history. First, faith was conceived as not standing in contradiction to understanding, religion as not opposed to secular knowledge. Second, yet despite this deep and deeply significant orientation to the harmony of faith and reason, a conflict between the claims and implications of the two became characteristic of the development of Christian thought forever after.

The first fruits of this coming together of Christian faith and the philosophical culture of the Greek world can be seen in the theological controversies of the fourth and fifth centuries. Here indeed "subtle theories" would appear to be both causing and expressing bitter division. The religious experience of the Christian Church had encountered God in three fundamental modes. It had met the transcendent God who revealed himself in history in the Old Testament and in the earthly career of Jesus of Nazareth. It had experienced God's Word become flesh and mediate the relationship between men and the Father. Finally, it had experienced what it saw as the Holy Spirit in the life of the Church itself. A transcendent, a mediational, and an immanent mode of God's self-revelation and of his relation to the world that he created were characteristic of the Christian experience. This found its formulation in the early Trinitarian formulae which we have already seen. But the intellectual mode of speculative philosophy which the Church had now adopted found such statements inadequate and demanding further explication. How was this fundamental Christian experience to be given adequate intellectual form as the Greek philosophical mind insisted it must? The distinctions between the three had been established by the end of the first century, but how could they be given precise and consistent definition and how were the relationships of the three to be stated in philosophical terms? By the third century there had evolved in the West a near unanimity on the answer to these questions but the East was divided. The East, moreover, was culturally more thoroughly Greek and more inclined to speculative theology than the West and much of the outstanding intellectual ability in the Church was found there.

The next century and a half saw the working through and fighting out of these issues. It was a process which exhibited three characteristics that remained with the Church throughout its history in one form or another. First, as we have already seen, is that mixture of faith and philosophical speculation which leads to the objectivized, formulated, intellectual statement of the content of faith, giving high salience to the element of intellectual assent. In the sixteenth century Martin Luther, himself a figure of intellectual eminence, challenged such intellectualization and presented faith as a more holistic acceptance of and dependence on Christ as Savior. This intellectual bent gave rise to the important status granted to the "correct" formulation and turned the understanding of faith into a sophisticated philosophy of religion accessible in this form only to a trained specialist. While the Church always admitted the equal personal worth of the faith (often implicit) of the simple believer, the intellectual statement became the accepted standard for official teaching and the measure of orthodoxy. A second characteristic long to be found in the Christian tradition also comes into existence at this time. When these theological conflicts reached their full force, the Church was no longer a community of the withdrawn, in the world but not of it, establishing and maintaining its own way of life alongside the life of the Roman Empire. Decius who became Emperor in 249 initiated the first really general persecution of the Church and sought to bring about its extermination. There followed both apostasy and heroic martyrdom. Such persecutions continued under the emperors Gallus and Valerian and reached the greatest proportions under Diocletian. But persecution came to an end with the Edict of Toleration in 311 "allowing Christians the right to exist again and to set up their places of worship" (Lactantius, *De Mortibus Persecutorum,* 24) and the identification of the new Emperor Constantine with Christianity in 312. Constantine saw in the Christian faith a means for constructing a foundation for unity and stability in the empire, a basis for developing that "consensus" which Cicero had seen as requisite to political order. Thus Christianity now became involved in the political life of Europe, subject to political pressures, and manipulated for political purposes, a fact of life for Christian existence which lasted until the nineteenth century and may still be seen in many parts of the world. A third element visible in these controversies is the amalgamation of religious points of view with the cultural interests of national and ethnic groups so that religious antagonisms often admit of analysis upon two levels—one concerned with the manifest content of religious thought, the other with the cultural, psychological, and political needs of various nationalities. In the post-Reformation period this aspect of religious phenomena became very prominent, and nowhere more palpable than in the history of the assimilation of European immigrants into American society in the nineteenth century.

The issue of how Christ was to be understood had already produced formulations considered heretical. There were those who identified Christ and the Father, saying "that the Father himself descended into the virgin, was himself born of her, himself suffered; in fact that he himself was Jesus Christ," a point of view Tertullian attributed to the devil (Tertullian, *Against Praxeas,* 1), or those following Sabellius, who held "that Father, Son and Holy Spirit are one and the same being in the sense that three names are attached to one substance" (Epiphanius of Salamis, *Against Heresies,* 42.1). There were also those who believed that Christ's humanity was not genuine but only an appearance (the Docetists) and those who saw Jesus only as a man chosen and adopted by God at the time of his baptism by John (the Adoptionists). The conflict came to a head in the formulation of Arius, a learned and pious priest of Alexandria, which stated that "the Son has a beginning, but God is without beginning," that before the Son "was begotten or created or appointed or established, he did not exist" ("Letter to Arius to Eusibius of Nicomedia," Theodoret of Cyprus, *Church History,* 1.5). He was opposed by Alexander, Bishop of Alexandria, and by the year 320 the conflict was widespread and bitter. Constantine desiring the unity of the Church as a basis for the stability of the empire called a council, which was held at Nicea in 325, the first in Church history, and presided over it although he was himself only in catechumen status—not yet baptised. There were some 308 bishops present with only about a half dozen of them from the West, where opposition to Arius was strongest. There were among the Council Fathers two small minorities, one supporting the Arian position and one holding with Alexander that the Son was eternal, of like essence with the Father, and uncreated. The majority were not deeply cognizant of the issues of the controversy. A creed was adopted using the terms "begotten not made" and "of one substance with the Father" (*homoousion*), representing the view of Alexander and of the West in general. The influence of the emperor was a decisive factor in the decision of Nicea and the Nicene formulation was almost immediately the subject of bitter controversy. Indeed, the real conflict only began with the Council's end.

There then arose Athanasius who became the champion of the Nicene formula, and bishop of Alexandria. He was a robust figure, strong in his convictions, and unlikely to be moved by political pressures or court considerations, and he led the Nicene party to ultimate success. Athanasius saw the problem as most intimately related to the understanding of salvation which he understood in harmony with the Johannine as well as the Pauline tradition: "He was made man that we might be made divine," "his task was to restore the corruptible to uncorruption" (Athanasius, *De incarnatione,* 53.3, 7). The conflict continued to rage for years, each side making use of and being used by political manipulation. Many of its leaders would see several terms of exile, including Athanasius who was exiled four times. At first it looked like a victory for the anti-Nicene party—a group made up of the Arians and a large conservative middle group which was not really of Arian convictions but disagreed with the Nicene use of the term *honoousion,* which sounded to them like Sabellius. This victory, like the earlier one of the Nicene group, was made possible by imperial influence. Moreover, the debate was broadened to include a discussion of the relationship of the Holy Spirit to the Godhead. Athanasius and his party saw that relationship as similar to that of the Son and the Father. With the death of Athanasius the leadership passed to the three great figures of the Eastern Church, Basil and the two Gregorys. These men were greatly responsible for the victory of the Athanasian point of view. In 380 an imperial edict was issued declaring that all should hold the faith as taught by Damasus, Bishop of Rome, and Peter, Bishop of Alexandria. Thus there was set up one religion in the empire and that was based upon the Nicene formulations. In 381 a synod, recognized as an Ecumenical Council, was held at Constantinople, which adopted the Nicene statements. A creed which became the standard belief of the Church came into general use and was finally approved by the Council of Chalcedon in 451. We reproduce it here as found in the writings of Epiphanius, in the lectures of Saint Cyril of Jerusalem, and as presumably read and approved at Chalcedon as the creed of "the 318 Fathers who met at Nicea and that of the 150 who met at a later time," that is, at Constantinople, and known since as the Nicene Creed or the Niceano-Constantinopolitan Creed,

> *We believe in one God the Father All-sovereign, maker of heaven and earth, and of all things visible and invisible;*
>
> *And in one Lord Jesus Christ, the only-begotten Son of God,*
>
> *Begotten of the Father before all the ages, Light of Light, true God of true God, begotten not made, of one substance with the Father, through whom all things were made; who for us men and*

> *for our salvation came down from the heavens, and was made flesh of the Holy Spirit and the Virgin Mary, and became man, and was crucified for us under Pontius Pilate, and suffered and was buried, and rose again on the third day according to the Scriptures, and ascended into the heavens, and sitteth at the right hand of the Father, and cometh again with glory to judge living and dead, of whose kingdom there shall be no end;*
>
> *And in the Holy Spirit, the Lord and Giver of Life, that proceedeth from the Father, who with Father and Son is worshipped together and glorified together, who spake through the prophets;*
>
> *In one Holy Catholic and Apostolic Church;*
>
> *We acknowledge one baptism unto remission of sins. We look for a resurrection of the dead, and the life of the age to come.*

In this creed we see the belief of the West in one God in three divine persons and the belief of Athanasius and his followers in the East in one essence (*ousia*) and three "subsistencies" (*hypostasis*) established as the faith of the Church. However, this decision did not set well in the East, where revolt threatened immediately. The creed of Chalcedon, in addition to enacting the Niceano-Constantinopolitan doctrine, further explicated it by speaking of "two natures," one of the same substance as the Godhead, the other of the same substance as our manhood (Council of Chalcedon, *Actio V, Mansi,* 8). Many in the East saw this as destroying the unity of Christ, and before long Palestine and Egypt were in revolt and there arose the Monophysite heresy and divisive religious and political conflict in the eastern empire. For more than two centuries the imperial government strove to adjust the ensuing controversies. These conflicts exhibited that combination of religious and national elements to which we have referred; non-Greek nationalities in the East struggled against the imposition and restraint of Greek ideas and against rule from Byzantium, the new Greek capital of the eastern half of the empire, as well as against the content of the religious ideas themselves. The exhaustion which resulted from these fierce struggles prepared the way for the conversion of most of the area to Islam, in which the non-Greek inhabitants of the region found a new religious form and one possibly much more in harmony with their indigenous culture than post-Chalcedon Christianity. Yet the definition of the triune God at Chalcedon became the faith of the overwhelming majority of Christians, the Eastern Orthodox, the Western Catholics, and most Protestant groups to this day. The West would, however, make one addition not accepted in the East. It would in the sixth century add the word *filioque* to the Latin creed, thereby declaring the Holy Spirit to proceed from the Father "and the Son." Monophysite (anti-Chalcedon) churches are still found, however, in Egypt, Ethiopia, and the Middle East.

In the Creed adopted at Chalcedon we see a combination of the sophisticated Greek philosophical ideas and the historical elements of the career of Jesus of Nazareth, a combination characteristic of Christian thinking in the centuries to follow. Moreover, we see an acknowledgment of the expected second coming and of the resurrection of the dead and the beginning of a new world-age. Together with this we see a growing reverence for the Church itself as the guardian of orthodoxy and the community of succor. This found expression by the end of the second century in describing the Church as a "mother." In the middle of that century we already see the Church appearing under various symbols, as for example in the *Shepherd of Hermas,* the brother of Pius, bishop of Rome (140–154), where among other forms that of an exhorting mother is to be found. By the end of the century we find Clement of Alexandria calling the Church "a mother" who feeds her children the spiritual food of the *Logos* (*Paedagogus* 1.6.42.1). The tradition of affection and respect for "Mother Church" had begun.

The Christological controversies had raised the question as to the genuineness of Christ's humanity, which involved some understanding of the role of his virgin mother, for the Church had very early accepted the idea of the virgin birth (Matt. 1:20 and 23; Luke 1:34 ff.). At the Councils of Ephesus (431) and Chalcedon (451) the title *theotokos* (Godbearer) for Mary, which had come into use by theologians by the fourth century if not earlier, was approved. This confirmed a growing attention to Mary's role and importance by Christian thinkers and a popular devotion to her and belief in the efficacy of her intercession which was already well established. This term was translated into Latin as *Dei Genetrix* (Mother of God). Thus was confirmed the devotion to Mary which would increase with the years and become a basic and central devotion in the Medieval Church and after the Reformation in Catholicism. Indeed, in the nineteenth century Pope Pius IX promulgated the dogma of her Immaculate Conception, the belief that she was born without the stain of original sin which Christians believe all men have inherited from Adam, although of natural parentage, and in the mid-twentieth century Pius XII promulgated the dogma of her Assumption—that is, the belief that after her death her body was miraculously transported to heaven. Indeed, some Catholic theologians have even conceived of Mary as a kind of mediator with Christ between God and man, a view never given dogmatic status. Protestantism rejected this emphasis upon Mary and the devotion to her as a nonscriptural accretion and as a kind of semiidolatrous activity.

**Head of the Virgin,** *a drawing by Leonardo da Vinci. (Courtesy of the Metropolitan Museum of Art. Harris Brisbane Dick Fund, 1951.)*

There also began early in the Church a devotion to martyrs and to other esteemed Christians, seeing them after their deaths as intercessors before God, that is, as those who offer prayers to God for the living and to whom the living pray to ask their intercession. This devotion spread rapidly from the fourth century on. It was approved by the later Fathers, the theologians of late antiquity, and in the Middle Ages was a prominent feature of popular and official worship and devotion. It found its way into the liturgy of the Mass, where Saint Augustine speaks of its presence in the fifth century (*City of God* 22.10) and the Divine Office of the monastic daily worship in which lives of the Saints were read. It has remained characteristic of Catholic practice but was repudiated thoroughly by the Reformation. Even the Church of England, although in some ways undecided on other Reformation issues, speaks of it as a "fond thing vainly invented" (*Thirty-Nine Articles,* art. 22).

HOW ARE WE SAVED?

The Christian East was concerned with problems of speculative theology and had centered its attention upon the Godhead and particularly on the character of Christ, as the pagan East had earlier been concerned with speculative philosophy. The Christian West was more humanistic in its emphasis as the pagan West had earlier been in its study and development of administration and law. The chief theological controversy in the West concerned the relations between God and man and the relation of each to the problem of the existence of evil and the nature of salvation. Moreover, in line with its humanistic emphasis the West was concerned with problems involved in the functioning of the Church, and the relationship between the Church and the secular world and particularly the state. The great figure who brought together and developed these themes was Augustine, Bishop of Hippo in North Africa. Augustine had been a Manichaean, a member of a religious group which held to a sharp dualism of good and evil, seeing an evil agency as an eternal part of the cosmos engaged in continual conflict with the good God. He later became a skeptic, taking up the ideas of the New Platonic Academy which denied the possibility of genuinely knowing truth. He then became a Neo-Platonist, which opened up to him a transcendent world of being and goodness above and beyond the material world he had previously conceived as total and ultimate. Neo-Platonism was most significant in preparing for his conversion to Christianity and in providing him with the philosophical concepts in terms of which he would develop his Christian theology after his conversion. He was converted in 387 after a personal religious experience of a semimystical character.

> *But when a profound reflection had, from the secret depths of my soul, drawn together and heaped up all my misery before the sight of my heart, there arose a mighty storm, accompanied by as mighty a shower of tears . . . I flung myself down, how, I know not, under a certain fig tree, giving free course to my tears . . . and weeping in the most bitter contrition of my heart, when, lo, I heard the voice as of a boy or girl, I know not which, coming from a neighboring house, chanting and oft repeating, "Take up and read; take up and read."*

He then picked up the copy of the scriptures which he had left nearby and opening it "in silence read that paragraph on which my eyes first fell" (*Confessions* 8). The paragraph which Augustine read was from Paul's Epistle to the Romans, "not in revelling and drunkenness, not in debauchery and licentiousness, not in quarreling and jealousy. But put on the Lord Jesus Christ, and make no provision for the flesh to gratify its desires" (Rom. 13:13–14). This experience was the culmination of a long period of interior suffering and it completely changed Augustine who had unsuccessfully up to then attempted to restrain his lusts and his ambitions. While Augustine was learned in scripture and ecclesiastical tradition, while he knew the philosophy of the age and was possessed of a towering intellect, his development of Christian theology was tremendously affected by the impact of that conversion experience. Augustine's thought evolved in the years before his conversion—from Manichaeism to skepticism, from skepticism to Neo-Platonism—but afterward he saw the whole of reality from one point of view, that of the supremacy of and centrality of God in human experience. Like Paul before him, Augustine reshaped theology in terms of his own profound experience of its meaning. Augustine's experience was whole and deep, involving both the profoundest emotion and the most sophisticated intellect and his theology reflected that experience. Moreover, Augustine considered his conversion and the transformation which he immediately experienced and which was to be seen and felt in his daily life, as a gift of God for which he himself deserved no credit.

In his life Augustine confronted three viewpoints either heretical or antagonistic to Christianity. He countered the first, Manichaeism, by asserting and explicating the infinite goodness of God, the creator, and the essential goodness of his creation. He saw evil not as a positive force, as did the Manichaeans, but as a privation of good, a lack in an essentially good creation. The source of moral evil he found in the human will. Classical philosophy had neglected the concept of the human will, which Augustine now subjected to brilliant intellectual analysis.

While he was Bishop of Hippo, Augustine came into conflict with the Donatist heresy. The advocates of Donatism, protesting immorality in the Church, held that sacraments administered by unworthy clergy were invalid. Augustine defended the objectivity of the Church's sacraments against this point of view, holding that they are not the work of men but of God and that therefore they do not depend on the spiritual condition of the minister. This conflict made Augustine examine the conception of the Church and the sacraments and to develop them beyond what had taken place up to his time. Augustine saw Baptism, the Holy Eucharist, and Holy Orders as the three chief sacraments, but recognized other ecclesiastical rites as sacraments as well. The Catholic Church would eventually define seven sacraments which it saw as outward signs instituted by Christ and endowing the communicant with God's grace—his gratuitous aid to the human spirit—operating *ex opere operato:* Baptism, Confirmation, Holy Eurcharist, Penance, Anointing of the Sick, Holy Orders (the ordination of the clergy), and Matrimony. The Reformation contested all of these except Baptism and Holy Eucharist, and the attitudes of various Protestant groups toward them differ. Moreover, Augustine emphasized the significance of the institutional church. He stands as the great prototypic example of that union of profound subjective religiosity and an objective ecclesiastical and sacramental system characteristic of the Middle Ages and the Catholic piety of the post-Reformation period. He felt that the "Holy Spirit may be said not to be received except in the Catholic Church" (*Baptism* 3.16), although he recognized that there were men outside the Church who were really within it in spirit (*Baptism* 5.28). However, "the church even now is the kingdom of Christ, and the kingdom of heaven" (*City of God* 10.9), though she contains both good and bad individuals who will not be separated out until the day of judgment. He also gave his attention to the relationship of the Church to the state. He accepted the state as part of God's providence but saw it as good only insofar as it was founded on the concept of justice. Yet he saw actual states as ambiguous, as the embodiments of human ambition and pride as well as God's instrument in punishing evil and maintaining peace and order. He felt that the state should support the worship of God and should help in counteracting heresy, although he rejected the idea of the death penalty for heretics. In his concepts of the Church and the sacraments and in his ideas of the function of the state and the relations of Church and State, Augustine was the great source of ideas for Christianity in the Middle Ages and indeed in modern times. His Platonic philosophy as he applied it in the explanation of Christian doctrines became the guide of Christian thinking up to the thirteenth century when St. Thomas Aquinas shifted the philosophical basis of theology from Platonism to Aristotelianism. Yet in Thomas himself the influence of Augustine and Augustinian Platonism is serious enough to be characterized as constitutive.

Important as these ideas of Augustine are, he is perhaps most significant in his ideas on grace and free will. Men were redeemed by Christ, but the question arose as to what role the individual performed in his own salvation and what part was to be attributed to divine initiative and support. Christ's death was the basis of salvation, but how? There are variations in Augustine's answer to this question—Christ had offered himself as our sacrifice to God; he had ransomed us by his death from the power of Satan; he had died in our stead and paid the human debt to God's justice. But of one thing Augustine was sure, basing himself upon the Scriptures and tradition viewed in the light of his own personal experience. The initiative was God's and the transformation was made by God. Salvation is the work of grace and it is neither deserved nor earned by man; it is God's free gift. All men fell in Adam's sin and all are in a sinful state until they receive God's grace. These ideas were formed in Augustine's mind early in his Christian life but they reached their full development and their most vigorous expression in the controversy with Pelagius and his supporters.

Pelagius was a Celtic, possibly Irish, monk who came to Rome during the time when Anastasius was pope (399–401). He and his followers, especially Celestius and Julian of Eclanum, taught that a man was himself responsible for both initiating and achieving his own salvation. The Pelagians insisted that the human race was not fundamentally damaged by the sin of Adam. Pelagius, who was a man of great ethical seriousness and shocked by the state of morality he found in Rome, believed that to say that a man was not responsible for his own deeds was to give him permission for self-indulgence and sin. Like the Stoics he saw most of the human race as bad in practice, but like them also he saw as paradigmatic the slogan, "If I ought I can."

What the Greek Fathers, the great religious thinkers of the Eastern Church, had taught about the relation of Adam's sin to the condition and guilt of the human race is far from clear. They seemed to hold that it had some effect making man corruptible, but their language is vague and there is no precise kind of statement on which they agree. In the West, however, Fathers such as Tertullian, Cyprian, and Ambrose were of the opinion that all men were somehow involved and implicated in Original Sin, an involvement transmitted to oncoming generations by heredity through the sexual act. Pelagius is said to have started his teaching in response to a sentence in Augustine's *Confessions,* "give what Thou commandest, and command what Thou wilt" (*Confessions* 10.29). Augustine soon replied and there followed a bitter controversy on the issue. In the course of this, Augustine set forth definite ideas on Original Sin and predestination.

It was Augustine's own personal experience that the transformation which came with and developed after conversion was not his own doing. He believed from all the depths of his fervent soul and with all the power of his vigorous mind that his own delivery had come from God. God had chosen and changed him, it was not his own initiative nor effort that was responsible. This was in harmony with the teaching of Ambrose, who had been influential in his conversion. It was in this light that Augustine read the Scriptures:

> *Sin came into the world through one man.*
>
> (Rom. 5:12)

> *For those whom he foreknew he also predestined to be conformed to the image of his Son . . . and those whom he predestined he also called; and those whom he called he also justified; and those whom he justified he also glorified.*
>
> (Rom. 8:29–30).

> *He destined us in love to be his sons through Jesus Christ according to the purpose of his will, to the praise of his glorious grace which he freely bestowed on us in the Beloved.*
>
> (Eph. 1:5–6)

The issue became a central one for the Church and the conflict saw the fortunes of both parties change from time to time. But the anti-Pelagian party eventually won the inner struggle and in 418 Pelagianism was condemned by an imperial rescript which ordered the exile of its adherents; a large council at Carthage was held that approved a moderate position, and Pelagius and Celestius were condemned by Pope Zosimus, who earlier had shown some sympathy for the Pelagians. Augustine's reassertion of the Pauline position established the doctrine of Original Sin as Church teaching, although it continued forever afterward to be a matter of controversy from time to time, and especially in the Reformation.

With respect to predestination, the doctrine that some persons are foreordained by divine decree to eternal salvation, Augustine developed the Pauline ideas. He felt that God had indeed foreordained to salvation and glorification and had given the gift of perseverance to those chosen. This depended not upon human attitudes of acceptance but on God's decree. Why God does as he does, Augustine saw as a mystery, beyond our human comprehension. God does not cause evil but he permits it for a greater good which we cannot understand here on earth. God is loving, generous, and just and the doctrine does not in any way impugn these divine qualities but may only seem to do so to our darkened intelligences. Moreover, man's will, though not responsible for his salvation but rather for his sin, is seen by Augustine as free and the doctrine of predestination as he teaches it does not violate the existence of free will. It is a subtle and difficult doctrine that Augustine develops and one which will cause great conflict in the future. Augustine and Pelagius seem to have been looking at different aspects of the general problem and from quite different points of view. Augustine was a man who has had a great religious experience which changed and transformed him, the impact of which ever remained fresh and clear to him. He also had a great theoretical mind, indeed he may be justly said to be the father of all Western theology, as Plato is the father of all Western philosophy. He saw the problem from a combination of a deeply personal and subjective and a lofty intellectual perspective. Pelagius, on the other hand, was a practical moralist concerned with developing ethical habits in individuals. To Augustine, Pelagius appeared to dwarf and parody the mystery and majesty of the conversion experience and the biblical doctrine of God as Lord of history electing and foreordaining crucial events affecting human destiny. To Pelagius, Augustine appeared to make sin man's normal condition and any goodness in him to be God's work, not his. This would make the achievement of virtue an extrahuman gift. The implication for Pelagius was that man is heartily discouraged from trying to be moral; in fact, he is encouraged to be what he is and to enjoy sinning since he cannot do otherwise of his own accord. Both points of view appear to be speaking of different levels of the problem which are brought together under a single conception. The issues they raised long continued to be a bone of contention in the Church.

The fifth century saw more moderate or "semi-Pelagian" positions (a word coined in the sixteenth century when the issues were again being debated) put forward. John Cassianus in 429 stated that "the will always remains free in man, and it can either neglect or delight in the grace of God" (Cassianus, *Collationes,* 12). In 434 Vincent of Lerins wrote a work which gave his oft-quoted and difficult definition of what the Christian tradition was—*Quod ubique, quod semper, quod ab omnibus,* "the faith that has been believed everywhere, always and by all" (*Commonitorium* 2.4)—and in which he characterized Augustine's distinctive ideas on grace and predestination as not meeting this criterion. Faustus of Rhegium declared in 473: "Man's effort and endeavor is to be united with God's grace;

man's freedom of will is not extinct but attenuated and weakened; he that is saved is in danger, and he that has perished could have been saved" (Faustus, *Epistle ad Lucidim,* P.L. 53.683). The Synod of Orange in 529 took the position "that through the sin of the first man, free choice was so warped and weakened that thereafter no one is able to love God as he ought, to believe in God, or do anything for God that is good, except the grace of God's mercy first come to start it in him (*Praeveniret*)."

In Pope Gregory the Great (590–604), the first monk to hold the papal office, an energetic, wise, and temperate man, who was the real ruler of Rome in secular as well as ecclesiastical affairs, we see a prefiguration of much of the Middle Ages. Although Gregory expected the world to come to an end before too long a time and felt he was living in the final age, he built the Church and the Papacy in a manner that would stand them in good stead in the difficult years ahead. His great practical wisdom may be seen in his advice on the conversion of the English—to disturb the indigenous culture as little as consonant with the new faith—and in his book *Pastoral Rule.* His theology is that of Augustine but with changed emphasis, and it reflects the growing loss of intellectual vigor of the declining Roman West. He accepts predestination but he often seems to see it merely as divine foreknowledge. He saw man truncated by Original Sin but rescued from this state by the death of Christ to which he becomes heir in baptism, an idea long accepted. For sins which a man commits after baptism, he must render satisfaction. This he can do by works of merit, which are done with the assistance of God's grace. The Church offers aids in this effort, especially the Eucharist, which he saw as a repetition of Christ's sacrifice. The prayers of the saints are also available and of help. Gregory put forward as a matter essential to faith an idea that began much earlier in the Church, the idea of purgatory. In some form this idea of a state after death in which those do penance who have not made adequate satisfaction and are still guilty of smaller sins was taught by various fathers. We find hints of it in Hermas, a clearer notion in Clement of Alexandria, and a more systematic treatment of it in the West, as in Ambrose. Indeed, the idea of purifying pains in the next life is also found in Augustine himself. Gregory declared, "It is to be believed that there is a purgatorial fire before the judgment for certain light sins" (Gregory, *Dialogues,* 4.30). Although the Eastern Church did not follow the West in such a precise and defined answer to the problem, it held a similar doctrine and continues to hold it, that some kind of intermediate state exists after death in which souls exist and can be helped, as they can also in the Western conception, by the prayer and sacrifice of the living. The doctrine became a basic one for the Middle Ages. Around it all sorts of abuses arose, including the sale of indulgences which set souls free from suffering in purgatory. It was completely repudiated by the Reformers of the sixteenth century, but was reaffirmed by the Catholic Church at the Council of Trent (1545–1563).

The Middle Ages accepted the doctrine of Original Sin as basic to Christian belief, and medieval theology was concerned with its implications and with its mode of transmission. They also were much influenced by Augustine's ideas on predestination but at the same time they held with the Greek Fathers that God desired and willed the salvation of all men. Moreover, they accepted, like Gregory, the idea that "the good that we do is both of God and ourselves" (*Moralia* 33.22). St. Augustine had seen man's fallen state as one in which the appetites of the flesh are no longer subordinated to reason. This was accepted in the Middle Ages but there was some question on how it was to be understood. St. Bernard (1090–1153), who was probably the most influential churchman of all Christian history, wrote in his treatise "On Grace and Free Will," "Remove free will, and there is nothing to Save; remove grace and there is left no means of Saving. The work of Salvation cannot be accomplished without the cooperation of the two." A more sophisticated and optimistic position was developed by St. Thomas Aquinas, who gives the matter considerable attention. Thomas, who made the great intellectual revolution of shifting Christian theology from a Platonic to an Aristotelian basis, recognized an autonomous nature which he separated from the sphere of the supernatural. Thus Adam before the Fall was not perfect in human nature only because that nature was brought to a perfection beyond itself by supernatural grace. In this state of grace there was in man a harmony between his supernatural end and his natural end and hence a harmony within his own composite make-up. The Fall deprived man of supernatural grace and hence of the internal order with which it had endowed him, thus wounding but not vitiating his capacities.

> *Hence in the state of the integrity of nature, man needs a gratuitous strength added to natural strength for one reason, viz., in order to do and will supernatural good; but in the state of corrupted nature he needs it for two reasons, viz., in order to be healed, and, furthermore, in order to carry out works of supernatural virtue which are meritorious.*
>
> (*Summa Theologica,* Part II, Ques. 109, art. 2)

Original Sin is thus a condition of the human race after Adam had lost the added gift of grace which put order and direction into man's make-up and behavior by relating him beyond the powers of his own nature to God and God's help.

The problems involved here rise again in full view at the time of the Reformation. Martin Luther, another great religious personality like Paul and Augustine, who combined knowledge of Scripture and tradition with profound personal religious experience, reformulated Christian tradition in keeping with his reading of the Scriptures in the light of his own profound inner struggles and religious experience. His deeply pessimistic view of man is to be seen in his denial of freedom of the will and in his affirmation of the total depravity of fallen human nature. Luther, who was himself an intellectual of impressive dimensions, suspected reason, considering it a harlot willing to serve any cause. Man is hopelessly sinful and is saved because God deigns to regard him as righteous because of the saving merits of Christ's death. As he said in his famous hymn, *Es ist doch unser Tun umsonst, auch in dem besten Leben,* "All we do is in vain, even in the best life." Justification of man is God's work and salvation is based upon faith alone—on man's total reliance upon God's mercy. This position had come to Luther as the solution of his own personal internal anguish which, like Augustine before him, he took as paradigmatic for the human problem as a whole. It was God attributing Christ's merits to man without human cooperation that brought salvation. Luther stood in the long medieval Augustinian tradition and he exaggerated its theological pessimism. However, he refused to teach the complete sinfulness of all human acts.

Augustinianism found its most radical and most intellectualized expression in John Calvin's *Institutes of the Christian Religion* (1536–1539). Calvin taught that before the Fall man could live in relation to God by his own natural powers. The Fall, however, which was willed by God for reasons that lie hidden in his transcendent inscrutability, so corrupted and vitiated man's nature that all he can do since is sin. He is no longer possessed of free will but follows of necessity either the attractions of his own fallen nature—his worldly desires and appetites of the flesh—or the call of divine grace. All human acts are sinful and all human glory is filth.

"Therefore original sin is seen to be an hereditary depravity and corruption of our nature, diffused into all parts of the soul." Moreover, this corruption is not just a weakening, for this sin we inherit possesses "positive energy." "For our nature is not merely bereft of good, but is so productive of every kind of evil that it cannot be inactive." Indeed, "whatever is in man, from intellect to will, from the soul to the flesh, is all defiled" (*Institutes of the Christian Religion,* Book 2, chap. 1).

This spirit of a hyper-Augustinian pessimism is found coming to the surface in the seventeenth century within the Catholic Church in a rigorous moralistic movement known as Jansenism and causing no little theological controversy. Its basic point of view is stated by Cornelius Jansen (1585–1638) in his book on grace and human nature entitled *Augustinus,* which was published after his death in 1640, and which is based upon the anti-Pelagian writings of Augustine. Five propositions extracted from this work were condemned by Pope Innocent X in 1653. Jansen and his followers held that obedience of God's commandments is impossible without a special grace from God, and that grace was irresistible by man. The problem of grace, how to understand its workings and its relationship to man's natural powers and psychological dispositions, gave rise to a large controversial literature in the seventeenth century. It was the subject of conflict between Protestants and Catholics and within the two groups themselves.

Paul had accepted predestination and free will but did not attempt to work out a rational theological context in which both positions were put together. Augustine also followed him in this, although Augustine presented considerable theological commentary upon the problems involved. The Middle Ages inherited these problems and attempted to put together the mystery of divine predestination with the belief in the universal saving will of God. In the ninth century we find a controversy over the meaning of the doctrine of which the leading figures were the monk Gottschalk (805–868) defending a hyper-Augustinian position and his chief opponents Archbishop Hincmar of Reims (806–882) and Johan Scotus Erigena (810–877). Here again Thomas, commenting on Romans 8:30, attempts a synthesis by viewing predestination as part of God's providence in which he directs men beyond the sphere of their own proper nature to eternal life. Behind predestination Thomas sees God's love, "all the predestinate are objects of election and love" (*Summa Theologica,* Part I, Ques. 23, art. 4). Most important is the fact that for Thomas God's predestination, his calling and electing of some, does not destroy free will.

> *Predestination achieves its effects most certainly and infallibly, and yet it does not impose any necessity, such that its effects should take place from necessity. For it was said above that predestination is a part of providence. But not all things subject to providence are necessary; for some things happen from contingency, according to the disposition of the proximate causes which divine providence has ordained for such effects. Yet the order of providence is infallible, as was shown above. So also is the order of predestination certain; and yet free choice, from which the effect of predestination has its contingency is not destroyed. Moreover all that has been said about the divine knowledge and will must also be taken into consideration; since they do not destroy contingency in things, although they themselves are most certain and infallible.*
>
> (*Summa Theologica,* Part I, Ques. 23, art. 6)

Luther had made salvation by faith alone (*sola fide*) the cornerstone of his theology and emphasized the all-pervading divine mercy which clothed the sinner with righteousness. Calvin, a man of stern temperament and logical rigor, insisted on pushing the notion of predestination to its logical implications without the saving qualifications which had long hedged its meaning. He indeed accuses his predecessors, not excluding Augustine himself, of a "superstitious fear" deriving "from motives of piety" which makes them "often shrink from the straightforward acknowledgment of the truth in this matter" and suggesting that biblical references to " 'hardening' and 'blinding' refer not to the operation of God, but to his foreknowledge" (*Institutes of the Christian Religion,* Book 2, chap. 5). Calvin says:

> *No one who wishes to be thought religious dares outright to deny predestination, by which God chooses some for the hope of life, and condemns others to eternal death. But men entangle it with captious quibbles . . . By predestination we mean the eternal decree of God, by which he has decided in his own mind what he wishes to happen in the case of each individual. For all men are not created on an equal footing, but for some eternal life is preordained, for others eternal damnation.*
>
> (*Institutes,* Book 3, chap. 21)

Thus Calvin denied the universal saving will of God and taught that Christ's atoning death affected only the elect.

The Westminster Confession of Faith in 1643 established this Calvinist doctrine as the credo of Presbyterianism. "By the decree of God, for the manifestation of his glory, some men and angels are predestined unto everlasting life, and others foreordained to everlasting death." Yet "neither is God the author of sin or is violence offered to the will of his creatures." Moreover, "neither are any redeemed in Christ . . . but the elect." The First Baptist Confession of Faith, drawn up by seven congregations in London in 1646 declared, "God hath, before the foundation of the world, foreordained some men to eternal life through Jesus Christ, to the praise and glory of his grace: leaving the rest in their sin, to their just condemnation, to the praise of his justice." The Quakers, however, took a different view of the matter. Robert Barclay presented their view in 1678 in *Apology for the Quakers.* While finding all men "fallen, degenerated and dead" as a consequence of Adam's sin, the Quakers emphasized God's "infinite love" and declared, "Therefore Christ hath tasted death for every man . . . even unto those who are necessarily excluded from the benefits of this knowledge by some inevitable accident."

A strong reaction against the Calvinist theory of predestination was initiated by Jacobus Arminius, a professor of divinity at Leyden, in 1603, when he put forth views similar to those adopted by the Catholics at the Council of Trent. He explained election by God's foreknowledge of man's merit. In 1618 these views were condemned at a synod of the Reformed Church at Dort and the Arminians expelled, but Arminianism increased in popularity in time and became a strong current in Protestant theology, greatly affecting the Methodists in the eighteenth century.

In the year 410 Alaric, a Visigothic noble and an Arian by religion, who had been commander of the barbarian troops of the imperial army, proved successful in his third seige of Rome and led his troops into the city. It was a shocking event to the men of that time and the cause of widespread consternation. In response to it Augustine wrote his *City of God.* The work was a reply to pagans who charged the reason for the fall of the city was the decay of the traditional religion. In it Augustine examined the relationship of Christianity to the world and set forth for the first time a Christian philosophy of history. Augustine presents human history as consisting of the careers of two cities, an earthly city and a city of God. In these two cities we find the key to an understanding of human destiny. "Accordingly, two cities have been formed by two loves: the earthly by the love of self, even to the contempt of God; the heavenly by the love of God, even to the contempt of self. The former, in a word, glories in itself, the latter in the Lord" (*City of God,* Book 14, chap. 28). The city of this world, the earthly city is self-oriented, the heavenly city, the City of God, is oriented to God. No institution can be wholly identified with one or the other, but the Church is seen as embodying in human terms the heavenly city. The real heavenly city is made up of those who have received God's grace and the Church contains others who have not. Yet the Church "even now is the king-

kingdom of Christ" (*City of God,* Book 20, chap. 2). Human history is the working out of the destiny of these two cities. Basing himself upon the Hebraic and Christian tradition, Augustine sees history as proceeding in a straight line and not a cyclical and repetitive process as had been held by Greek thought. In this work which consists of twenty-two books, Augustine presents not only a view of history but a discussion and explanation of Christian doctrine, and a consideration of other philosophical opinions. This involves Augustine's presentation of world history, a history in which the City of God is gathered together and triumphs in its ultimate peace and in its final glory. But before that time it is a society of pilgrims. Yet "in its pilgrim state the heavenly city possesses this peace by faith" (*City of God,* Book 19, chap. 17).

# THE JEWISH RELIGIOUS TRADITION

The God who loved Israel was also the God who had punished it. The conviction remained that it was only because of Israel's heavy sin that the suffering of exile had been imposed. "Because of our transgressions we were exiled from the holy land and banished from its borders." Exile and redemption—the one, reality, and the other, expectation—were crucial concepts in the consciousness of the Jew and quite essential notions in the development of Judaism. To account for its historical destiny, Israel looked inward. Its deeds and the will of God, not external political forces, had determined its fate. The exile was viewed as a time of terrible suffering and penance which the Jews had to endure in order to atone for the sin of forgetting God's law and will. At the same time, just as living in exile accomplished atonement for Israel's sin, it was also thought to be part of the process of atoning for the sins of the world. Jews saw their own suffering as redemptive for mankind, in the image of the servant of God according to Isaiah. The task of the Jewish people was to suffer in humility and with patience. Their despised and rejected condition, the condition of degradation and suffering, testified to the fulfillment of their mission and the consequent hastening of the redemption.

Thus the pain of exile could be considered a positive blessing, since it was the opportunity God offered to realize the historic role for which Israel had long ago been chosen. According to the Jewish conception, world history depended upon Israel's fulfilling that role, and hence responsibility for the course of world history devolved upon the shoulders of the individual Jew. Knowledge and acceptance of this responsibility constituted the spiritual power of the politically powerless people. Of course, the Jews knew that they could not force the redemption, as had been shown by the crushing of their rebellions and the failure of their pseudo-messiahs. But Israel could pray, could study, and could perform righteous acts—behavior prescribed by the Lord and pleasing unto him—and thereby move history closer to its end station.

The actual reality of exile was often bitter and difficult to bear. In times of persecution the question as to God's intention had to arise. "God, do tell me why I suffer, for I am no doubt unworthy to know why, but help me to believe that I suffer for your sake." Rabbi Akiba believed that sufferings were a gift of God. They served to bring man to a recognition of his own sins, to cause him to repent, and then to bring him to an unquestioning love of God. Akiba refused to challenge divine justice, believing that whatever God did must be for the good. "One ought not criticize Him who said 'let the world be.' Everything He does in justice and truth . . . the judgment is just" (*Avot* 3:20). Although there were many who did not accept Akiba's position and did question the ways of God, the notion that suffering ennobled and was hence a positive value penetrated the Jewish consciousness and brought consolation to the nation. "According to Rabbi Azariah: David said before God: show me the way of life! God said to him, if it is life you seek, seek suffering" (*Pesikta Derekh Kahanna,* p. 152, l. 7). It is this view of suffering which led Jews to accept martyrdom willingly. During the Crusades, which at times led to Christian attacks against Jews, martyrdom became the ideal act of devotion to God. This period witnessed numerous cases of self-slaughter, in which the victims, identifying themselves with Isaac, sacrificed themselves ritually to God, in the belief that this was his wish and part of his divine plan. The Jews of Mayence, attacked by the soldiers of the first Crusade,

> *declared with their whole heart and willing soul, After all one must not have any doubts concerning the ways of the Holy One blessed be He who had given us His Torah and the commandment to suffer death in behalf of the unity of His holy name. Happy are we if we fulfill His wish and happy is he who is slain and slaughtered for the unity of His name. Such an one will be prepared to enter the world-to-come. . . . More, he will have exchanged the world of darkness for a world of light, a world of suffering for a world of joy, the transitory world for a world enduring forever.*
>
> (*Chronicle, Solomon*)

The Jews lived, in a certain sense, ahistorically and apolitically. They had no share in actual political power, and hence were not very much interested in it. Throughout the Middle Ages, in Christian lands, the Jews lived in the status of "Serfs of the Kingdom." This meant that they were considered serfs of the ruling power and that their residence and privileges were entirely dependent upon the will of that power. As long as they were useful, in an economic sense, they could remain. However, if their economic value declined, or if, for some reason, ecclesiastical authorities objected to their presence, the residency right was withdrawn and the Jews exiled. Completely dependent upon the will of the sovereign, the will of the

Church, and often the threats of the townsmen or peasants, the Jews lived in a state of constant insecurity. They were unable to determine their own fate, and hence did not really participate actively in the making of contemporary history. Their historical world was that of the past, of the Bible and the Tradition, which was a spiritual world out of time but in the midst of time. The condition of exile led the Jew to live with his eye toward the future, when existence in this world would end and all would be changed. Understanding of the present and hope for the future is summarized in the following statement of Rabbi Judah ha-Levi:

> *If his mood is disturbed by the length of the exile and the diaspora and the degradation of his people, he finds comfort in acknowledging the justice of the divine decree . . . then in being cleansed from his sins; then in the reward and recompense awaiting him in the world to come, and the attachment to the Divine Influence in this world.*
>
> (*Kuzari* II.33, 36)

The belief which sustained Israel and was of primary significance in Judaism was messianism, that is, the certain conviction that in God's appointed hour a messiah would come to deliver Israel and the world from travail. "For the vision is yet for the appointed time. And it declareth of the end and doth not lie; though it tarry, wait for it, because it will surely come and not delay" (*Sanhedrin* 97b). Every day the Jew prayed for the speedy fulfillment of the messianic promise. "Manifest to us the dawn of the Messianic deliverance and cause it to flourish by the grace of thy salvation. Thy redemption we want every day. Praised be Thou, O Lord, who causest deliverance to arise." Restoration of self-rule, of the ancient city of David, Jerusalem, return of the exiles, and the return of God himself to Zion—these were the ardent desires of the expectant nation. Jews also prayed for universal deliverance, for the day

> *When we shall behold the triumph of thy might, when idolatry will be uprooted and falsehood utterly destroyed. We hope for the day when the world will be perfected under the dominion of the Almighty and all mankind will learn to revere thy Name; when all the wicked of the earth will be drawn in penitence to Thee. O may all the inhabitants of the earth recognize that unto Thee every knee must bend every tongue vow loyalty.*

The messianic age would be filled with glories. First, Israel would be gathered together and restored as a national entity to its homeland to enjoy there the bounties of political freedom and material wealth. Following this age of material and national prosperity, the world-to-come would dawn. Conditions would be totally changed and a new order instituted. According to Jewish belief, at this time a universal judgment would take place and the righteous of all nations would be rewarded with eternal bliss. Descriptions of all stages of the future world and golden age abound in Jewish literature, providing hope and comfort to a people discredited in the eyes of the world and suffering the grave anxieties of exile.

The apex in the development of Jewish messianic thought is to be found in the doctrines of the Lurianic school of mysticism, which flourished in the mid-sixteenth century in the small Palestinian town of Safed. The devotees of this school, followers of Rabbi Isaac Luria, reinterpreted the traditional concepts of exile and redemption in light of their intense mystical experience and gave a radically deepened meaning to these keystones of Jewish belief. In 1492 the Jews had been exiled from Spain. This event had profound consequences upon the religious consciousness, manifested in the bursting forth of mystical speculation and activity concerning redemption, and the wide response to it. Around the time of the catastrophic exile and immediately following, messianic expectations ran high. Jews felt that the cruel events of reality could only be the signal and birth pangs of the long-promised ultimate deliverance. It is told that a group of Spanish Jews, confident of immediate redemption, marched headlong into the ocean, expecting it to part and let them pass. As late as 1560 a rabbi wrote that "No Jew has lived in Spain for seventy years, and we are sure that no Jew will ever pitch his tent there, for God will soon gather together the scattered remnants of his people of Israel" (*Baer* 69). However, when it became clear that the exile of 1492 was but another link in the chain of tribulations and not the beginning of the redemption, when the depth of the tragedy penetrated the Jewish consciousness, an explanation was sought. Why had the new darkness descended upon man? What had brought the evil fate? The Lurianic school of mystics, engaged in this inner process of soul searching, developed a doctrine of redemption which both offered an explanation of the external reality of intensified suffering in exile and presented a new path for internal spiritual salvation.

Lurianic mystical thought rested upon the notion that God, in order to create the world, had to impose limits upon himself. He had to retreat into himself in order to make space for the creation of the universe, so that in the very first act of creation a negative element was present. When God created the world he sent out his divine light, which was contained within form-giving vessels or spheres. However, the light was too much for the vessels to hold, and they burst, allowing the divine light to be scattered. Some of the sparks managed to return to God himself, but some descended to earth, to be diffused in the evil of the world and imprisoned below. Thus, in the process of creation, God himself went into exile. First, he exiled himself when he imposed limits on his being, and second, he was exiled when the spiritual and pure light was mixed in the impure world of man.

Through this mythological sketch of creation, the mystics revolutionized the Jewish concept of exile by giving it cosmic proportions. With God in exile, with exile built into the very nature of the universe, the exile of Israel became merely one sign of a total cosmic condition. The world had been broken from its very inception. Being itself had been distorted, had been ruptured, and the divine source of all suffered constantly from loss of wholeness. Exile, in this conception, was seen as a phenomenon characterizing all being, a matter of the inner nature of the universe. And redemption consequently was to be deliverance of the entire universe from its broken state of being. In the hands of Lurianic mystics, the traditional Jewish concepts of exile and redemption were deepened, interiorized, and universalized.

According to this school of mysticism, the task of the Jew was still to participate in the process of redemption, but in a new way. Within the framework of the traditional paths, of fulfilling the commandments, engaging in study, and devotion to prayer, the Jew had to now work for the inner salvation of the entire cosmos. He acted with a new intention, knowing that he participated in a universal process and that his deeds had cosmic power. The Jew had to help to redeem the fallen sparks and thus restore God to himself. It is this labor which he had to intend when he performed a religious commandment. With this concept, Lurianic mysticism radicalized the value of religious practice and the role of the individual Jew. The regimen of prescribed Jewish law would now be performed with the inner knowledge that such performance effected a cosmic change because with the fulfillment of commandments the diffused sparks were uplifted and returned to God. Man was thus a necessary agent in the process of reuniting God with himself and in healing the rift in creation. Through his actions he either hastened or delayed redemption.

The Lurianic mystic, when he observed the commandments and when he engaged in mystical prayer, believed that he helped to free his own soul from the bonds of earthly existence, and at the same time, that he helped to free the world itself. The great power of this doctrine lay in its awarding each man a vital role in the process of cosmic redemption and thereby the highest worth as a man. For the Jew who lived in the darkness of disappointment, in the brokenness and impotence of exile, Lurianic mysticism gave nobility and power. It enabled him to reach a new spiritual dimension of meaning and validation. To be sure, he and his people were defeated and unsuccessful when judged according to the standards of the external world. But he and his people alone possessed the internal spiritual power to redeem that exile. Thus, when judged according to the truth of inner reality, the Jewish condition was an elevated one. In the suffering of exile, reflecting the broken state of the cosmos, lay the opportunity to redeem the sparks and restore the world.

The concepts of Lurianic mysticism caught on and had great influence among large segments of the Jewish people. The rise and widespread acceptance of Sabbetai Zevi, the false messiah of the mid-seventeenth century, was made possible by the messianic expectations which Lurianic doctrines had encouraged. And in Hasidism, the great modern mystical movement, certain Lurianic notions live on, still providing great spiritual strength to those who participate in the hidden inner reality of the redemptive process. In Hasidism the emphasis is on the individual and his subjective religious experience. But his relationship with God is one which involves the act of redeeming the sparks and contributing to the restoration of the world. To the *hasid,* as to every traditional Jew, the basic fact of existence was exile, and redemption the basic need. In hasidic prayer ecstasy, the individual came close to God, achieved a degree of inner redemption, and returned to lead others to the same reality.

Judaism is a religion of revelation, in which ultimate authority resides in the word of God as found in Scripture and interpreted by legitimated scholars. The meaning of Jewish life and the order of its society was determined by an understanding of the revealed word. Religious ideas, values, and ways of behaving provided the framework for the total existence of the Jewish community throughout exilic history. However, the Jewish community was not a completely self-contained closed-off world, but was part of a larger environment and was subject to influences from it. In the hellenistic period, Greek ideas and values penetrated the Jewish consciousness and had a marked influence upon several levels of Jewish society. It was when the Jews came under Muslim rule, however, during the Arab conquests of the eighth and ninth centuries, that they were most deeply affected by outside influences. Through Arab writers and thinkers, the classical tradition of Greece and the traditions of the Hindus and Persians were presented to Jewish readers. In natural science, medicine, astronomy, history, literature, and philosophy Jews learned and responded to new ideas and new forms. The centuries under Islam proved to be among the most creative in Jewish cultural and religious history, producing a vast literature of a religious and secular nature.

The rise of Islam and the claims of the new religion challenged Judaism to respond in defense of its own claims to possess the original and true revelation of God and hence to be the one true religion. Rivalry with Christianity at other times evoked similar controversy and polemical activity. Jews were spurred to justify the beliefs and practices of their tradition in the rational philosophic language which would be understood by exponents of challenging beliefs. Influenced by the writings of Muslim philosophers and theologians, Jews were often themselves perplexed, and sought to examine the biblical tradition in the light of reason. From the ninth century to the eleventh, Jewish philosophic activity flourished in the Arabic lands.

The issues with which Jewish philosophers dealt were those which concerned all philosophical proponents of biblically derived religion, who attempted to integrate the doctrines of revelation with the ideas of Plato and Aristotle. There was the primary question of the role of reason within the structure of revealed religion and the relationship of philosophy and religious knowledge. Then questions as to the existence and nature of God, his relationship to man, and the role of man in the world were most significant. For the Jew in particular, proof of the eternal and absolute truth of the Torah, and validation of the election of Israel, were of great concern. An understanding of the commandments, both ritual and ethical, was also demanded as part of the attempt to rationalize the entire traditional way of life.

The first great Jewish philosopher of the Islamic period was Rabbi Saadia Gaon, who became head of the Academy at Sura in

*The Dome of the Rock of the Temple Mount in Jerusalem, a sacred Moslem and Jewish site. The Dome marks the site of Solomon's Temple and is believed to be the place where Abraham prepared Isaac for sacrifice. (Courtesy of the Israel Government Tourist Office.)*

Babylonia in 928, and who wrote his major work, *The Book of Beliefs and Opinions,* in 933. Saadia was impelled to write this work not only because of the challenge of Greek and Islamic ideas but also because of the internal threat posed by the Karaites, a Jewish sect which denied the authority of rabbinic interpretation, and hence the validity of the definitions, concerning law and ideas, handed down in the Talmud. Saadia was most influenced by the Aristotelian, the Mutazilite school, within Islam, and his defense of Jewish beliefs, such as the existence of God, was Aristotelian in nature. Saadia claimed that the truths of reason and revelation were completely harmonious. What God had revealed to the Jews, the content of the Torah, could not be contradicted by the knowledge which man would attain through reason. The specific value of revelation in contrast to reason was that revelation offered the truth to all men, many of whom could not otherwise attain it, and revelation, because of its final absolute nature, offered this truth in a form free of the inconclusiveness and uncertainty inherent in the process of reasoning. For these reasons, God's gift of revelation was necessary for man. Saadia believed that the exercise of reason in pursuit of the same basic truths was also a necessary, and indeed, a religious act. The philosopher is charged to engage in philosophical inquiry, with the assumption that he has already accepted the truths of revelation and hence knows the end to which his reasoning will lead. Saadia was as certain of the identity of natural knowledge and revelatory knowledge, as he was of the truth of Israel's special revelation. The indisputable historical fact that the Mosaic Torah, unlike any other revelation, was disclosed in a public event to an entire people guarantees its validity.

The writings of Saadia enjoyed widespread circulation among Jews in the Islamic lands and encouraged the development of Aristotelian philosophic thinking. Among the many figures to participate in this philosophic movement, the greatest by far was Moses ben Maimon, or Moses Maimonides (1135–1204). Maimonides was born in Cordova, Spain, fled with his family from anti-Jewish attacks to Fez, and finally settled in Fustat, outside Cairo, where he practiced medicine and served as the head of the Egyptian Jewish community. In his life and in his writings, Maimonides harmonized the Greek and Jewish traditions. He was pious in his religious practice, engaged in the rabbinic tasks of teaching and study and legislating, advised the Jewish community on public affairs, and at the same time was interested in general cultural ideas, devoting himself to bringing together Greek philosophy and biblical revelation. The first literary task which Maimonides undertook was a commentary on the Mishnah, followed by a systematic compilation of Jewish law. These works reflect his basic concern with traditional pursuits, and his desire, derived from acquaintance with Greek forms, to impress a logical order upon the traditional legal material. In the *Commentary,* Maimonides explained the concepts necessary for understanding the contents of each of the six volumes of the Mishnah, and prefaced the entire work with a chapter on the nature of Jewish tradition as it developed from the original Mosaic revelation into the halakic and aggadic writings of the rabbis. In the *Mishneh Torah,* Maimonides summarized the voluminous legal material of the Oral Law and codified the law in fourteen parts, corresponding to the fourteen types of legal commandments. He intended his work to be a lucid authoritative compilation of the law. Its merits were soon recognized and the *Mishneh Torah* became a basic guide to practice and a subject of study for all later generations.

It was in the *Guide to the Perplexed* (1190) that Maimonides expounded his philosophical ideas, which were decisive in the development of Jewish thought and which greatly influenced Christian Aristotelians, such as St. Albert the Great and St. Thomas Aquinas. As its title indicates, Maimonides composed the *Guide* for the perplexed of his time, for those troubled by the challenges which philosophy presented to biblical faith and concepts. He addressed the book to his student, Joseph, and intended it to be read only by those trained in traditional Jewish disciplines, mathematics, logic, the sciences, and who were thus fully prepared for the perils which philosophical speculation presented. Free rational inquiry was not

Mishneh Torah *by Moses Maimonides, showing the title and contents.* (*Courtesy of the British Museum.*)

to be pursued by all Jews, but only by an elite, whose minds and spirits could bear the doubts which such inquiry inevitably aroused.

The first concern of Maimonides was the relation of faith and reason. Like Saadia, he argued that natural knowledge and revelation were identical, and hence that there existed a harmonious relation between religion and philosophy. He did not propose that all philosophic knowledge was contained in Revelation, but that philosophic knowledge was the highest and truest way to reach an understanding of the content of Revelation. To Maimonides, philosophy was a religious task, and the pious man one whose faith has been understood and thereby deepened. He considered the greatest good of man to be the attainment of knowledge, for through metaphysical knowledge of the divine reality and divine truths, man entered into a relationship of love with God and achieved communion with him.

Therefore, contemplation, reflection, and the pursuit of understanding were the highest values of the religious life.

This view of Maimonides as to the value of contemplation and philosophical speculation represents a distinct shift in emphasis from the traditional Jewish evaluation of religious virtue. While contemplation was never disregarded, the traditional Jewish emphasis has been upon positive action, based upon loyal acceptance of the law. Maimonides' evaluation of intellectual activity and the internalization of divine knowledge, as the main activity of the religious life, does not imply a rejection of practice nor a denigration of tradition. On the contrary, Maimonides prescribed complete faithfulness to the ceremonial and ethical law of the Torah and assumed that philosophical study would be based upon mastery of the religious tradition. Further, he was himself involved in practical rabbinic tasks and wrote two major works on rabbinic tradition. His God was always the moral Lord of the Bible, who was concerned that men follow in the divine paths. Yet, despite this obvious loyalty to tradition, there is no doubt that Maimonides did shift emphasis when he postulated that knowledge would lead men to imitate God, and that this knowledge ought to underlie external conformity to religious imperatives.

Recognizing that most men were incapable of a life devoted to philosophic speculation, Maimonides postulated certain basic beliefs, which he felt were religious truths available to everyone and necessary for the salvation of every man. These thirteen creedal articles, listed in the *Commentary to the Mishnah,* include the existence of God, the unity of God, his incorporeal nature, his eternity, the obligation to worship God, the existence of prophecy, the recognition of Moses as the greatest of all prophets, the acceptance of the Torah revealed to Moses as divine in origin, the acceptance of the eternal validity of the Torah, the notion that God is omniscient, that he will reward and punish men on the basis of their actions, that he will deliver men through his messiah, and finally, that he will resurrect the dead. The ordinary Jew was required to affirm these beliefs and follow the commands of the Torah, whose purpose it was to lead men to an ordered moral and social life.

In the *Guide* Maimonides presented concise discussions and definitions of the classical religious questions. His doctrine of the attributes of God, based upon the notion that only negative attribution is possible in predication about God, was brilliantly presented, and became highly influential in later philosophical discussion of this problem. Altogether, his rational explanation of Jewish beliefs and practices is the most thorough and complete in Jewish literature. Its greatness was immediately recognized by his contemporaries and the *Guide* met with much success among those who felt the challenge of rationalism to their faith and experienced the need to work out a harmonization between reason and revelation. However, the intellectualization of Judaism accomplished by Moses Maimonides, his elevation of philosophical knowledge to the rank of the greatest perfection over the virtues of traditional study and practice, offended certain sectors of the Jewish population and eventually stirred protest against the entire philosophical enterprise. The basic motive of the protest was the desire to delimit reason and the autonomous activity of man. It was felt by the antiphilosophical party that human rationality could not go beyond a certain point. Maimonides and his followers were said to have exceeded the boundary, thereby distorting the simple precepts of Judaism and introducing alien forms and ideas into Jewish consciousness. Tradition could not be subordinated to the intellect and piety relegated to a position secondary to intellectual endeavor. During the thirteenth and fourteenth centuries the controversy between the advocates of philosophy and their opponents raged. It was the latter who eventually won out, and Jewish philosophical development was largely stemmed. However, the work of Maimonides was not lost and the attempt to rationalize faith was continued by many individual thinkers. The great work of Rabbi Nahman Krochmal (1785–1840), *The Guide for the Perplexed of Our Time,* indicates in its very title the influence of Maimonides and represents a significant attempt to do in the nineteenth century what medieval Jewish philosophers had attempted from the tenth through the fifteenth centuries.

Another development in Jewish religious thought, related to Neoplatonism rather than Aristotelianism and much closer to distinctly Jewish ideas and sentiments, is presented in the writings of Judah Halevi (1085–1141/42), the greatest poet and one of the greatest thinkers of the medieval period. In his major philosophical work, the *Kuzari,* Halevi endeavored to prove the uniqueness and truth of Judaism in opposition to Christianity, Islam, and philosophy. He did not base his claim on metaphysical proof, but rather denied that rational method could achieve absolute certainty in this area at all, calling attention to the innumerable differences between philosophers on all critical issues. The single proof for the truth of Judaism is a historical one, according to Halevi, namely, the historical facts of God's mighty deeds, his public revelation to the Jewish people, and his providential care for them. It is thus that Halevi stated his position:

> *I believe in the God of Abraham, Isaac, and Israel, who led the Israelites out of Egypt with signs and miracles; who fed them in the desert and gave them the Holy Land, after having made them traverse the sea and the Jordan in a miraculous way; who sent Moses with His Law, and subsequently thousands of prophets, who confirmed His Law by promises to those who observed, and threats to the disobedient. We believe in what is contained in the Torah—a very large domain. . . . I made mention to thee of what is convincing for me and for the whole of Israel, who knew these things, first through personal experience, and afterward through an uninterrupted tradition, which is equal to experience.*
>
> (*Kuzari* I.11, 25)

Halevi denied that the rational intellectual efforts of man could ever reach knowledge of God. Such knowledge is available only when God discloses himself because of his own desire to communicate with man. God has chosen and revealed himself to Israel, the object of his greatest affection. He has given Israel a special religious sense, a faculty to perceive the divine, which is of course superior to any other faculty with which man has been endowed. However, this special faculty is not fully actualized even in Israel, but must be nurtured by obedience to the divine law. And even with the religious faculty, not all Jews can come really to understand God, to see him fully, but only the prophets among them. To these men God reveals himself directly and sensually. The knowledge of the prophet cannot be reached by the philosopher, and the latter can never enter into the relationship of love and communion which the prophet has with God.

According to Halevi, Israel is essentially different from all other human groups in its religious endowment, and has a crucial role to play in history because of this endowment. The ultimate redemption of the world is dependent upon the relationship of Israel to God. The pious Jew who cultivates his religious faculty, who sanctifies his life by fulfilling the word of God, not only ascends toward communion with the Lord but hastens the salvation of all men. In the messianic age, what Israel alone possesses will become the property of all, and all men will enter into communion with God.

Halevi's views on the peculiarity of religious as distinct from philosophic truth and the peculiarity of Israel as bearer of this truth, essentially distinguished from all other religions, provided answers to the dilemmas which rational speculation and the rival claims of seemingly more successful faiths presented to the Jews of his time. Further, the historical stress of Halevi and his emphasis upon the uniqueness of the religious sense appealed to the traditional Jew greatly. Yet, despite the differences between them, Halevi and Maimonides both represented the philosophical strain in Jewish spiritual life. Of much more significance for the common man, and consequently of greater popularity, was the developing pietistic literature. In the Middle Ages, the greatest work in this area was Bahya Ibn Pakuda's *Duties of the Heart,* which became a standard guide to the meditational, devotional, and ethical life. In the spirit of his time, Bahya expounded proofs for the existence of God and presented a discussion of the divine attributes. However, his main concern was not with such rational doctrines nor with external ethical behavior, "duties of the limbs," but with the development of the inner soul, which was the relation of man's heart to God. In his central chapters on worship, trust in God, submission to God, humility, repentance, self-examination before God, withdrawal from the world, and finally, on love of God, he attempted to direct man toward the most intimate relationship with God which the soul could attain. Although man must labor in the world and live a life of righteousness, Bahya taught inner withdrawal and concentration upon the true task, which was ascent to God in order to communicate with him and serve him more perfectly. It was the appeal to the soul of the pious man which drew Bahya's writings to the soul of the Jewish people. His stress on the life of devotion and meditation, his emphasis upon the sentiments of trust and love rather than knowledge and wisdom, responded to the needs and exercised lasting influence upon the Jewish religious spirit.

Concentration upon the inner life, the life of the soul in relation to God, was most highly developed in medieval Jewish mysticism, known as the Kabbalah. Literally, the term *kabbalah* means "tradition," and refers to the mystic's claim that his knowledge of divine mysteries has been received through revelation. The tradition of mystical speculation and mystical practice was a continuous one from the days of *merkavah* mysticism. However, it was only during the thirteenth and fourteenth centuries that kabbalistic ideas spread to large segments of the Jewish population and became for many as significant a force in religious life as was traditional learning and practice. The classical kabbalistic work, the *Zohar,* assumed a position alongside the Bible and Talmud as a basic religious text of the people and maintained this position for three hundred years. The desire to understand the mysteries of God's being, the mysteries of his creation, and the secret relation of man's soul to God was a powerful one shared by all levels of the Jewish population. The *merkavah* mystics, the German *hasidim,* the Spanish kabbalists, the school of Isaac Luria, the Eastern European *hasidim,* and other groups form a continuous chain. A vast literature on theory and practice emerged from this mystical tradition, which aroused the soul of the Jewish people and drew many into participation in the inner religious life of mystical learning and into the intense social life of a mystical community.

The great development of the Kabbalah, which carried mysticism outside small esoteric circles to large numbers of the people, began in 1200 in southern France and Spain. Leaders of the movement were more often laymen than rabbis and were not committed to a life devoted to talmudic learning. They could approach the Jewish tradition from a new perspective and find in it new depths of spiritual insight and meaning. Largely uninfluenced by non-Jewish cultural forms or ideas, the kabbalists developed their tradition in the typical exegetical manner, but probed to hidden levels and interpreted scriptural passages in a novel, and often mythical, and highly imaginative way.

The *Zohar,* the *Book of Splendor,* is the most significant work in the kabbalistic corpus. The book was issued anonymously, and its authorship has been clouded in mystery. However, modern research has attributed it to Moses de Leon, a Castilian Jew, who is said to have composed the main body of the work c. 1280. The form of the *Zohar* is quite complex. It consists of many sections, not systematically ordered and not unified, which include homiletical interpretations of biblical passages, dramatic descriptions of persons and places, and epigrammatic revelations of divine mysteries. The use of Aramaic, and the ascription of large parts of the work to the first-century sage and saint Rabbi Simon bar Yohai, add further to the *Zohar*'s mystery and difficult nature.

The *merkavah* mystics had attempted to ascend to the throne of the Lord and to contemplate the majesty of the divine presence in the palace, throne, and garments of the seventh heaven. The kabbalists sought to go beyond this level of appearance in order to see the Lord himself. They perceived levels closer and closer to the real being of God, and penetrated deeper and deeper into his very essence. The kabbalists called the levels of divine being which they perceived the *sephirot,* the spheres. They were the manifestations of the hidden God, the *En Sof,* embodying specific attributes of his nature. According to the kabbalists, men could grasp God in the *sephirot* and could thereby enter the hidden and true reality of the divine being.

The kabbalists believed that the Torah contained a hidden meaning, which could be discerned if the text were interpreted in the mystical mode. Delving into the mysteries of revelation in order to penetrate to the mysteries of the universe, the kabbalists constructed, through their homilies, a world of mythical symbols to describe the divine mysteries and the mysteries of the spheres. They disclosed these secret meanings to the initiated, a group which grew steadily as men sought new paths to understand the ways of God. The mystical search for the beginning and the end, the search of the soul to reach God himself, has been embarked upon by generations of pious Jews, in the hope that this quest would lead to ultimate understanding and ultimate redemption.

During the long history of Judaism, many streams of religious thought and religious life developed. Rabbinic learning, rabbinic values, and rabbinic definitions of practice always constituted the mainstream and were the base from which innovative ideas and forms emerged. At the foundation of Jewish life was the original revelation to Moses and its interpretation by the successive schools of rabbis. Every Jew knew the Scripture and was acquainted with the most lucid and brilliant commentary upon it, that of the great French scholar Rabbi Solomon bar Isaac (1040–1105), known as Rashi. Rashi's commentary transmitted to the student, by way of exegesis upon the biblical text, an understanding of the literal meaning of that text and an understanding of its religious insights. With a knowledge of the Bible and Rashi, the Jew was anchored in the sacred traditions of his people, and had absorbed the religious ideas which gave meaning to the life of the community in which he participated.

Study of the Law and cultivation of the spirit were handmaidens in the history of Judaism. The ideal man was a saint and a scholar, who neglected neither mind, soul, nor body in the attainment of religious perfection. "Simon the Just was one of the last of the Great synagogue. He was wont to say: Upon three things the world stands —upon the Torah, upon worship, and upon the doing of righteous deeds" (*Avot* 1:2). The embodiment of this precept is to be found in innumerable heroes of Jewish tradition, one of whom, Rabbi Joseph Karo (1488–1575), may be taken as exemplary. Karo was recognized as the leading legist of his day and his legal writings have become classics in the rabbinic heritage. He composed the *Bet Joseph,* four large volumes tracing the sources and development of the Law, and the *Shulhan Aruch,* a concise summary and codification of the Law. The latter became the most widely used legal guide throughout the Jewish communities of the exile. However, legal activity was only one side of Karo's complex personality. On the other, he was constantly engaged in mystical experiences, which are recorded in a diary of his spiritual life, the *Maggid Mesharim.*

Karo had studied the Law intensely and had wrapped himself in his work in a most profound way. He had been devoted particularly to the Mishnah and had somehow become part of that code himself, so that the angel which appeared to him is identified as the Mishnah. This Mishnah-angel came to Karo during the night to advise, admonish, encourage, and teach him the mysteries of the tradition. Karo was commanded by the angel to devote himself more to the Kabbalah and to the devotional study of Bahya's *Duties of the Heart.* The greatest rabbinic scholar and authority of his day lived a double existence, always in contact with the inner world of the angels and the heavens. He believed that in his own work on earth he reflected in microcosm a heavenly reality, which the angel-mentor expressed in his greeting, "Peace from the College of Heaven." Karo labored on his legal tomes in the shadow of the heavens and in anticipation of the world to come, where he would sit with the righteous in the presence of God.

Karo's rabbinic school was established in Safed. At the same time and in the same town, the greatest school of Jewish mysticism arose and thrived, the school of Rabbi Isaac Luria. Karo had taught Moses Cordovero, leader of the Safed mystics before Luria, and Karo and Luria were in contact during the latter's years in Safed. This association of the mystics and scholars was certainly not unique, for it was common in Jewish history that the same man was both a rabbinic sage and mystic, while mystical movements arose and lived alongside rabbinic centers. Thus, in the eighteenth and nineteenth centuries the main center of talmudic learning was in Vilna, in Lithuania, where the great scholar Elijah Gaon lived and studied. Refusing any official position of authority, the Vilna Gaon was still recognized as the leading figure in rabbinic interpretation and was regarded by his contemporaries as a great saint, whose guidance was to be sought on all matters. In his personal life the Gaon was totally absorbed in his studies and dedicated his entire life to them. His example and his method inspired many disciples, and the great yeshivah at Voloshin owes its foundation to the work of Elijah of Vilna. This school stands as a symbol of the heights to which rabbinic learning in Eastern Europe rose. Here hundreds of boys and men submitted themselves to the discipline of talmudic study, laboring from early morning till late in the evening throughout the week, in the belief that such labor lifted the mind, deepened the spirit, and was a service to God.

At the same time that the Vilna Gaon wrote his commentaries and rabbinic studies flourished in schools throughout Eastern Europe, the mystical movement of Hasidism developed and captured the hearts of thousands among the simple pious folk and among the educated. In the figure of the Baal Shem Tov, the founder of Hasidism, one sees a complete contrast to the Vilna Gaon, for the Baal Shem (1760–1810) was an unlearned enthusiast, a wonder-worker, as his name indicates. He was a simple man, whose miraculous powers and marvelous character attracted followers and soon led to his being elevated to the position of a popular saint and legendary figure. The Baal Shem and his followers created a dynamic revivalist movement which encompassed large parts of Polish and Russian Jewry, arousing deep devotion and piety. Hasidic mystical activities regenerated a religious life which had become alien and ossified for many.

Although in its initial stages Hasidism's emotional subjective religiosity was in part a protest against the objectivity and intellectualism of rabbinic Judaism, and did represent the virtues of the simple and pious in opposition to the learned and aristocratic, the movement did not become antinomian, and did not long maintain an opposition stance. Hasidic leaders were also rabbis and the rabbinic tradition was integrated with hasidic ideas and practices in the formation of new vital religious communities. The *Habad* movement within Hasidism represents the coming together of subjective enthusiasm in worship, deep devotion to traditional subjects and methods of study, and dedication to mystical doctrines and practices, the enthusiastic revival of immediate religious experience, and the reaffirmation of popular mysticism. The Hasidic movement occurred within the structure of rabbinic Judaism, demonstrating the continuing ability of the traditional ideas and forms to develop and accommodate the multiple needs of the religious spirit.

# MAN'S RELATION TO GOD

## WORSHIP AND PRAYER IN CHRISTIANITY

We have been considering here the chief elements of the Christian tradition as they developed from the messianic career of Jesus of Nazareth and the primitive Church. In considering tradition, we naturally concern ourselves with what is believed, for it is beliefs that make up traditions, and the content of beliefs that tradition transmits from past to future. But we must remember that important though belief indeed is, it derives from something more basic and more central to the religious life. Most basic to religion is the religious experience, the believer's experience of God. Man responds to what he experiences above and beyond the mundane happenings of his workaday life—to an aspect of the environment which he neither comprehends nor manipulates, but which calls to him and is related to him in an intimate way. That response is the central religious act—the act of worship.

Worship is a universal human response found in all cultures and traditions. It embodies and expresses man's basic relationship to what really is—to what is apprehended as real, fundamental, and in some way constitutive of all reality. Worship is a response in depth which points beyond experience to a realm of being and mystery. It points toward and expresses a relationship to transcendence. In worship men feel related to the source and origin of their own being, and of all being, and to the deepest end and goal of their own existence. Worship places man in a subject-object relationship to the Beyond, but it is an unequal and asymmetrical relation. Before the mystery which he confronts in the religious relationship, man feels a vast reverence, a kind of fear, mingled with an experience of being called to a closer intimacy. This complex attitude finds its expression in the acts of adoration which become the religious practices of the various religious traditions.

In the Judeo-Christian tradition this Beyond is revealed as the creator of the world and the Lord of history, the author and sustainer of nature, and the God who reveals himself in historical time. It is he to whom all honor and worship are due. "I am the Lord your God, who brought you out of the land of Egypt, out of the house of bondage. You shall have no other gods before me" (Deut. 5:6–7). Christianity finds the progressive revelation of this God in the history of the Jewish nation brought to its fulfillment in Jesus. "In many and various ways God spoke of old to our fathers by the prophets; but in these last days he has spoken to us by a Son, whom he appointed the heir of all things, through whom also he created the world" (Heb. 1:1–2). Jewish and Christian worship is centered on God and in it man is believed paradoxically to find his highest self-expression and fulfillment in relating himself to God and making God the center of his life. This worship has taken two general forms. It has found communal expression in a corporate form, a public prayer of the community, as seen in the early Temple sacrifices and the later worship services of the Jewish synagogue and the Christian church. It has also found an individual expression as seen in the importance attached to individual prayer. This individual expression reaches its highest development in mysticism.

The central act of worship for Christianity is the celebration of the Eucharist, called the Mass in the Latin church. In this service we have the ritual repetition of the last supper which Jesus ate with his disciples on the night before he was put to death, a ritual in which it is believed that his presence is experienced again. The New Testament contains four accounts of the institution of the Eucharist by Jesus and tells of its celebration in the early Christian community. From the beginning two things appear to have been held generally concerning it: It involved a real present relationship with the risen Christ and it was instituted by Jesus himself. From the first centuries it was generally accorded that it brought to the receiver the body and blood of Christ as stated in the words of Jesus quoted in the celebration. The Eucharistic celebration is a public external act of worship which is held to reenact and re-present the Last Supper of Jesus and his sacrificial death upon the cross of Calvary the next day. The Mass is held to be not only the reenactment of and sharing in the sacred Passover meal of Jesus with his disciples but also an unbloody re-presentation and participation in the mystery of Christ's redemptive death—his offering of himself as the sacred victim to his Father for the redemption of men, his blood shed for the "remission of sins." Jesus was the Suffering Servant of Deutero-Isaiah and this death was his great redemptive act. It is in this that all share in the Mass. It is this public corporate act which provides to the worshiper the occasion for his own deepest subjective interior relation to God. The Eucharistic service of which the consecration and reception of the sacrament are central and basic involves also preparatory prayers and readings of Scripture obviously influenced by the synagogue as well as final prayers of thanksgiving. Indeed, the word "Eucharist" means thanksgiving and the celebration is also considered a thanksgiving service. At once individual and collective, both ritualized and eliciting spontaneous participation, objective and shared and subjective and individual at the same time, the Eucharistic celebration remains the central dramatic expression and fulfillment of the religious response in Western Catholic and Eastern Orthodox Christianity. Protestantism simplified much in the years following the Reformation, yet the meaning of the Eucharistic service remained in some sense central for most of the Reformation churches.

It is remarkable that although theological precision has been so prominent a Christian concern and the resulting controversy so prominent a feature of Christian history, the first several centuries of the Church witnessed hardly any real attempt at precise Eucharistic definition or any real controversy concerning Eucharistic faith. We find Cyprian stating that Christ "first offered himself as a sacrifice to the Father, and commanded this to be done in remembrance of himself" (Cyprian, *Epistle,* 63.14), Ignatius saying that "the Eucharist is the flesh of our Saviour Jesus Christ" (*Epistle to the Smyrnans* 6), and Irenaeus proclaiming that "the bread of the earth, receiving the invocation of God, is no longer common bread but Eucharist, consisting of two things, an earthly and a heavenly" (*Against Heresies* 4.18.6). From the fourth century on we find a general use of terms indicating that the elements of bread and wine are transformed into Christ's body and blood (anticipating the later Catholic definition), while some writers speak of a continued presence of the natural elements as well as of the body and blood of the Lord in the consecrated sacrament (anticipating Luther's later definition). It was not until the eleventh century that a significant conflict is to be found on these matters which will become so controversial in the Reformation period. At that time Berengarius denied the generally taught and accepted doctrine of the Real Presence but twice retracted his denial under pressure before his death in 1088. Some of his followers held a doctrine of a kind of hidden and obscure presence of Christ's body and blood covered and concealed by the presence of the bread and wine. Peter Lombard, who was the theologian who most influenced education in the Middle Ages, held that Christ was substantially present in the Eucharist but conceded the difficulties involved in any precise definition. In 1215 the Fourth Lateran Council declared in a dogmatic definition that "the body and blood are truly contained in the sacrament of the altar under the species of bread and wine; the bread being transubstantiated into the body and the wine into the blood by the power of God." Later in the same century this doctrine was given detailed definition in the works of Thomas Aquinas, who held in Aristotelian terminology that the elements were changed into the substance of Christ while the accidents of bread and wine remain and are present to our sense perception.

The Reformation saw great controversy on the meaning of the Eucharist. Luther found that transubstantiation "must be considered as an invention of human reason, since it is based neither on Scripture nor sound reasoning." He proposed a doctrine of consubstantiation which held that in the sacrament both the bread and wine and the body and blood of Christ coexist—"the bread and wine are really bread and wine and the true flesh and blood of Christ is in them." Ulrich Zwingli (1484–1531), the great Swiss Reformer, took the most radical view of the Eucharist of any major Reformation figure. Zwingli denied any doctrine which affirmed a real flesh-and-blood presence of Christ in the sacrament, and the differences between him and Luther on this question prevented any unity of the Reform efforts in Germany and Switzerland. Unlike Luther, Calvin had no sympathy with the worship practices of the old Church. He was overwhelmed by the transcendence of God, a God "wholly other," who "hath no image." Calvin reacted negatively and radically against all ceremonial and gestural symbolism and saw himself called to purify the Church. To him the Roman Mass was composed of "a criminal godlessness." For him there was not really a present and spontaneous here-and-now relation to God enacted by the worshiper aided by God's grace. Nor was a sacrament an established medium for this kind of present relationship. It was rather an "external symbol by which the Lord attests in our consciences his promises of goodwill towards us to sustain the inferiority of our faith, and we on our part testify to our piety towards him as well." Of the Eucharist Calvin says that as "the visible sign is offered to us to attest the granting of the invisible reality, then, on receiving the symbol of the body, we may be confident that the body itself is no less given to us." Calvin really did away with the old act of consecration, yet he saw the Eucharist as a "holy mystery" and was convinced that it involved a real relation to the Divine Presence, though this presence was not "enclosed in the bread and wine." He held that the recipient of Holy Communion received the power or virtue of the body and blood of Christ.

The Roman Catholic Church at the Council of Trent reaffirmed the Real Presence, the doctrine of transubstantiation, and the idea of the Mass as a sacrifice. The last doctrine also went back to the earliest times of the Church but like the Eucharist itself it was not given any precise definition for many centuries. From the fourteenth century on, however, a tremendous literature developed concerning the matter. In 1551 Trent declared that it has always "been held in the Church of God, and this holy Synod now declares anew, that through consecration of the bread and wine there comes about a conversion of the whole substance of the bread into the substance of the body of Christ our Lord, and of the whole substance of the wine into the substance of his blood." The tridentine declaration used the term "transubstantiation," but it did not give the Thomist definition of the term as part of its own statement. Most Reformation theologians tended to deny the element of sacrifice or to explain it away. The Westminster Confession drawn up in 1643, which became the basic document of Presbyterianism, rejected the idea of the "Popish sacrifice of the mass" and stated that "In this sacrament Christ is not offered up to his Father, nor any real sacrifice made at all . . . but only a commemoration." Reformation churches and the Church of England, which often hesitated before decisions on Reformation issues, also generally rejected the idea of sacrifice. Although Cranmer had used the word "Mass" in his first Book of Common Prayer, the term came for most Protestants to signify those aspects of Eucharistic worship which they had rejected as unwarranted, unscriptural "accretions."

In the Roman Catholic Church attendance at Mass on Sundays and on certain feast days is obligatory. The tendency for the observance of the first day of the week, or the "Lord's Day," in place of the Jewish Sabbath began in New Testament times and was based upon the commemoration of the Resurrection. From the fourth century we find both ecclesiastical and civil regulation of this observance, as in the decree of Constantine in 321 which commanded observance and forbade all nonagricultural work. Increasingly strict legislation continued in the Middle Ages. The Reformation churches also emphasized the importance of Sunday rest and worship, and in England and Scotland gave rise to that form of rigorous enforcement known as "sabbatarianism." Under the Puritan Commonwealth in England the observance was imposed by legislation which prohibited all kinds of recreation, including taking a walk. This strict tendency took its start with the book of Nicholas Bound, published in 1595, *True Doctrine of the Sabbath,* which proposed and defended a strict observance of Sunday comparable to the Jewish observance of the Sabbath. It became a political issue in 1618 when James I issued his *Book of Sports* which enjoined abstention from work but permitted and advocated recreational activities. The Puritans were particular rigorists in this respect and in 1643 the Puritan parliament, having beheaded James's son, proceeded to burn his book.

As Christians followed Jews in observing one day a week as holy, they also followed the Jewish practice of marking the passage of the year by special days of prayer. In the Western Church a liturgical year developed characterized by two chief seasons, that of Easter and that of Christmas. The former, centered on Easter Sunday itself, involves also forty days of penitential preparation following the example of Jesus' forty days' fast in the desert, and known as Lent; the feast of Pentecost, commemorating the descent of the Spirit as described in Acts, and Ascension Day, fifty and forty days after Easter, respectively. The latter, the season of Christmas, begins with the first Sunday of Advent, which comprises four weeks of penitential preparation commemorating the four thousand years which by traditional reckoning the world waited for Christ's coming and includes the feast of the Nativity or Christmas itself, the feast of Jesus' circumcision, January 1, and the feast of the Epiphany, January 6, which commemorates the showing of the child to the Magi. Easter is a movable feast, originally connected with the Passover, and hence is still observed on the lunar calendar, showing its link with the Jewish year. Christmas was fixed on December 25 in the fourth century to coincide with the pagan celebration of the solstice and thus follows the solar calendar and is linked with the ancient Roman year. Moreover, during the year thus commemorating the life of Christ there is a continual celebration of the feasts of saints, the most solemn being those dedicated to the Virgin Mary. These days and seasons all have their own special prayers which are incorporated into the Mass. A similar liturgical calendar is followed in the Eastern Church, divided into three parts: *triodion,* the fourth Sunday before Lent to the Saturday before Easter; *Pentacostarion,* Easter to the Sunday after Pentecost inclusive; and *Octoechos,* the remainder of the year.

Besides the Eucharistic celebration the Western and Eastern churches recognize another public prayer, the Divine Office, which is required of priests and many others in formal religious life. It is recited or sung at various times of the day and night in monasteries and religious houses, but more individually and informally by others. Those prayers which have variations according to the season and day are found in the Breviary and are composed of psalms, hymns, and readings. The psalms which make up the present psalter in the Jewish Scriptures are basically liturgical prayers, and the Book of Psalms has often been called the "Hymnal of the Second Temple." It is not surprising that Christians put it to similar use from the earliest times. Outside of its use in such public prayer where it is completely recited once a week (or once a month in the office of the Church of England), the Book of Psalms has been a favorite for private devotion not only in the Western Catholic and Eastern Orthodox communions but among the Protestant churches as well. Among Roman Catholics another popular prayer since the late Middle Ages has been the Rosary. A tradition which goes back at least to the fifteenth century holds that this prayer was introduced by Dominic, the founder of the Dominican Order, in the thirteenth century, but actually it seems to have developed gradually under the influence of both Dominican preachers and Cistercian monks. It consists of saying three sets of five "mysteries" composed of the recitation of ten Ave Marias, preceded by the Lord's Prayer and followed by a doxology praising the Trinity. The mysteries themselves commemorate important events in the salvation history of man from the Annunciation of the Angel to Mary that she would bear a son, through the Passion, death, and resurrection of Jesus, to Mary's own Assumption and coronation as "Queen of Heaven." This form of devotion was rejected by the Reformation as at best a pious accretion, but it has remained extremely popular among Catholics. It is said privately and in a semipublic setting as in homes and other informal gatherings as well as in devotions held in churches.

Like Jewish prayer the prayer of Christians receives its specific characteristic form from the belief in a God at once transcendent and personal, a God who although "wholly other," at the same time calls men to a profound personal relationship. In the prayer of Christians this relationship is centered upon the redemptive and mediating figure of Christ, who comes to us as God and who as fellow man leads us to the Father. We have seen that in the prayer life of Catholic and Orthodox Christians, devotion to saints to implore their intercession and to honor them is a significant form of religious expression, and most especially devotion to the Blessed Virgin Mary. Yet the official prayer of the Church in the Mass and in the Divine Office is christocentric and offered through Christ to the

The Journey of the Magi *by the Quattrocento painter Sassatta.* (*Courtesy of the Metropolitan Museum of Art. Bequest of Maitland F. Griggs, 1943.*)

Father, in the majority of cases, although prayer directly to the Father as taught by Jesus, to Christ himself, and to the Holy Spirit is also considered proper. Prayer to the saints possesses a different character than prayer addressed to the Godhead. It represents rather a communion between the members of the church in heaven (the church triumphant) and the church on earth (the church militant), in which the former intercede for the latter before the Divine Presence. Jesus taught prayer to his disciples by both precept and example. The one prayer he taught as recorded in the gospel remains a most significant model of prayer and is found prominently in the public and private prayers of Christians.

The Lord's Prayer contains the basic elements of prayer—adoration and praise together with petition for earthly and spiritual needs, including the penitential request for forgiveness. All prayer is an expression and often a combination of these elements. Another important element in prayer is thanksgiving. Moreover, Christian prayer is meant to be an activity of the entire person—of mind, will, and affection. But prayer is not simply a spontaneous expression, it is a duty, and it is moreover an art. This is recognized in the Christian exclamatory petition: "Lord, teach us to pray!" Moreover, in more profound prayer, adoration of God as the supreme and ultimate good and thanksgiving to him as the author of being and life are intimately related. In the words of the great prayer giving glory to God in the Mass:

*Glory to God in the highest,*
*And on earth peace to men of good will.*
*We praise thee, we bless thee.*
*We adore thee, we glorify thee.*
*We give thee thanks for thy great glory.*

Perhaps the most significant distinction made concerning prayer is that between vocal and mental prayer. St. John of Damascus, the great theologian of the Eastern Church, gives one of the earliest and clearest formulations. "Prayer is either the ascent of the mind to God, or the decently beseeching him" (*Concerning the Orthodox Faith* 3.24). By mental prayer is meant practices of meditation and contemplation which though rejected by many Protestant groups are of tremendous significance in Catholic and Orthodox religious life. Mental prayer is often classified as ordinary and extraordinary. The former refers to discursive meditation, forms of affective prayer, and finally contemplation—a more advanced, nondiscursive mode of lifting up the whole person to God. The latter refers to such prayers when they are marked by authentic mystical elements culminating in true mysticism.

Mysticism is the name given to a profound personal relationship between man and God in which man achieves a real experience of the relation—a vision or union with God in this life. In the Christian tradition this union does not lead to the annihilation of the individuality of the human person; the ontological gulf between creator and creature remains. Yet God's grace and love is felt by the great mystics as bridging that great chasm, and individuation is in some sense transcended. What is involved is a relationship in which God gives himself to man and man aided by God gives himself to God. It is a relationship of love. Whether in the Judeo-Christian tradition or in the other religious traditions of the world, mysticism must not be thought of as some kind of vaporous and unreal state characteristic of some adepts at psychological self-manipulation or self-hypnosis. It is a relationship which is achieved fully only by a few, and if achieved at all, only after long and rigorous preparation involving difficult mental prayer and ascetic exercises. In all true mysticism a difficult state of purification precedes the achievement of understanding and enlightenment, and the final relationship of vision or union achieved by the great religious geniuses of the mystical tradition is a final crowning of a long process. Moreover, in Christian mysticism the genuineness of the mystical experience is seen by the mystics themselves as attested to by its effects in the attitudes and actions of those involved—in an increase of such virtues as humility, patience, and charity. Accompanying phenomena such as visions and the hearing of voices have long been recognized as accessory and secondary. What is basic is the relation to God—the experience, in the words of Jacopone da Todi, of God's Presence, "ineffable love, imageless goodness, measureless light." What exhibits the marks of authenticity are its fruits. "What fruit dost thou bring back from thy vision?" asked Jacopone.

Institutional religion has often suspected mysticism as a kind of religious individualism outside its sphere of effectiveness, and indeed in periods when the institutional church has faltered for one reason or another in its ability to provide for men's religious needs, mysticism has increased in popularity. But mysticism needs and is a part of the institutional church, for without an authentic religious tradition and the religious environment provided by the institution there would be a severely truncated basis for its own development. Yet the suspicions are not without some basis nor are they all based upon institutional self-interest by any means. Mysticism offers the most profound fulfillment of the religious experience but it is a difficult path and its demands and the attendant strains can give rise to various illusions and to dangerous temptations. There is the temptation to extreme emotionalism, to antinomianism and immorality, and of fascination with secondary psychological phenomena. There is an old talmudic story of four rabbis who set out to study mysticism. One lost his mind, a second lost his faith, and a third died. The fourth one, Rabbi Akiba, came out a better Jew.

Protestant thinkers and writers have taken various positions on mysticism and in the Reformation period both the Catholic and Protestant institutions derived considerable inner strength from the mystics within their ranks. In our day men such as Emil Brunner and Reinhold Niebuhr have considered mysticism to be Neoplatonic rather than Christian and have characterized it as actually unchristian and antichristian; whereas a member of the Church of England such as Dean Inge and an Orthodox thinker like Nicholas Berdyaev consider it to be the essence of Christian religiosity. In the Western Catholic and Eastern Orthodox churches mysticism has remained an important element of religious life into our own times.

That Christian mysticism owes much to Neoplatonism is undeniable, but it has used what it has received to seek a relation to God on a profound level which would be consonant with the New Testament tradition. The Fourth Gospel and the Pauline Epistles, not to mention the Book of Revelation, all show mystic elements. The great theological rethinking of the Western tradition by St. Augustine was deeply affected by the mystic element in his experience. Such elements are found in many early Fathers. It is true that Christianity is a historical religion based upon a historical revelation now considered to be closed. It is true that morality—personal righteousness and social justice—are of the very essence of biblical religion. But it is also true that man's relation to God is central to all religion and that religion must in all ages base itself in experience. The mystical tradition has provided that experience and that relationship at its highest point of God's gift and man's achievement. The great mystics are to the religious life what the great artists are to the life of the senses and the great philosophers to the life of the mind.

The choice is not between a morally committed Christianity and a withdrawn mystical one. We have innumerable examples from Paul to our own time to illustrate the superficiality of such a distinction. The biblical tradition is one of both morality and a personal relation to God as part of one undivided religious attitude. "You shall love the Lord your God with all your heart, and with all your soul, and with all your mind." This is the great and first commandment. And a second is like it, "You shall love your neighbor as yourself" (Matt. 22:37–39). The mystical tradition has deepened the first side of this unity for us to the immense enrichment of the second.

## WORSHIP AND PRAYER IN JUDAISM

The Jewish communities, in exile, without political power and dependent upon internal religious order for their continuity, relied upon the cultivation of the spirit and the mind, upon the constant dedication to conserving and upbuilding of religious sources, for their survival. Therefore, the school, the *yeshivah,* was a vital institution for the maintenance of Jewish life, and the rabbi, as teacher and exemplar of the tradition, society's most honored man.

Alongside the school, the synagogue as house of prayer and assembly was a crucial institution in the continuity of communal life and in the enrichment of that life. Soon after the destruction of the Temple in A.D. 70, the task of establishing a fixed order of prayers and rituals, which would be surrogate for the Temple worship, was completed. The time of the daily services—morning, afternoon, and evening—substituted for the Temple sacrifices which were offered at those hours. A supplementary service on the Sabbath and festivals filled in for the special sacrifices which would have been made on those occasions. In addition to set prayers, scriptural readings were incorporated into the service on Mondays, Thursdays, the Sabbath, and festivals. The full development of the prayer service enabled Israel to find a new outlet for its deeply felt emotions in relation to the divine. Joy, adoration, praise, and also sorrow, question, and anger could be expressed within an institutional framework. Israel was certain that this was in conformity with the will of God, who desired to relate to his people, and who was listening to their cries.

Prayer is an obligation upon every Jew. At the same time as it is a required matter, a duty to be performed at fixed times and according to a fixed ritual, it is also a matter of subjective intention: ". . . to love the Lord your God, to serve Him with all your heart . . ." (Deut. 11:13). "What is the service of the heart? It is prayer" (*Taanit* 2a). The quality of one's prayer, its intentionality (*kavannah*), is considered of supreme importance. "Better is a little with kavannah than much without it" (*Tur Orah Hayim,* p. 61). "Let him who prays cast his eyes downward but his heart upward" (*Yebamoth* 105b). In prayer the worshiper addresses himself to God and attempts to participate in the reality of the divine. He praises, he offers thanksgiving, and he petitions the Creator and Ruler of the world. Prayer is not to be used as a magical technique whereby man automatically receives what he requests. Rather, it is an act through which man can establish contact with God. In prayer man opens his heart, trusting that God does come near, that he hearkens, and that he understands the words of his creature. It is even suggested that God longs for the prayers of man, considering them more beautiful than sacrifices and even than good works. Hoping that God is present and listening, man turns toward him, seeking to go beyond his self to participation in the beyond. He seeks to establish a living vital relationship with the divine, and this is the essence of Jewish prayer. The Jew, throughout the ages, sensed that God guarded his people, took an interest in the concerns of each individual, and could be moved by prayers which expressed the joys, hopes, and agonies of these men. "O Lord our God, hear our cries!

*Late thirteenth-century miniature in North French style showing Aaron the High Priest filling the Menorah from a Bible and prayerbook. (Courtesy of the British Museum.)*

Have compassion upon us and pity us. Accept our prayer with loving favor. You, O God, listen to entreaty and prayer. O King, do not turn us away unanswered, for you mercifully heed your people's supplication. Praised are you, O Lord, who is attentive to prayer." The outpouring of the heart found in the Jewish liturgy attests to the profound conviction that God was present, that he cared, and that he would answer the address his people directed toward him.

The scriptural Book of Psalms and the *siddur,* the prayerbook of later Judaism, have served to bridge the gulf between man and God, enabling the Jew to expose his most profound feelings to the deity and to sense that God responds. Prayer has been the fundamental religious act of piety, both preceding and going beyond rational reflection and speculation. The Jew who stands before God blesses, sanctifies, and magnifies a reality which he knows instinctively is present. Knowledge of God's infinite transcendence exists, while "God is near in all kinds of nearness" (*Jerusalem Talmud, Berakoth* 13a). One kind of nearness is the nearness of prayer. ". . . when a man enters a synagogue and prays, God listens to him, for the petitioner is like a man who talks into the ear of a friend" (Ibid.). Throughout the centuries prayers were added to the liturgy, and reflected the ever-evolving piety and religious consciousness of the people. The *siddur* expresses in poetic form the soul of the Jewish people as it stood before God, and hence contains the highest thoughts and deepest sentiments of the religious spirit.

The life of the religious man is devoted to sanctification, to the act of making ordinary events and ordinary things holy. He is engaged in transforming the profane into the sacred by allowing a reality beyond the level of ordinary appearance to enter and to transform that appearance into something beyond itself, into something holy. The entire ritual order of Judaism serves to accomplish this act of sanctification in as many areas of man's life as possible. Reciting a blessing over food and drink transforms the mere intaking of food into a sacred act. Reciting a blessing over crops, over a house, over children, are acts which transform the ordinary into the extraordinary, the secular into the sacred. Whether it be the most mundane and trivial areas of life or the most significant and elevated, this process of transformation lifts the existence of the religious man into the dimension of the holy and the divine.

The religious year is a sanctification of time, in which precious moments are consecrated through ritual celebration and reenactment. Judaism, a religion founded upon the experience of God's appearance in time, possesses a full sacred calendar, in which the moments of divine revelation and the moments of sacred acts are recalled and relived. The year is marked by religious holidays, during which the eternal, the transcendent, is felt to enter time and thereby to transform it. The secular or profane cycle is raised to the dimension of the sacred. The pious Jew lives in the world, in secular time and space, but constantly anticipates the moments when, through participation in religious holidays, he will enter into another world, the world of the eternal and of the holy. He looks forward to the holy days, prepares for them, and longs to taste of their reality, which to him seems to be alone truly real and truly ultimate.

The Jewish ritual year is founded upon the Sabbath, the weekly sanctification of Creation. The entire spiritual year is marked off by the sequence of the Sabbaths. They provide a constant source of renewal and sanctity to the pious man, who in some way is re-created himself as he celebrates the creation of the world. "Wherefore the children of Israel keep the Sabbath, to observe the Sabbath throughout their generations, for a perpetual covenant. It is a sign between Me and the children of Israel forever, for in six days the Lord made heaven and earth, and on the seventh day He ceased from work and rested" (Exod. 31:12–17).

The Sabbath is thus a memorial to the work of God's creation. It is also a day of rest, in which the toil of the workweek is to be laid aside for prayer, celebration, and reflection. The rules of Sabbath observance have been prescribed in order to preserve its character as a day of rest. They allow man to separate himself from the cares of daily ordinary existence and thereby free himself to participate in the sanctification of time. According to Jewish tradition, participating in the Sabbath, celebrating God's own deeds of creation and rest, is of supreme importance. "Rabbi Levi said: If the Jewish people would observe the Sabbath properly even once, the son of David [the Messiah] would come. Why? Because it is equal to all the other commandments in importance" (*Exod. Rabbah* 25:12).

There are three festivals in the Jewish year, which are agricultural in origin, but which have been transformed into historical holidays marking sacred events in the religious history of Israel. The first is the feast of Deliverance, the Passover, or *Pesach,* which recalls the miraculous redemption from Egypt. Yahweh had revealed himself to the people in this mighty act of Exodus, personally leading them out of the house of bondage into freedom. Therefore:

> *In every generation a person is obligated to see himself as though he personally came out of Egypt, as it is written, "You shall tell your son on that day saying: This is because of what the Lord did for* me *when I left Egypt." It was not our ancestors alone that the Holy One, praised be He, redeemed, but he redeemed us as well, along with them. . . . Therefore we are obliged to thank, praise, laud, glorify and exalt, to honor, bless, extol, and adore Him who performed all these wonders for our fathers and for us.*
>
> (Passover *Haggadah*)

This great event, which was so engraved upon the consciousness of the Jew, is celebrated in the *seder,* a ritual meal in the home preceded by a recitation of the Exodus narrative. By participating in the recitation and the meal, the Jew returns and participates in the historical events. He feels himself one of the redeemed, and praises the Lord for the gift of freedom.

The festival of Weeks, *Shavuot,* occurs in late spring, forty-nine days after Passover, and celebrates the revelation of God at Sinai, when the Ten Commandments were presented to the newly formed nation. The third festival, called *Sukkot* (Booths), is an autumn harvest holiday, and marks the historical incident of the forty years' wandering in the wilderness when the children of Israel dwelled in booths. The final day of this festival is the day of Rejoicing in the Law, because on this occasion the yearly cycle of Torah readings is concluded with the last chapter of Deuteronomy and is begun again with the first chapter of Genesis. All three festivals are joyous holidays in which man recalls God's interventions in history. In so doing he participates in these symbolic events which are the core of Israel's religious history.

Two other holidays are of major significance in the ritual year and they are the High Holy Days of *Rosh Hashanah,* the New Year, and *Yom Kippur,* the Day of Atonement. *Rosh Hashanah* occurs on the first and second days of the month of Tishri, corresponding to September in the Gregorian calendar, and on the tenth day of Tishri is *Yom Kippur.* These are the Days of Awe, the most solemn period in the Jewish year, for it is thought that at this time each Jew is judged by God and his destiny for the coming year determined. In legend, God is pictured as sitting over a book and inscribing in it the fate of every individual, according to that man's actions of the past year. Judgment is thus not reserved for a final day at the end of life, but is meted out every year during these critical days, which are set aside for self-examination, repentance, and reconciliation, both between man and man and between man and God. At this time the individual stands alone, as he seeks forgiveness for his sins, purifies himself, and prays that he be judged favorably.

*Rabbi Kruspedai said, quoting Rabbi Johanan: On Rosh Hashanah, three books are opened in the heavenly court; one for the wicked, one for the righteous, and one for those in between. The fate of the righteous is inscribed and sealed then and there: Life. The fate of the wicked is inscribed and sealed then and there: Death. The fate of those in between lies in doubt from Rosh Hashanah until Yom Kippur. If, during those days, they show their worth through their deeds, they are inscribed and sealed for Life; and if not, they are inscribed and sealed for death.*

(*Rosh Hashanah,* 16b)

On *Rosh Hashanah,* the day which celebrates the creation of the world, the process of judgment begins:

*The great shofar is sounded, and a still small voice is heard. Angels are seized with fear and trembling as they proclaim: This is the Day of Judgment! The hosts of heaven are to be arraigned in judgment, for in your eyes even they are not free of guilt. All who enter this world pass before You as a flock of sheep. As the shepherd musters his flock, causing each one to pass beneath his staff, so You pass and number, record and visit every living soul, setting the measure of every creature's life and decreeing its destiny.*

*The shofar, or ram's horn. Played in synagogues at Rosh Hashanah and Yom Kippur, the shofar was blown by the ancient Hebrews in battle and at high religious observances. (Courtesy of the Israel Government Tourist Office.)*

On the most solemn day of the year, the Day of Atonement, which is given over completely to prayer and fasting, the judgment is concluded.

*On New Year's Day the decree is inscribed and on the Day of Atonement it is sealed: How many shall pass away and how many shall be born, who shall live and who shall die, who shall attain the measure of his days and who shall not, who shall perish by fire and who by water, who by the sword and who by the beast, who by hunger and who by thirst, who by earthquake and who by plague, who by strangling and who by stoning, who shall have rest and who shall wander, who shall be at ease and who shall be disturbed, who shall become poor and who shall become rich, who shall be brought low and who shall be exalted. But Repentance, Prayer, and Righteousness avert the severe decree.*

From *Rosh Hashanah* through *Yom Kippur,* the Jew has repented and sought mercy. He has confessed his sins innumerable times, and has layed himself open before the righteous Judge.

*What shall we say before You, who dwell on high, and what shall we recount before You, who abide in the heavens? You know all things, hidden and revealed. You know the mysteries of the universe, and the hidden secrets of all living. You search out the innermost reasons and probe the heart and mind. Nothing is concealed from You or hidden from Your sight. May it therefore be Your will, O Lord our God and God of our fathers, to forgive us for all our sins, to pardon us for all our iniquities, and to grant us atonement for all our transgressions.*

After a full day of prayer, the worshiper, humbly trusting in God's mercy and goodness, finally bursts out in joyous affirmation: "The Lord is God, this God of Love, He alone is God!"

Thus ends the most sacred day of the religious year. Man reenters the cycle of life, purified and hopeful, but with the knowledge that he will sin again, that he is again embedded in the evils inherent in profane existence, and that his only salvation lies in reliving once again in the coming year the entire cycle of holy days, experiencing through them renewal and redemption. The meaning of the ritual year in the life of the Jew is summarized in the following statement taken from the closing prayers of the Sabbath:

*Praised are You, O Lord our God, King of the universe, who has endowed all creation with distinctive qualities and differentiated between light and darkness, between sacred and profane, between Israel and the nations, and between the seventh day and other days of the week. Praised are You, O Lord, who differentiates between the sacred and the profane.*

Throughout its religious history, Israel has been certain of two things: that the transcendent God was present in history and that he had singled out the Jews to participate with him in bringing redemption to the world. God was understood as the Creator and Universal King, but also as the Father who had selected Israel to be his son. This choice was one of love, and is Israel's greatest blessing. "Beloved are the Israelites because they are called sons of God; still greater love that it was made known to them that they are called sons of God." (*Avot* 3:14). The traditional Jew felt God's presence in nature and in history. The great Hebrew poet and thinker of medieval Spain, Judah Halevi, wrote, "Lord where shall I find thee? High and hidden is thy place and where shall I not find thee? The world is full of thy glory. I have sought thy nearness; with all my heart have I called thee. And going out to meet thee, I found thee coming towards me." It is true that the Jews had been exiled from their holy land and had been chastised by God for their sins. However, even in exile, God was near. His *shekhinah,* his "presence," had followed Israel into exile and abided there, sharing in its suffering and homelessness.

Israel sensed that although God was not man, he shared the feelings of his creatures. "In the hour that the Temple was destroyed, and Israel exiled, and the Sanhedrin uprooted, God wept bitter tears" (*Pesikta Rabbati* 28). Judaism accepted the paradox of the infinite omnipresent Lord who is still found in specific places, the God who is totally other than man but who chooses to come close to man and to be involved in his fate. Jewish tradition stated that God actually needs man, and this is implied in the concept of Israel's election. "And you are my witnesses," said God, "and I am God" (Isa. 43:12). "When you are my witnesses, I am God, and when you are not my witnesses, I am not God, as it were" (*Pesikta Derrabh Kahannah, Bahodesh,* 102.6). It was said that God derived pleasure from hearing the prayers of man and from seeing his righteous deeds. This sense of God's abiding presence and his involvement in the particular fate of Israel was summarized in the statement, "My Torah is in your hands and the end is in my hands, so that the two of us need each other. As you need me to bring on the end, so I need you to keep my Torah and to hasten the rebuilding of my house in Jerusalem" (*Pesikta Rabbati* 31.144b). It was such faith in their election and in the critical role assigned to them in realizing God's plan, which inspired Israel and gave purpose to their struggle in exile.

# ECCLESIA SEMPER EST REFORMANDA

PROTEST, REFORM, REVOLT

Christianity brought to Western man a new insight into and the possibility of a new relationship to transcendence, gathered to itself the parallel and sympathetic philosophical thrusts of antiquity, especially Neoplatonism and Stoicism, reworking them in relation to the Bible, and thus became the religion of Europe. It was a religion that could move simple folk and at the same time inspire great minds and sublime spirits. This biblical religion showed itself capable of great interior development and of receiving the insights and meeting the needs of the Teutonic and Celtic peoples of the North, who by and large had remained outside the civilization of Mediterranean antiquity. It was this religion that remained when the civilization of antiquity went down, brought low by the onslaught of the barbarian and its own inner decay and fatigue. It was this religion which nurtured the rise of the new Europe which, beginning in the tenth century, has had such an enormous influence upon the entire globe. It is this religion that provided Western man with the basic dimensions of his world view and the fundamental elements of his personal consciousness. The fact that Western men were the first to reach out and explore first the globe and now to begin the exploration of space, the fact that they first developed science with its transcendent and manipulative mental leverage over the elements of the human situation, the fact that they first developed a marked secularization of thought and a demythologization of their understanding of man and the world, the fact that they first built an enormous secularized social structure based upon commercial rationality and scientific technology and thereby changed irretrievably the character of life on this earth, have all been seen by many scholars as closely related to the religion of the Bible and as representing to a considerable extent a further working of insights already embryonic within it in Patristic times. That these complex developments were also often achieved in conflict with religious institutions and religious faith does not seriously detract from the fundamental character of the religious background which for so many centuries was the training school of the Western mind and spirit. Biblical religion rested upon the foundation of breakthrough and transcendence. It taught man to see himself seriously engaged in history but at the same time not enclosed within it. It brought him to a sense of universality. It showed him an ethical ideal which could not be attributed to his own creations and which raised his critical acumen above all mere localisms and provincialisms. It gave him a sense of individual worth and dignity. It taught him the rationalism of the Greeks which it had incorporated into itself. Though Western men honored these insights as much in the breach as in the observance, they had their effect upon the formation of minds and characters and became the basic core-meaning structure of Western culture.

When we use the word "religion," we may use it in three distinct but interrelated senses. First, it may designate that inner relation to the Beyond, however characterized and understood, which lifts man above himself and the effort of men to sustain and live by the implications of that relationship. Second, it may also be used to refer to the beliefs and practices which give objective intellectual and ritual expression to the meaning and significance of that relationship, making it available to men in general and transmissible from one generation to the next; or it may refer to the religious tradition as developed and passed on within a religious group. Third, it may denote the organizational and institutional framework which evolves as the communal structure providing a community for the individual believer and a social basis for the tradition. While the first usage points to the most basic and profound religious phenomenon, to that which gives rise to and nurtures the others, it is not accessible to direct observation and to scholarly study. It is the real essence of religion and we can know it directly only in our own inner lives and indirectly insofar as we are capable of appreciating the reports of others who have known it directly themselves. What we can know and study is the objectified and available second and third aspects. In this presentation so far we have drawn heavily upon the second in the attempt to suggest to the reader the quality and character of the religious experience with which biblical religion is concerned. We must now examine briefly the institutional framework.

We have already noted the importance of this side of religious life in the significance which is to be seen in the precise form of organization and life in the world characteristic of the people of Israel in the biblical period. We also noted the significance for the continuation and development of the Christian tradition of the rise of defined and stable ecclesiastical organization in the second century. It is the Church which acts as the institutional expression and instrument bringing the message of Christianity to men. Problems of the Church therefore become significant problems of the Christian tradition.

The Church came to see itself as the institutional continuation of the life and mission of Jesus, performing through its liturgy and sacraments his mediating role between heaven and earth. Its original emphasis upon transcendence and on man's destiny beyond the mundane here and now was transformed by the experience and spiritual affinities of late antiquity into a pronounced other-worldly point of view. The Church mediated between heaven and earth, and man was here below on probation in preparation for a better life in the world beyond. These tendencies of the declining ancient world were strengthened in the centuries which followed its fall—centuries of near barbarism in which the Church alone attempted to hold up spiritual ideals and maintain a degree of civilized order, efforts which bore fruit in the rise of the medieval civilization.

The Church came to the world to bring to it its message of salvation, and in entering that world to convert it, it was itself in the process unable to remain "unstained from the world." As in all social institutions, men brought to the Church a great variety of motives and sought from it a variety of satisfactions. Ambition, desire for esteem, will to power—such motives came in to qualify and corrupt the orientation to the meaning and propagation of the gospel. Like all social organizations the Church represented both the concrete expression and application of the values it preached and their compromise and indeed corruption at the same time. Already in the second century we saw lukewarmness and a superficial formalism alongside fervor and authenticity. From the first we find immorality alongside asceticism and moral rigor. The separation of clergy and laity into two distinct estates turned the latter into passive participants in important respects, while it gave the former opportunities for psychological and often material aggrandizement not conducive to a high level of religious performance. The picture within the Church was in fact a spotty one and we see an enormous variety from heroic sanctity to harsh political manipulation. The Christian community was never without moving witness; it was also never without an ever-present need for reform. It is a permanent continuing condition of the Church—to be in need of reform. *Ecclesia semper est reformanda.*

*Plaster casts of two Apostles from the chancel arch of Kilpeck Church, England, c. 1125. (Courtesy of the Victoria and Albert Museum. Crown Copyright.)*

We have already noted that protest is a significant category of religious behavior. Such protest is directed against conditions in the Church. Monasticism was in part a protest against increasing worldliness. The Patristic age saw many movements of protest—in Montanism, in some Gnostic movements, etc. The Middle Ages saw the rise of protest movements and the secession and driving out from the Church of groups embodying such protest. The role of protest, however, is an ambiguous one. It is a necessary element in the forward movement of the Church in time, which places obstacles in the way of the Church's deserting or neglecting its basic mission, and calls it back from the varied temptations of the world. But it may also reveal itself as standing in the way of developments and innovations which have become necessary under new conditions. It is always the significant question whether protest is against what actually is corruption and vitiating compromise or whether it is directed against justifiable development and necessary adaptation.

The distinction between the two in many historical cases may be anything but clear-cut, and conflict and contention on such issues play a prominent part in Christian history. We may ask this question in another way. We may say that the real issue is always this: Is protest the expression of authentic reform? To reform the Church means to alter its internal condition so that under the circumstances of its existence it is able to bring the basic message of Christianity to men. Consequently, efforts for reform always involve definite convictions concerning what is basic and central to that message. The history of the Church is at the same time the history of efforts to reform it, and contention concerning which aspects of its religious message are most basic.

Elements of protest and reform were often found in the Church to be related to apocalyptic ideas and their millenarian expectations. They also were at times embedded in situations of social and economic frustration so that the impulse for protest and the desire for reform were often both religious and social and political at the same time, but the reality of their religious aims and motivation is not to be doubted. The Middle Ages saw the founding of a whole series of new monastic orders, such as the Carthusians founded by St. Bruno in 1084, the Cistercians by St. Robert in 1098, and the Premonstratensions by St. Norbert in 1120. Perhaps most significant were the Mendicant Orders, the Franciscan Order founded by St. Francis of Assisi in 1209 and the Dominican Order founded by St. Dominic in 1220. These two orders, based in towns and not in the countryside as were the older monastic groups, became the dominant religious influence of the late Middle Ages. The Franciscans emphasized poverty and the issue became the cause of a bitter internal struggle ending in the excommunication of the "Spirituals," the party which advocated maintaining the early ideal of corporate as well as individual poverty as the rule of life. The chief interest of the Dominican Order was educational and it produced Thomas Aquinas, the greatest Christian thinker of the entire medieval period. Such monastic and mendicant groups brought a new spiritual vigor to the Church and affected the religious life of many among the laity. Such groups by precept and example advocated a reform of religious life. The most impressive example of the reform role of religious orders is to be seen in the history of the famous Benedictine monastery at Cluny in Burgundy. Cluny was established in 910, and by the power of its high example of the religious life, and its reform of financial and economic management, it grew to be the center of some 314 affiliated establishments and came to exercise a decisive influence in the Church in the eleventh and twelfth centuries. The reforming efforts of this group reached their culmination in the election of the cluniac monk Hildebrand to the papal office as Gregory VII, a pope who repressed simony, enforced clerical celibacy, and removed numbers of offending churchmen from office. Religious orders appealed chiefly to upper-class youth who gave up the world of the nobility (and later the bourgeoisie) to dedicate themselves to the call of the gospel. The protest and reform carried out by such groups did not usually challenge the established ecclesiastical and social order, although this was definitely not the case in the Franciscan struggle in which the demand for poverty had significant social and political implications.

The Middle Ages also saw protest and the demand for reform of a sort that was not contained within the Church and which sooner or later resulted in an antiecclesiastical stance. The Cathari of the eleventh century, encouraged by Pope Gregory VII and his agitation for reform, rose in revolt against the political-ecclesiastical establishment in the cities of Lombardy. The thirteenth century saw the rise of the Waldensians or Poor Men of Lyons, whose advocacy of poverty and simplicity of life also contained serious social implications. The fourteenth century saw the rise of the Lollards—precursors of the more radical groups of the Reformation—and Hussites, in which nationalist expression and religious interests would be found together. The two figures perhaps most significant in connection with protest and reform efforts thoroughly challenging the form in which Church polity and doctrine had evolved were Huss and Wycliffe. John Wycliffe (1329–1384) wrote on the concept of "dominion" or legitimacy of rule and found that only those in a state of grace could legitimately exercise ecclesiastical and even civil office. Considering the condition of the Church a sinful one, he suggested that the Church should be disendowed and deprived of all temporal properties. He advocated the centrality of the Bible for faith and its translation into English, and accepted predestination. He also attacked the Papacy, monasticism, and transubstantiation, as well as abuses in the Church. His teachings were popularized by the Lollards in England and became popular in Central Europe. John Huss (1369–1415) was attracted to Wycliffe's doctrines, especially their political implications of the abolition of property and the hierarchical structure of society. The teachings of these men were condemned and Huss was burned at the stake as a heretic. The teachings of Wycliffe appealed to the poor and oppressed in English medieval society, and although he had nothing to do with the 1381 Peasant Revolt his doctrines may indeed have had their effect in it. In these figures we see protest and reform passing over into revolt.

Another significant figure in medieval Christian thought with respect to the relation of Christian teaching to Church and society was Joachim of Fiore (1132–1202). Joachim's ideas had a tremendous impact upon many in the centuries following his death, who often, like the Franciscan Spirituals, tended to act on their revolutionary implications, although he himself was quite submissive to duly authorized ecclesiastical authority. Joachim wrote three chief works in which he put forth the idea that the history of the world was divided into three periods. The first was the age of the Father, which was a social and political order of the laity and lasted from the Creation to the end of the Old Testament period. The second was the age of the Son, which was an order of clerics and a period of grace which began with the New Testament period and in which he and his contemporaries still lived. This age of clerics he predicted would last for forty-two generations of about thirty years each. It would be followed by an age of the Holy Spirit, which was to be an order of monks and a time of freedom and blossoming of the spirit of man in relation to the Holy Spirit. He expected this age to begin in 1260. In this third age, new religious orders would arise and convert the whole world and would thus inaugurate the time of the spiritual Church. In these movements of protest, reform, and revolt we see the way in which Christian ideals and influences entered into the evolution of Western man's aspirations and his responses to the problems of various ages.

CHURCH VERSUS STATE

The people of Israel had considered themselves a "holy people" set apart and chosen by God, and the Church had inherited this idea, which it accepted and applied to itself. Israel was at first, and for long aspired to be, a national and political as well as a religious entity, but by the beginning of the Christian era the Jews of the diaspora tended to be a confessional group with ethnic identification rather than a nation, the tendency which the defeat of A.D. 66–70 would implement and increase. The Christian Church, seeing itself as the new Israel, was in the first centuries a community within the general community. It did not even in the times of the bitterest persecution question the legitimacy of the Roman state. Its response to the world it rejected was a peaceful one as was that of the rabbinical Jews after 70. Hence, when it became the general and established religion of the empire, it did not challenge the political authority structure but merely posited its own ecclesiastical authority alongside it. Even when Rome fell and the Church became the ruler in fact in much of Europe, it never sought to supplant the idea of civil rule with one of a total monocratic theocracy. What resulted was a community in which there were two authority structures, each granted to be legitimate, but one of them, the Church, claiming more ontological value and religious dignity. Both historical experience and religious beliefs seemed at first to confirm this superior position of the Church, but it became increasingly questioned. Hence, in the Middle Ages there took place within Christendom a conflict between these two structures, a struggle to define their spheres of competence, to separate their powers, and grant the primal position to one or the other of them. It took European man a long time to work out these problems in any generally satisfactory way.

The European community had two authority structures; that is to say that it was really two communities, but that the membership of the two communities was the same. One was organized around religion—around the hierarchically organized and functioning mediational role between God and man carried out by the Church in public worship, teaching, and the administration of the sacraments. The other was organized around the secular state, maintaining political order as the requisite social context for civil life with its this-worldly pursuits. The New Testament insistence on the supremacy of religious values had come to mean in this situation the supremacy of the religious institution and its sacerdotal authority structure.

The conflict between Church and State—pope and emperor, bishop and king—was also a conflict to define the proper ends of man's communal life, although the Christian theological language used by both sides most often kept this element potential and implicit. From the spokesmen for secularization of authority, ideas of reform were also forthcoming. The most celebrated work in this respect was the *Defensor Pacis* of Marsiglio of Padua which appeared in 1324 in the middle of a war between pope and emperor. It presents a proposal for a radical disestablishment of the Church and placing of it under the civil rule of the state. It was of course a radical statement in line with the interests of one party to the conflict, but at the same time it shows how severe the problem had become. The Church, now a hierarchically organized community of prayer and mediation, was ruled by a clerical structure far removed from the lives and interests of the laity in many respects. What was seen by churchmen as a conflict between the Church and the world—between the spiritual understanding of man and his end and the ambitions and pleasures of the world—was seen by others as a conflict with a vast institutional structure inhibiting the normal development of the European political community. Indeed, such issues were subtly and inextricably intertwined. Marsilgio cut through them with his radical proposals.

The *Defensor Pacis* states that the civil government is the proper unifying authority in society. It derives its authority from the people, an authority institutionalized in the emperor, who may be criticized and even deposed by popular action. The Church should be subject to the civil power. It has no rights of its own but only those given it by the state and which the state may withdraw. It has no right to own property, but only to use that which is lent to it by the state. The book also denies the divine origin of the ecclesiastical hierarchy and that the primacy of the Church was given to Peter. Marsiglio suggested that the rule of the Church belonged properly to a general council which should be composed of both clergy and laity. This work contradicted the basic presuppositions of the Middle Ages with respect to civil authority and its relation to the Church, but it anticipated much that was to come.

The fourteenth and fifteenth centuries however saw an attempt to make use of the general council to reform the Church. The Church was an old organization deeply involved in the world in terms of its interests, though having developed few new ideas to aid it in adapting Christianity to the needs of the new complex commercial and political society which was developing in Europe. This Church stood in need of reform on several levels—in thought, in organization, and in religious practice. Moreover, internal fighting in the Church—the existence of two rival popes, for example—made the situation all the more difficult and discouraging. At several councils, efforts at reform were made, often combined with efforts to place a general council above the papal office. At the Council of Constance (1414–1418) there were considerable efforts in this respect. Here a schism over the papal office was finally healed, but three commissions appointed to propose reforms accomplished little. The Council did however adopt some reform measures against simony and other abuses. It also condemned Huss as a heretic and handed him over to the secular power for execution. It has been said by many historians that the failure of the conciliar movement and of the Council of Constance to affect real reform in the Church was one of the main causes of the Reformation.

## THE RELIGIOUS AND ECCLESIASTICAL CRISIS OF THE SIXTEENTH CENTURY

Despite a degree of secularization, despite the reality of political conflicts, Europe was still at the beginning of the sixteenth century an entity not inaccurately described as Christendom, a *Republica Christiana,* but it was a Christendom in severe crisis. All the problems of the medieval civilization—problems of religious faith, its meaning and significance, problems of the value and worth of the lay life, problems of the functioning of an overstructured and often corrupt ecclesiastical organization, problems of the relation of the Church to the new national consciousness developing in places like Germany and England, and problems of the relation between Church and State as two separate but necessarily interrelated authority structures—remained unsolved and exacerbated by time, and the resulting internal ferment brought tremendous pressure against the institutional structures of the old Church. The last half of the fourteenth century and the entire fifteenth century was a time in which religious life in Europe was in shambles, if by religious life we mean the functioning of the Church organization and its relationship to the civil power. In these years the moral prestige of the Papacy waned, and this together with its claims to authority and the widespread and often contradictory feelings of discontent throughout the lands of Christendom made it a central target for attack. At the beginning of the sixteenth century all literate Europe agreed that the Church was sadly in need of reform; all knowledgeable Christians saw the need for some kind of change in the structure and functions of the ecclesiastical institution. But as we have seen, how the Church should be reformed was a question that could be answered only in relation to another more basic and fundamental question: What aspects of the Christian faith are central and should be given emphasis? Hence, while all agreed on the need for reform, while all cried out against abuses, in many cases one honest Christian's abuse was seen by another equally honest as a necessary and defensible practice. When churchmen spoke of the need for reform, they did not usually mean change of belief as that belief was represented and taught by the Church and even by the pope. It was the Church's legal system, its bureaucracy with its inefficiency, its corruption and graft, and the worldliness and immorality of important and unimportant clerics alike to which they referred. Some who were interested in humanistic culture and were effective in the development of that intellectual phenomenon known as the Renaissance—the revival of ancient humanistic letters, the flowering of art, and the continued development of science—desired intellectual changes as well. What was desired was an organizational, a moral, and an intellectual reform and renewal. To bring that about within the structure of the old Church, so deeply embedded in the secular civilization to which it had given rise, proved impossible. Yet down to the very beginning of the great Reformation movement in the sixteenth century radical anticlericalism and deep divergence from Catholic doctrine were unusual in any open or pronounced sense.

In the course of its development as a separate and even primary authority structure, the Papacy had become a political power in the complex Italian political situation and in Western Europe. Its needs for revenue increased tremendously in the new commercial society and it made use of its bureaucratic system to collect money and bring it to Rome. These efforts often involved highly questionable practices, such as the sale of indulgences which originally aroused the protest of Luther. Moreover, Rome had been greatly affected by the new Renaissance flowering of art and architecture and had become its most lavish patron. As a part of this, the papal court had become the most magnificent of any ruler in Europe, a fact seemingly not inappropriate to many for Christ's vicar and the visible ruler of Christ's Church. The abuses of papal finance and the demands upon Northern Christians to support the political and artistic requirements of the Papacy proved to be important elements leading to a new protest movement and strategic to the outbreak of revolt and schism.

Yet the Church had become elaborated in such a way that it would be difficult to sustain any movement for reform that penetrated to the grass roots of the Christian population without a considerable amount of dismantling on all levels—doctrinal, organizational, and cultic. As we noted before, men brought a variety of motives to the Church and sought the fulfillment of a variety of needs within it. Now two decades into the sixteenth century, men would divide in terms of these complex internal alignments of their values and interests and give rise to equally complex external arrangements among friends and foes. When Luther in 1517 protested against Tetzel's sale of indulgences to raise money for the support of the pope's renovation of the basilica of St. Peter's in Rome, his expression of such grievances was not in itself an unusual phenomenon. But when he developed his protest to involve far-reaching theological changes issuing in his basing Christian faith upon the outcome of his own deep interior spiritual experience of salvation by faith alone, he opened the way for impulses to reformulation which had lain deep beneath the surface of European religious life.

Many of the basic ideas of the Reformation had already been expressed by the sectarian protests of the Middle Ages. Indeed, in the revolt of the laity in the eleventh century, a revolt supported and aided by Gregory VII, we see in anticipation many of the chief phenomena of the Reformation and post-Reformation periods, including lay preaching, rejection of the sacraments from corrupt clergy, an emphasis upon poverty of worldly goods, abrogation of taxes and tithes, indifference toward the state, advocacy of independent study of the Bible, and the raising of the example of the primitive Church as the standard for ecclesiastical life. The idea that the sacraments possessed no objective validity was as old as Montanism. Moreover, the medieval sects often advocated the doctrine of predestination in radical form, and when this was combined with some moralistic doctrine of signs of election in those who lead "good lives" the whole sacramental structure of the old Church became unnecessary at best, a spurious and evil development at worst. The revival of immediate eschatological expectations gave rise to an atmosphere of crisis and urgency which made the institutional church seem irrelevant, and if unreformed in its abuses, about to be condemned. Medieval sectaries also rejected the Mass and the sacraments and thereby questioned the central mediational function which the Church understood as constitutive of its earthly mission. Together with this they often attacked Church authority.

Moreover, developments in intellectual life in the fourteenth and fifteenth centuries contributed to a further weakening of the ground and sense of sufficient reason concerning the Church's doctrines. Nominalism had become the philosophical viewpoint of the late Middle Ages, and denying the existence of universal concepts with significance in reality, it severed the relation between faith and reason which the earlier medieval thinkers, and Thomas preeminently, had labored to build. For Ockham, the originator of this point of view, human knowledge consisted merely in conventions which though of practical use possess no objective value. The consequence was a radical skepticism. Nominalism became the accepted view of the leading theologians of the pre-Reformation period, and thus theology was cut off from any rational justification and from any positive rational criteria of judgment as well. Religious truth could only be held by faith, a faith no longer seen as harmonious with, though going beyond, reason. Hence authority was in certain respects enhanced, being freed from the critical oversight of rational thought, a kind of freedom likely to prove most detrimental to its functioning. Moreover, the critical and skeptical spirit of Nominalism undermined authority even as based upon faith. Since universals did not exist but were only conceptions, the Church as such did not exist but was only a collection of individuals so far as being a repository of truth is concerned. Truth was not in the Church but in individuals. But which individuals? Ockham stated that the pope was not infallible and composed a compendium of errors which he attributed to Pope John XXII with whom the Franciscan Order, of which Ockham was a member, was involved in profound conflict. He held that since Christ promised that the gates of hell would never prevail against the Church, someone in the Church would always be right but we cannot know unerringly who it is. We can only rely on the Bible. However, in the decades before Luther the Bible for the first time was being subjected to critical study, as may be seen in the work of Erasmus, who however rejected Luther and remained in the old Church. Moreover, there developed at this time a revolt against the sterile hyperintellectualism of the late medieval university and its academic theology. This movement, known as the *devotio moderno,* called for a simple piety and an end to theological subtleties. Its most famous expression was found in Thomas à Kempis' *Imita-*

*tion of Christ* (long a devotional work among Catholics and Protestants alike) and the Brothers of the Common Life to whom Thomas belonged. It elicited the sympathy of such humanist intellectuals as Erasmus.

Luther's protest was one more protest and Luther's break with Rome was one more schism, yet for subtle and complex reasons on which historians are by no means in agreement they turned out to be much more. Although Luther's general cast of mind was conservative and medieval and although even the most radical reformers saw themselves as bringing back the pristine purity of the primitive Church rather than making innovations, the Reformation turned out to be a quite new phenomenon in European religious history. In its complex development, conditioned by the specific historical circumstances which it encountered, the Church had responded on both the doctrinal and organizational level to the problems which time and place presented. In meeting these problems it gave shape and form to itself and to its beliefs. The faith of the early Church gradusually assumed the form of a sophisticated and elaborate philosophy of religion whose development we have already followed, especially with respect to the doctrines of Christology and grace. The Church was gradually transformed into a vast hierarchical structure administering a highly objectified system of worship and sacramental mediation. This structure was functioning badly as the sixteenth century began. Change in it was necessary, but change in it could not but involve a more and more radical questioning of the whole system and the specific form it had assumed in the course of its long history.

## CHRISTIANITY AND JUDAISM

The traditions of biblical religion had assumed a fixed form which would be thoroughly challenged in the modern age, which began in the sixteenth century. Those traditions which we sketched here split early into two strands, a minority strand which became the majority in Christianity and a majority strand which became the minority in Judaism. These two communities, grounded in a common past and common basic religious premises, differed over the significance to be attributed to the life and mission of Jesus. Judaism rejected the claims of Christianity with regard to the messiahship and meaning of Jesus, the doctrine of election, and the abrogation of the law. To the Jews it appeared that redemption had not come. None of the changes which were expected to accompany the coming of the Messiah had taken place. The Jews themselves remained defeated, paganism continued, and the world was still evil. They rejected the Christian belief that Jesus' suffering and death had brought redemption and saw in the Trinitarian ideas and Christological conceptions of the Church something like idolatry. The claim of the Church to be the true Sarah now chosen over the synagogue which it saw in the role of Hagar was sheer usurpation in Jewish eyes. Israel, they felt, could not be superseded, since the promises to it were eternal. Because the world had not been redeemed, the Law was still absolutely binding. The kingdom had not come and therefore men must live under the Law's yoke, fulfilling Gods commands in the attempt to purify themselves and to remain obedient. The Jews did not claim to be justified by their obedience, but only to be approximating the realization of God's will. "The congregation of Israel spoke before the Holy One, blessed be His name: Lord of the universe, though I am poor in meritorious acts yet nonetheless I belong to thee and it is within thy power to help me" (*Pesahim* 118b). They held that the Torah, in its entirety, was an everlasting guide to the way of life which God expected from his chosen people and that through faithfulness to its commands they were brought close to him. The growth of Christianity was not seen by them as an evidence of the truth of Christian faith but rather as the continuing dominance of a power outside the covenant over the defeated and scattered people of Israel reduced to a tolerated and too often abused minority within the confines of Christendom.

Two communities, a vast majority and a small minority, professing faith in God and an ethic in which love was central, lived together in a strange combination of hostility and symbiosis. Underneath their differences there remained the fundamental elements of agreement and similarity. Yet to members of the two groups it was the differences which were salient to their consciousness. Differences, especially since it was a matter of differences within a common tradition, meant rivalry and competition, and all the antagonism to which they give rise. Differences, especially since it was a matter of differences concerning profound religious beliefs, made that antagonism abiding and often bitter. To many Christians, Judaism was not merely a rival but a blasphemous one, since it rejected Christ; to many Jews, Christians came close to idolatry in placing a human figure next to God and were themselves guilty of blasphemy. As the majority group with political power in its hands, the Christians could make the rules. As a large majority, it contained groups who would make an unpopular minority a scapegoat. In popular thinking the existence of Judaism was often seen as an affront to the religious sensibilities of Christians, and Jews a people punished for Christ's death. To the Jews such conditions were a continuation of their exile and they looked for God's deliverance.

In periods of social and political unrest from the late eleventh century on, the Jews found themselves the victims of pogroms from time to time. Such matters of religious identification and antagonism as always became inextricably intertwined with other more mundane interests and the outbreak of anti-Jewish violence reflected this. Yet the history is not one of complete antagonism, for despite controversy and opposition Jews in practice had friendly contact with Christians in certain areas of life and in theory did develop a more tolerant attitude toward Christianity. Thus in the Paris debate of 1240 Jews stated that the talmudic restrictions on the relations of Jews to idol worshipers did not apply to Christians and that the negative evaluation of the seven foreign nations found in the Bible and the Talmud did not refer to contemporary Christians. At the end of the thirteenth century the great French Jewish scholar Ha-Meiri enunciated the principle that Christianity is not idolatry and that

Christians share with Jews basic ethical and religious truths evident to all men of reason. In the developed Jewish view the seven Noahide commandments are universally binding and all men who fulfill them will be recognized by God and share in the redemption to come.

In the early Christian Fathers we find harsh language used in expressing hostility to the synagogue and those who worship there. Yet the Fathers, despite the hostility of rivalry, saw the Jews as somehow continuing their testimony to God's revelation—indeed, to what the Fathers saw as the Christian fulfillment of that revelation. Augustine, who could see the Jew in the image of Judas Iscariot, could also recognize the importance of his continued existence.

> *Today, if the Jews are dispersed through all nations and lands, that is due to God's design; so that if idols, altars, sacred groves and temples are destroyed all over the earth and the sacrifices forbidden, it could still be seen from the Jewish books that all this was prophesied long ago; and although the prophecies, fulfilled in the Christian religion, may be read also in our own holy books, no one can accuse us of having composed them ourselves after the event.*
>
> (*City of God* IV.34)

Moreover, more profound Christian thought beginning with Paul was aware of a continuing special religious meaning and destiny for Israel. For Paul things happened as they happened by God's providence. The Jews now stand aside that the gentiles may be gathered. "Through their trespass salvation has come to the Gentiles"; but Paul asks, "have they stumbled so as to fall?" He answers, "By no means!" (Rom. 11:11). For Paul, "a hardening has come upon part of Israel, until the full number of the Gentiles come in," but when that is accomplished "all Israel will be saved" (Rom. 11:25–26). He says to gentile Christians, "As regards the gospel they are enemies of God, for your sake; but as regards election they are beloved for the sake of their forefathers. For the gifts and call of God are irrevocable" (Rom. 11:28–29).

Following Paul, the Christian view saw the Jews as both acting out God's will and subjectively unfaithful, and granted them a kind of secondary legitimacy. They should be permitted to exist, since that is God's will, and since they bear testimony to the truth of Christianity. But they should exist in a subject condition since they rejected the fulfillment of the truth and this subjection was the sign testifying to their infidelity. Proselytism of Christians by Jews continued well into the Middle Ages but it was forbidden by law; Christian attempts to convert Jews were of course perfectly legal. Jews were forbidden to hold public office in the Christian society of the Middle Ages and the public character of their worship was limited, as was the number of synagogues they could build. In the eleventh century the ghetto or special Jewish quarter arose as a pattern of residence and in the fifteenth century Jewish residence there was made compulsory, especially in Spain and the papal domain in Italy.

And the modes of contact between Jews and Christians were regulated by Church law. They were also regulated by Jewish law, and a strange symbiosis grew up in which the regulations of both communities worked to maintain Jewish identity and separateness. The condition of the Jews worsened greatly during the Crusades, when they were often victimized and massacred by adventurers and mobs.

St. Thomas held that although the Jews were in the status of bondsmen to the civil powers of Christendom, they did not by that fact lose their natural rights nor their special religious rights to practice their own religion. He held also that Jewish children could not be baptized without the consent of their parents (*Summa Theologica* Part II, ques. 10, art. 12, and Part III, ques. 68, art. 10). The policy of the Church followed Thomas in this, but there were those who disagreed with it and it was violated in practice at various times. The Church and the civil power did act at times to protect the Jews, but the policy of restricting their influence in a Christian society was generally accepted by all. As Malcolm Hay said: "The Popes of the Middle Ages often intervened, not always effectively, to defend the Jews against personal violence, but seldom wrote a line to condemn the ill-will which made such violence inevitable." Religious rivalry and the sense of threat which each group offered to the other left little room for their seeing each other as neighbors whom they were commanded to love by the commandment they both accepted.

Geography and history rather than the content of faith led to a further split in the majority tradition, and finally in 1054 Eastern and Western Churches split into two distinct groups, each considering the other to be schismatic. Several attempts were made to heal this rift but they failed. Finally in the Reformation, Western Christianity itself split again, unable to compose its differences, and the Protestant camp split up still further into numerous denominations as time went on. Medieval Europe had gradually and toilsomely built the foundations of a secular society within the confines of a sacral civilization with its institutions justified by their own functions and rationale. That this was the case would become apparent by the mid-seventeenth century, but the great changes would begin their long process of development at the commencement of the sixteenth.

## THE REFORMATION

The Europe that saw the beginning of the Reformation was still religious and the Reformation was a religious movement. But once the issues had been joined on basic questions of Church reform, including questions of belief itself, it was unavoidable that all other aspects of European life would be drawn into the struggle. The Reformation could not help become at the same time a political phenomenon. It was in part a conflict of princes against the pope. It was in part a revolt of the Teutonic North against the Latin South; it was in part a revolt of new middle classes against the older aristocratic society and culture. And although it sought to deepen the religiosity of European man, it eventuated in a marked secularization of culture and a frank admission on the part of strategic classes in

Europe of the practical primacy of this-worldly aims and aspirations in politics and in business. Over a century of religious wars following the Reformation began with wars in which religious interests were dominant although intertwined with worldly interests, and ended in palpably secular struggles for power and wealth. There are times in the development of societies and cultures when the social structures and the modes of comprehension of man and his destiny which have evolved are no longer appropriate. The new situation which has slowly developed and the old forms which have been carried over into it from the past no longer fit. Men in such situations are for long unaware of the true dimensions of their problems, but as they seek to act on them they act as though forced to more and more extreme positions by the logic of the situation itself. Perhaps we live in such a situation in our own day. Certainly the men of the sixteenth century did, and what they started as a return to an imagined and idealized past eventuated in a greatly changed society and culture, although it would take some two or three centuries before all its implications would make themselves apparent.

The Reformation may be said to have begun in 1517 with the protest of Luther against the sale of indulgences and to have expanded in the next three years as he took a position against the validity of "good works" as aids to salvation, denied the primacy of the pope and the infallibility of general councils, attacked clerical celibacy, transubstantiation, and the indelibility of priestly ordination, and demanded far-reaching reforms of religious orders. By 1520 Luther had broken with the old Church, and after a period of pronounced religious conflict in Germany, Rome excommunicated him on January 3, 1521. Although at first placed under ban by the Holy Roman Emperor, he attracted sympathy from a number of rulers of German states, and his support of authoritarian secular government during the Peasant War ensured that he would be backed by powerful princes. In 1524–1526 the German peasants rose in rebellion, demanding the abolition of serfdom and certain taxes, as well as certain religious privileges, such as the right to elect their own pastors. It was another of those movements of mixed socioeconomic and religious motivation and it soon led to extremes of violence in the burning of castles and monasteries. Luther at first tried to mediate, but this proving unsuccessful he turned against the violence of the lower orders and wrote his own intemperate denunciation of them, advocating that they be stabbed and killed to extermination, a stand that effectively reduced his popularity if it brought him powerful support. Yet Luther's ideas spread throughout Germany, and popular religious enthusiasm as well as official protection and support brought many victories. The old order crumbled in many places as priests married and religious deserted the cloister. Many Catholic religious practices were given up. In 1524 Luther put aside his monastic habit and married a former Cistercian nun.

What had developed was a new form of Christianity designated as Lutheranism. Its basic doctrines proclaimed salvation through faith alone and the priesthood of believers. It tended to follow Luther in seeing all men totally depraved and human reason as useless in the search for religious truth. It emphasized the centrality of the Bible and had Luther's magnificent translation into German as its own vernacular scripture. Lutheranism became the faith of about two-thirds of Germany and all of Scandinavia.

In 1523 under the leadership of Ulrich Zwingli, who claimed that he took no ideas from Luther, but who brought forth many similar notions and some far more radical as in Eucharistic and social doctrines, reform gained control of the city of Zurich. There, with the backing of the civil authorities, Zwingli broke with Rome and abolished the ecclesiastical hierarchy and monasticism. The Zwinglian Reformation made rapid advances in many Swiss cantons and in South Germany as well.

The most dynamic of the Reformation tendencies came forward in Geneva under John Calvin, who replaced Zwingli as the reform leader in Switzerland when the latter was killed fighting against the Catholic cantons. Calvin was an austere and intelligent man; he was a logical expositor of doctrine and often extreme in his views, some of which we have already considered. Here for the first time the new religious agitation produced a massive, rigorously argued, and intellectually constructed theological system based upon predestination by a transcendent God far beyond the reach of man's understanding and saturated with a hyper-Augustinian pessimism. Calvin held that the Bible contained all we need to know about God and the moral life. He denied freedom, held that all human acts were sinful, but that in those who were of the elect they were covered over by the merits of Christ's death. He emphasized God's inscrutable and transcendent omnipotence and unlike Luther paid little heed to his mercy or his justice. In 1541 Calvin took over control of Geneva, which had become the center of the Swiss Reformation. Here he established a rigid theocracy and used the most coercive supervisory and repressive measures to keep people in line. He enforced an austerely ascetic life, and all forms of mere pleasure such as dancing and game playing were outlawed.

Calvin was the father of ascetic Protestantism which advocated a strict ascetic mode of life characterized by a high degree of self-control. Calvinism imparted a dynamic quality to the Reformation, which Lutheranism never really achieved. Whereas the latter rested content to concern itself with the inner life and left government and the worldly pursuits to the state, thereby effecting a kind of passivity which long remained one of its distinguishing characteristics, Calvinism set out to create Christian communities after the Calvinist model and under the supervision of Calvinist leadership. This austere ascetic religion appealed to the rising middle classes of a Europe experiencing commercial expansion and its consequent social change. It also combined with the national interests and sentiments of such groups as the Dutch and the Scots. Even more than Lutheranism it became involved in the political struggles of the time, as may be seen in France, in the Netherlands, in West Germany, in Scotland, and in England. It has been said that Calvinism provided the new rising bourgeoisie in many places with a form of Christianity which fitted the psychological and religious needs of rising individualists cut off from meaningful participation in the old Church, whose modes of worship and ways of belief they found as barriers to any religious experience and against which they turned in fury, and from real involvement in traditional national life as well. It is one of the unexplained ironies of the Reformation period that the religious point of view which most appealed to the highly activist and energetic capitalist classes was one that held man to be unfree and incapable of good by his own efforts. Yet the notion of election must have given a profound basis of inner security, providing it could be maintained. To maintain it was in fact difficult, and various compromises with it soon developed. Indeed, wherever the bourgeois classes got the upper hand they tended radically to reform the notion of predestination or to reject it entirely, although it remained the official doctrine of the United Presbyterian Church in the United States until 1965.

In England the Reformation got its opportunity when a small group of clerical intellectuals took advantage of the marriage problems and dynastic worries of a conservative Catholic king to bring about a break with Rome and to introduce change in doctrine and church structure. There evolved the Church of England, governed by bishops, but with its headship vested in the monarch. That church, in the settlement under Elizabeth I which gave it its definitive form, held to a kind of middle way on most of the controversial issues of theology. Yet Calvinism made important inroads in the Church of England in which, however, a Catholicizing tendency also remained important. Outside the established Church in England, Calvinism became an important force. In the Puritan Revolution (1640–1660) it abolished the monarchy and established a Commonwealth controlled by the more extreme religious groups. This movement split into numerous competing sects and led eventually to the restoration of the king and the established Anglican Church. It was never able to convince the English as a whole to accept its more extreme positions, not to mention its rejection of the monarchy.

The idea of the Church as it emerged in the Reformation took varied forms, and the working out of a definition of what the Church was became an important task of Protestant theologians. Whatever it was seen to be, it is obvious that it was conceived quite differently from the way it had been viewed in the preceeding centuries. The vast overarching superstructure of the medieval Church with its objective means of grace and its elaborate theology had to be replaced by other conceptions. All Protestant variations had one thing in common; they all rejected to one degree or another the Catholic emphasis on a centralized teaching office and an objective sacramental system. A new emphasis upon the Bible was characteristic and preaching came to take up a large portion of the time given to Sunday worship. Despite the variations to be found in reformed conceptions of the Church, perhaps three general tendencies may be distinguished. There was first a more traditionalist tendency which held that Christ intended a visible universal Church, but because that Church had been corrupted by ignorance and sin, national schisms in the interests of reform were justified. This conception gave some significant place to an objective, at times hierarchical, ecclesiastical institution. A second tendency held that the Church was really an invisible body comprised of the elect or those saved by a personal act of faith, and its true membership was known to God alone. Yet it also held that the Church needed a visible social organization as a means of existence in this world. This outward Church should enforce high standards so that its membership would correspond so far as possible with the inward Church, though there would never be a one-to-one correspondence of the two. It held that this visible organization would ideally be universal, but in fact, since that was now impossible, national churches and churches coterminal with political entities and established by law in them should be sought. Hence the Lutheran and Calvinist churches took hold in Germany and Sweden and in Holland and Scotland.

A third tendency may be seen in those who substantially agree with the second tendency respecting the ideas of the visible and invisible Church but who held that no form of unity between congregations was necessary, and some who even held such unity to be evil. This view may be best described as a sect ideal, which held up as the true model of the Church of God a small austere brotherhood withdrawn from the world or militantly hostile to it. In the Puritan Revolution the original aim of the Commonwealth was to establish a Calvinist Church, and in 1643 an Assembly of Divines convened for that purpose drew up The Westminster Confession as its basis. But the composition of the supporters of the Commonwealth, especially in the army, was decidedly of independent and sectarian stamp, and sectarian freedom had to be given legal approval.

The more extreme Reformation movements have often been lumped together under the label of "Left-Protestantism." They present a varied array but they all approach to one extent or another to the sect ideal. They are often radical in both theology and social ideas and apocalyptic at the same time combining communitarian social ideas, emotional enthusiasm, and millenarian expectations. Though often condemned by the great reformers and the official Reformation churches at least in their more extreme forms, these groups, at times made up of the poor and oppressed, represent a genuine and significant religious phenomenon. Just as sectarian and semimystical groups emerged in the pre-Reformation period, becoming either religious orders or excommunicated sects, and affected the life of the Church as a whole, so they emerged in the Reformation and post-Reformation periods as well. From the start such groups were present and the tendencies they embodied were widespread. Official Protestantism, however, was conservative in important respects and moreover needed time to work out its conception of the Church, and under those circumstances such groups found little place. From the middle of the seventeenth century, however, these groups began to have an increased effect on the more conservative Protestant churches. Among the important and quite varied groups of which we speak are Levellers, Mennonites, Diggers, Millenarians, the so-called Anabaptists, and the less extreme Congregationalists, Independents, Baptists, and Quakers.

## THE CATHOLIC COUNTER-REFORMATION AND ATTEMPTS AT UNITY

Luther's original demand for reform may indeed be viewed as part of the religious revival which was developing in the Church, a revival which was to be seen in the founding of such lay groups as the Brothers of the Common Life and in a marked renewal of religious fervor in the religious orders. New religious orders were founded in the 1520s, the Capuchins, the Theatines, and the Barnabites, and in 1540 the Jesuits, established by the austere militant Basque Ignatius Loyola who soon became the vanguard of the movement to defend, reform, and extend Catholicism in Europe, in the Americas, and in the Far East. A small but highly influential group founded in Rome in 1517 was the Oratory of Divine Love, made up of men who were of contemplative mind and who put together many humanistic ideas of the Renaissance with their Catholicism to produce an authentic Christian humanism. They led lives of prayer and devotion, as well as of responsible thought and action. Two of their prominent members, Cardinals Contarini and Pole, attempted to mediate between the Catholics and Protestants and to negotiate a compromise which would reestablish the unity of the Church. This idea of compromise and union appealed to important figures on the Protestant side as well, for after all had not Christian unity always been the ecclesiastical ideal, and wasn't it supported by men as significant as Bucer and Melanchthon? These leaders sought such a compromise at the Colloquy of Regensburg (or Ratisbon) in 1541. Pole and Contarini had agreed that the formal statement of Lutheran faith, the Confession of Augsburg, need not be an obstacle. Two groups of three each—for the Catholics Eck, Pflug, and Gropper; for the Protestants Bucer, Melanchthon, and Pistorius—drew up a statement on justification by faith which was agreed upon. It mentioned neither freedom of the will nor subjective certainty of salvation. Evidently other doctrinal matters proved negotiable in a similar manner but not the Mass, invocation of the saints, and papal supremacy. Bucer brought about a second Regensburg meeting in 1546, but it got nowhere. Luther was unfriendly to the whole affair, and Calvin who was present at one of the meetings was less willing to compose differences than the other reformers. The compromise party of Pole and Contarini was suspect by other Catholics, and Protestant princes were against any reunion being effected. Catholic and Protestant opinion had diverged widely in the two decades of separation and conflict, and vested interests had become invested in continuing disunity.

This effort after unity was but one expression of the reform tendency which had been gathering strength and energy in the old Church since the beginning of the sixteenth century. The other sought to combine an effort to combat the spread of Protestantism with the renewal of religious life and the promotion of austerity, discipline, and devotion within the Church. This tendency found its spokesman in Gian Pietro Caraffa who also had been a member of the Oratory and later became Pope Paul IV. Pope Paul III, whose personal life was far from presenting a model to churchmen, but who was however an effective promoter of reform in the Church, sympathized with both tendencies but sided with the more militant approach of Caraffa, partly perhaps in response to the aggressive expansion of Calvinism. Orthodoxy was enforced by a renewed Inquisition (1542) and the so-called Catholic Counter-Reformation began. In 1540 the Jesuit Order was formally established. It attracted much Catholic idealism eager to strive and suffer in defense of the Church. This new order gave the Catholic side a dynamism and a militancy to match that of the Calvinists. Largely through Jesuit efforts South Germany and Poland were won back to Catholicism and Catholic foreign mission work vastly stimulated. The battle between Protestants and Catholics was joined and Europe would now pass through an awful period of the religious wars. As well as efforts to mend the split in the Church at large, there were also efforts to bring about Protestant unity. A number of conferences were held, many of them initiated by Bucer, but they were unsuccessful. The ideal of Church unity was held by many, but it was not possible any longer. For nearly all it involved imposition of belief. One man, Sabastian Castellio, whom Calvin had expelled from Geneva, suggested toleration of differences in belief, but this found little favor among reformers trying to reestablish some kind of religious order and to domesticate the religious individualism which had been released by reform and rebellion. Consequently the seventeenth century saw a greater division among Protestants and the formation of the so-called Left-Protestant groups.

The Council of Trent also represented an attempt at unity in that Protestants were invited, but after appearing they soon left, refusing to take part in a meeting led by the pope. What Trent actually did was to provide a tighter formulation of Catholic doctrine and to increase the significance of strict and proper belief as the criterion of orthodoxy. Also, Trent carried out significant internal reform. After Trent there continued a magnificent flowering of the religious life within the Catholic fold. Yet it is another great irony of the religious history of the West that this most authentic and most long-lived renewal of spiritual life took place within the confines of a Church which was defensive in posture, closed to rethinking of its doctrinal positions, and now with its renewed purity of intention even more rigid in its structure. Trent indeed stamped upon Roman Catholicism the imprint of an intolerant age; Trent imparted to the Catholic mentality a sense of being under siege and of facing Protestant Christians as adversaries to be fought to the end. This feeling was of course reciprocated from the Protestant side but there disunity kept uniformity and rigidity of structure from dominating the entire religious scene.

## SECULARIZATION AND SCIENCE

Europe had seen from the twelfth century a rise of secular states, which though Christian asserted their own competence and autonomy, and a vast development of commerce which carved out of rural and traditional medieval society an autonomous market becoming ever larger and more ramified. By the outbreak of the Reformation, Antwerp was the Wall Street of Europe and many modern business practices were to be found there. The break in Christian unity, which yielded to no attempts at reunion, gave the secularizing tendencies favorable conditions for their further development, and the consequent secularization of culture made religious unity seem less urgent and less important. It could loom large in the mind of Leibnitz in the seventeenth century, as can be seen in his correspondence with the French Catholic Bishop Bossuet, but it never again took on such significance with such an illustrious intellectual figure. The most significant element in these developments came in the seventeenth century in what is called the rise of modern science. The stage had been set for a far-reaching secularization of culture, and the revival of humanism in the late Middle Ages and early Renaissance led to an eventual break between humanistic and religious thought and feeling. There was no longer a grand overarching Church with its largely undisputed doctrines whose leaders could realistically hope to be the key influential elite keeping the conscience of a whole civilization. Now with science would come an element radically solvent of traditional thought and feeling. What commerce was doing to disenchant the world of human relations by introducing quantitative calculation as a dominant mode of relationship, scientific thought would do to the intellectual cosmos. The scientific development of the seventeenth century was a complex process and represented the continuation of a long development going back to the university life of the High Middle Ages and the numerous useful inventions which were made in Europe in the medieval period. When Luther began his protest, Western Europe was in fact the most technologically advanced society the world had seen up to that time. But in the seventeenth century there came a breakthrough in the scientific development—from Galileo to Newton—which justifies being described as a scientific revolution. It was much more than a continuation of the use of experiment and mathematics which had taken place since the thirteenth century. Nor was it merely the consequence of new data gradually accumulated and slowly changing men's outlooks. It was an abrupt and radical shift in ways of thinking which led men to look at their world in a new kind of abstract way. Moreover, in this development the earth itself had been thrown out of center and a new heliocentric astronomy became accepted. This development threatened religion directly, for the older geocentric view was held, at least superficially, to harmonize with religious ideas and to reinforce them with common pragmatic prejudices. The scientific endeavors of centuries came to sudden fruition and men found themselves with a new mathematized mode of thought which gave them distance from their world and a means of manipulating it symbolically in their heads. To the already proceeding secularization of culture was added an incomparably more powerful solvent of tradition which in less than two centuries would transform both man's world and his way of thinking about it. Thus there began a new and tragic division of the Western mind—a conflict between science and religion, a conflict in which religion was often reactionary and obscurantist despite the fact that the great pioneers of science, its greatest founding figures, were sincere Christians. It took a long time—even until our own day—for

*The chapel at Ronchamp. Designed by Le Corbusier, it replaces a war-damaged church built in the thirteenth century. The structure is so fashioned that mountain winds playing between the columns under the roof and through archways make musical sounds heard for miles. (Religious News Service Photo.)*

the idea to become evident that science and religion see experience from different standpoints, respond to their worlds in different modes of response, and require different languages to express their meanings. There is here a vast field yet to be explored and understood. The fact is, however, that by the year 1800 Christianity existed in a world which was increasingly secularized for dominant classes and in which science provided more and more the model of thinking for the literate. Religion was definitely on the defensive, though numerically most Western men were still believers; it was in fact definitely in retreat. Yet traditional religion would remain in a secularized world the repository of the riches of the religious heritage and the source of the profoundest Western values and aspirations.

## THE JEWISH RESPONSE TO SECULARIZATION

This breakdown of a unified Catholic Europe and the emergence of a secularized bourgeoisie meant also the creation of a neutral public sphere free from the domination of religious values. This led to a gradual but drastic change in the status of churches in society, as can be seen in such countries as England and Sweden which officially still have established churches but are in fact about the most secularized in the world. But perhaps the greatest changes to result were found in the traditional Jewish communities of Europe. New ideas penetrated the ghetto and influenced the minds of many. The entire structure of exilic existence, which rested on the foundation ideas of election, exilic suffering, and ultimate redemption, was threatened by a rationalistic reconsideration of accepted truths. What Christianity was undergoing in the larger world was now coming with more sudden impact to be a fact within the Jewish communities themselves. The new secular spirit penetrated the ghettos and captivated sections of the Jewish population, challenging the religious framework of the community. In the eighteenth century, the so-called age of reason, the values of this world, especially material values, were elevated above the values of the next. Bourgeois man tended to dedicate his efforts to the pursuit of gain and the betterment of his mundane condition, using his autonomous reason to do so. The bourgeois Christian had little need of the God of the Bible, and the Church's inability to speak to him in any depth left the matter to take on its own shape and form. What developed was the notion, seemingly confirmed by the facts of bourgeois existence, that realistic, practical rational activity would lead to continuous progress in the betterment of human life. Such ideas now penetrated the Jewish community and as a consequence some Jews adopted this rational spirit and found that for them too the God of the Bible was obsolete. They rejected the Torah culture and the religious values of traditional Judaism. No longer could they be satisfied to live in expectation of a future redemption while fulfilling the religious duties of the present; no longer would they look upon worldly success and the practical activities that led to it as secondary to religious activity with its future expected reward. Jews affected by this new modern spirit and its attendant ideas dedicated themselves to ending Jewish exile by achieving prosperity and success in this world. The emerging Jewish bourgeoisie, embodying this spirit, soon abandoned the religious practices which hindered its progress. Abrogation of the Law was common, and such abrogation rent the fabric of the traditional community. The emerging Jewish intellectual stratum, espousing secular ideas, abandoned religious beliefs and practices which could not be justified according to the canons of reason, and thus attacked the very foundations of Jewish life. Desiring to become part of the developing secular society of Western Europe, to become one socially and culturally with the general secular European world, now replacing what had once been Christendom, these Jews rejected self-segregation and the all-encompassing cultural world of the Torah tradition. They sought to share in the open society of European rationalism and humanitarianism.

The history of Judaism in modern times is a history of response to the challenges which the scientific and philosophical ideas of the past three centuries and the social, economic, and political changes in European society presented to the biblically derived religion and those which opportunity for assimilation into the new kind of general society presented to the isolated self-enclosed exilic community. The Jewish religious reforms proposed by German Jewish reformers offered one solution to these challenges by developing a system of religious beliefs and practices which conformed to the spirit and ideology of their time. This system legitimated the separation of the secular and the sacred and the truncation of Judaism and its relegation to one fragment of the individual's life. It also sanctioned a definition of Judaism which denied the necessary link between faith and the Jewish people as an ethnic unit, and thus justified the assimilation of the Jews and the end of their existence as a separate national community. In opposition to the radical reform movement, a more conservative trend developed, which did not reject whatever could not be rationalized according to contemporary standards, but which sought to accommodate tradition to the present without completely destroying what had been sanctified by the past and had long been considered essential to the sacred nature of Judaism. The more conservative reformers did not oppose ceremonial practices as irrational, nor did they reject the ethnic base of Judaism, yet they did make adjustments in belief and practice to render Judaism more viable under modern conditions. The efforts at reform along both radical and conservative lines have continued so that within Judaism today, Conservative, Reform, and Reconstructionist movements exist alongside many Orthodox groups to offer alternative definitions of belief and practice.

Another response of Jews to secularization has been the total abandonment of traditional religion and the substitution of nationalism for religion as the basis of Jewish unity. As Christendom broke up, the importance of the national group for men's basic identity and its significance as their basic community was greatly enhanced. Although such national developments offered rivalry to traditional Christianity, they did not usually seek to replace it. The Jewish proposal was more radical, reflecting perhaps how thoroughly challenged was Judaism by the conditions of modernity. Moreover, the rise of Jewish nationalism took place mainly in Eastern Europe, where ethnic group life was the dominant pattern and where assimilation into the general society was never a realistic possibility. Within Russia and Poland, Jews found themselves necessarily identified as Jews by external forces, but often at the same time lacking the religious convictions that had grounded that identity in the past. No longer accepting the traditional religion, these men sought a new ground for Jewish unity and identity and suggested national loyalty to a common past and present community now seen in secularized terms. They maintained that national sentiment, rather than religious belief, had always really been the primary factor in Jewish exilic survival and that now this same sentiment would continue to give purpose to Jewish existence and preserve Jewish unity. Nationalism as a political and cultural movement has provided a secular substitute for religion to many Jews, grounding their identity in a secular ideal and an ongoing community. As secularization continued in Western Europe, nation-states provided similar contexts for community and common values to lands and peoples where traditional Christianity was waning. In these conditions, biblical religion, both Judaism and Christianity, both Catholicism and Protestantism, remain as the embodiments of the great religious tradition of the West. Each and all they face vast problems of reinterpretation to bring their spiritual riches to a greatly transformed world so much in need of them. A first step of such reinterpretation is certainly understanding. Jewish attempts at restructuration offer many lessons whose meaning requires comprehension and which once understood may point out important general lessons.

THE CHRISTIAN RESPONSE TO SECULARIZATION

Catholic efforts to retain the integrity of the tradition, though distorted by the defensive post-Tridentine mentality, revealed an important lesson for all Christian institutionalism—the necessity of preserving the many-sidedness and the universality of the Christian tradition and its connection with the past as well as its expression in liturgical worship of great aesthetic value and capable of tremendous impact upon the interior psychological make-up of men. The internal renewal of the Roman Catholic Church in the period following the Reformation, although closed in upon itself and avoiding the real issues which history was presenting to Western man—in a word reactionary, despite its indubitable spiritual worth and beauty—remains a model for certain aspects of Christian life. In St. Francis de Sales, St. Teresa of Avila, St. Charles Borromeo, St. John of the Cross, and many others we see an austere yet human Christian piety which provides authentic examples of religious experience. The Protestant efforts to rework the tradition and to shed accretions which stood in the way of its contemporary relevance and to develop a Christianity cognizant of the changing world of the sixteenth and seventeenth centuries and its demands revealed another lesson no less significant. It demonstrated with the irrefutable confirmation of history itself that a great religious tradition could not become identified with any single intellectual expression or any one institutional form and remain a living flexible spiritual reality providing guidance and meaning to an evolving human society. It showed that all human realizations are relative to time and place, that even when they represent the realization of ultimate values and the expression of an ultimate religious relationship, they are realizations of ultimacy conditioned by specific historical and cultural circumstances, and cannot not be regarded as absolute. It is one of the tragedies of the period that if Catholicism rejected this Protestant principle, Protestantism itself failed to understand it.

THE CONTEMPORARY SITUATION OF BIBLICAL RELIGION

Indeed the Reformation conflict may be seen in retrospect as the manifest and surface expression of a great problem which man did not recognize as a whole and in the round, let alone solve. That problem is still to be formed, still to be stated, and the effort to solve it still to be begun. The tradition of biblical religion is one which tells us that God is central to man's fulfillment and that only through a relation to God can authentic human existence be cultivated. Man is called to live in that relationship, to grow in it, to prosper in it, to have life more abundantly in it. For the Hebrews and for the earliest Christians that was understood as awaiting, in the tension of hope and in the practice of the commandments, God's intervention into human history to redeem it and to lead human life to its apotheosis. When that hope receded under the specific conditions of declining antiquity, another interpretation developed. Jews in isolated communities, often persecuted for their loyalty to their religious convictions, awaited the end of God's strange exile and his sending of his Messiah. They combined this with other doctrinal adaptations to make life possible in the prolonged interim of this-worldly existence. Christians spread their good news throughout the European world and gave central place to a here-and-now relation to God through Christ and through the Church which continued his mediational mission. In this situation men also lived in the world. The world was a sinful place and Christians and Jews were sinners. But the world was more than this. It was also a place of human achievement and accomplishment, a place where men rose to nobility and towering human stature in spite of their offenses. European man built a civilization which incorporated many of these values, although being human it was also permeated by avarice and ambition. Yet while European man built that civilization, drawing his values from his religious tradition to provide its foundation, the religious tradition itself did not recognize the genuine worth of men's this-worldly accomplishments. By 1500, as we have seen, Christianity had become overelaborated in its doctrines, overrigid in its liturgies, and corrupted in its social organization. It was moreover formed and conditioned by earlier ages and presented its religious truths encapsulated in the ideas and expressive forms of the past. It was this situation which demanded reform; it was this condition that called for renewal. Nominalism attempted to dismantle the old elaborated intellectual forms and Marsiglio to give the this-worldly community a proper value. Protestantism tried to find a new way to state the implications of Christianity and render it contemporary. But a new and satisfactory solution was not found. Yet it was more than this that lay at the root of the trouble. The conditioned form which biblical religion had assumed was incapable of proclaiming its own values and at the same time recognizing the true worth of building a human community, a human culture, and a human civilization in this world. It was incapable of providing men in the world with a view at once religious and worldly, at once showing man his way in history and raising him above it in relation to transcendence. This problem neither the Catholics nor the Protestants nor the Jews were able to formulate explicitly in a form that would enable them to work for its solution. In the aftermath of the conflict Catholicism became even more set in its original form of other-worldliness, while Protestantism in disunion and disagreement with itself gradually experienced a vast secularization of thought and life which led to a recognition of the world but also a loss of religious consciousness, and the impact of modernity on self-enclosed traditional Jewish communities commenced a ferment whose end is not yet evident. As a consequence in the modern period of European history, civilization and culture have continued to rest unconsciously and implicitly upon the secularized versions of the values of biblical religion, while men have spent their efforts in mastering their environments and in emancipating themselves from all tradition so far as possible. Yet the tradition of biblical religion remains with its immense spiritual worth to confront that secularized world now in profound crisis and torn asunder by its own unbridled ambitions. Biblical religion remains to confront that world with that still unformulated question: What should man be doing on this earth being called to a living relation with God? Biblical religion remains confronting the modern secularized world to which it must explain the profound implications for a life of authentic value of the greatest commandments: You shall love the Lord your God with all your heart, and with all your soul, and with all your mind. You shall love your neighbor as yourself.

**BIBLIOGRAPHY**
Judaism in Historical Perspective

*God's Call and the Covenant with Israel:*

Bright, John, *History of Israel,* Philadelphia, The Westminster Press, 1959.

DeVaux, Roland, *Ancient Israel: Its Life and Institutions,* New York, McGraw-Hill, 1961; also available in paperback.

Eichrodt, Walther, *Theology of the Old Testament,* trans. J. Baker, 2 vols., Philadelphia, The Westminster Press, 1961 and 1967.

Kaufmann, Yehezkel, *Religion of Israel,* ed. M. Greenberg, Chicago, The University of Chicago Press, 1960.

Noth, Martin, *The History of Israel,* 2nd ed., New York, Harper & Row, 1960.

Orlinski, Harry M., *Ancient Israel,* 2nd ed., Ithaca, N.Y., Cornell, 1960; also available in paperback.

Ringgren, Helmer, *Israelite Religion,* Philadelphia, Fortress Press, 1966.

Speiser, Ephraim, ed., *Genesis,* Anchor Bible Series, Garden City, N.Y., Doubleday, 1964.

Von Rad, Gerhard, *Old Testament Theology,* 2 vols., New York, Harper & Row, 1965.

*Kings and Prophets: Disappointment and Hope:*

Buber, Martin, *The Prophetic Faith,* New York, Macmillan, 1949; paperback ed., New York, Harper & Row, 1960.

Frankfort, Henri, *Kingship and the Gods,* Chicago, The University of Chicago Press, 1948.

Heschel, Abraham J., *The Prophets,* New York, Harper & Row, hardcover and paperback eds., 1962.

Scott, R. B. Y., ed., *Jeremiah,* Anchor Bible Series, Garden City, N.Y., Doubleday, 1965.

*The Exile: Israel's Abiding Faith:*

McKenzie, John L., ed., *The Second Isaiah,* Anchor Bible Series, Garden City, N.Y., Doubleday, 1968.

*Restoration:*

Bickerman, Elias, *From Ezra to the Last of the Maccabees,* New York, Schocken, paperback ed., 1962.

Meyers, Jacob M., ed., *Ezra and Nehemiah,* Anchor Bible Series, Garden City, N.Y., Doubleday, 1965.

Tcherikover, Victor, *Hellenistic Civilization and the Jews,* Philadelphia, Jewish Publication Society of America, 1961.

*The Emergence of the Apocalyptic Spirit:*

Charles, R. H., ed., *The Apocrypha and Pseudoepigraph of the Old Testament,* 2 vols., New York, Oxford, 1913.

Klausner, Joseph, *The Messianic Idea in Israel,* New York, Macmillan, 1955.

Rowley, Harold H., *The Relevance of Apocalyptic,* London, Oxford, 1944, rev. ed., New York, Associated Press, 1964.

Simon, Marcel, *Jewish Sects at the Time of Jesus,* trans. J. H. Farley, Philadelphia, Fortress Press, paperback ed., 1967.

Christianity in Historical Perspective

*The Beginnings of Christianity:*

Barrett, C. K., ed., *The New Testament Background: Selected Documents,* New York, Harper & Row, paperback ed., 1961.

Bultmann, Rudolf, *Primitive Christianity in Its Contemporary Setting,* trans. R. H. Fuller, New York, World Publishing, paperback ed., 1956.

Grant, F. C., *Roman Hellenism and the New Testament,* New York, Scribner, 1962.

Grant, Robert M., *Gnosticism: A Sourcebook of Heretical Writings from the Early Christian Period,* New York, Columbia, 1959, 1966; paperback ed., *Gnosticisim and Early Christianity,* New York, Harper & Row, 1966.

Jonas, Hans, *The Gnostic Religion,* Boston, Beacon Press, paperback ed., 1963.

Nock, Arthur Darby, *Early Gentile Christianity and Its Hellenistic Background,* New York, Harper & Row, paperback ed., 1964.

*Jesus of Nazareth:*

Cross, Frank Moore, Jr., *The Ancient Library of Qumran,* Garden City, N.Y., Doubleday, paperback ed., 1961.

Daniel-Rops, Henri, *Daily Life in the Time of Jesus,* trans. Patrick O'Brian, New York, Hawthorn, 1962; paperback ed., New York, New York, New American Library, 1964.

Davies, W. D., *Sermon on the Mount,* New York, Cambridge, paperback ed., 1966.

Enslin, Morton Scott, *Christian Beginnings,* New York, Harper & Row, paperback ed., 1956.

———, *Literature of the Christian Movement,* New York, Harper & Row, paperback ed., 1956.

Flusser, David, *Jesus,* New York, Herder & Herder, 1969.

New Testament.

Smith, D. M., Jr., and R. A. Spivey, *Anatomy of the New Testament,* New York, Macmillan, 1969.

*The Early Church:*

Bettenson, Henry, ed., *Documents of the Christian Church,* New York, Oxford, 1947.

Cadbury, H., *The Book of Acts in History,* New York, Harper & Row, 1955.

Lebreton, Jules, and Jacques Zeiller, *The Emergence of the Church in the Roman World,* New York, Macmillan, paperback ed., 1962.

———, *Heresy and Orthodoxy,* New York, Macmillan, paperback ed., 1962.

Walker, Williston, *A History of the Christian Church,* rev. ed., New York, Scribner, 1958.

*The Gentile World:*
Bultmann, op. cit.
Jonas, op. cit.
Nock, Arthur Darby, *Conversion,* New York, Oxford, paperback ed., 1961.
Tcherikover, op. cit.
*The Religious Temper of Later Antiquity:*
Bultmann, op. cit.
Jonas, op. cit.
Nock, *Conversion.*
Nock, *Early Gentile Christianity and Its Hellenistic Background.*
*The Understanding of Christ: Paul and John:*
Beare, F. W., *St. Paul and His Letters,* Nashville, Tenn., Abingdon, 1962.
Brown, Raymond E., ed., *The Gospel According to John, One to Twelve,* Anchor Bible Series, Garden City, N.Y., Doubleday, 1966.
Dodd, C. H., *Historical Tradition in the Fourth Gospel,* New York, Cambridge, 1963.
———, *The Interpretation of the Fourth Gospel,* New York, Cambridge, hardover ed., 1959; paperback ed., 1968.
Nock, Arthur Darby, *St. Paul,* New York, Oxford, 1938; paperback ed., New York, Harper & Row, 1963.
*The Making of the Institutional Church:*
Bettenson, op. cit.
Dawson, Christopher, *The Making of Europe,* New York, World Publishing, paperback ed., 1956.
Heer, Friedrich, *The Medieval World: Europe 1100–1350,* trans. Janet Sondheimer, New York, New American Library, paperback ed., 1964.
Southern, R. W., *The Making of the Middle Ages,* New Haven, Yale, hardcover and paperback eds., 1961.
Walker, op. cit.
*The Rise of Monasticism:*
Daniel-Rops, Henri, *The Church in the Dark Ages,* trans. Audrey Butler, Garden City, N.Y., Doubleday, 1962.
Duckett, Eleanor Shipley, *Monasticism,* vol. 3 of *The Gateway to the Middle Ages,* Ann Arbor, Mich., University of Michigan Press, hardcover and paperback eds., 1961.
Verheyen, Boniface, ed., *The Holy Rule of Our Most Holy Father Benedict,* Atchison, Kans., The Abbey Student Press, 1949.
Waddell, Helen, *The Desert Fathers,* New York, Barnes & Noble, 1936; paperback ed., Ann Arbor, Mich., University of Michigan Press, 1957.

Second Exile: Israel Reconstitutes Itself

Baeck, Leo, *The Essence of Judaism,* New York, Schocken, hardcover and paperback eds., 1961.
Baron, Salo W., and Joseph L. Blau, *Judaism: Postbiblical and Talmudic Period,* New York, Liberal Arts, 1954; also available in paperback.

Cohen, D. Gerson, "The Talmudic Age," in Leo Schwarz, *Great Ages and Ideas of the Jewish People,* New York, Random House, 1956, pp. 143–212.
Ginzberg, Louis, *Legends of the Jews,* 8 vols., Philadelphia, Jewish Publication Society of America, 1919–1925; rev. ed., hardcover and paperback, New York, Simon and Schuster, 1961.
Goldin, Judah, "The Period of the Talmud," in Louis Finkelstein, *The Jews,* Philadelphia, Jewish Publication Society of America, 1956, vol. 1, pp. 115–215.
Guttmann, Julius, *The Philosophies of Judaism,* trans. David Silverman, New York, Holt, Rinehart and Winston, 1954; paperback ed., Garden City, N.Y., Doubleday, 1964.
Katz, Jacob, *Tradition and Crisis,* New York, Free Press, 1961.
Maimonides, Moses, *The Guide to the Perplexed,* trans. S. Pines, Chicago, The University of Chicago Press, 1963; paperback ed., M. Friedlander, trans., New York, Dover.
Scholem, Gershom, *Major Trends in Jewish Mysticism,* New York, Schocken, paperback ed., 1954.
Scholem, Gershom, ed., *Zohar the Book of Splendor,* New York, Schocken, paperback ed., 1963.
Zangwill, Israel, ed., *Selected Religious Poems of Solomon Ibn Gabirol,* Philadelphia, Jewish Publication Society of America, 1923.

Man's Relation to God

*Worship and Prayer in Christianity:*
Cullman, Oscar, *Early Christian Worship,* London, SCM Press, 1953.
O'Brien, Elmer, *Varieties of Mystic Experience,* New York, New American Library, paperback ed., 1965.
Otto, Rudolf, *Mysticism East and West,* trans. Bertha L. Bracey and Richenda C. Payne, New York, Collier, paperback ed., 1962.
Underhill, Evelyn, *The Essentials of Mysticism,* New York, Dutton, paperback ed., 1960.
———, *Mysticism,* New York, World Publishing, paperback ed., 1955.
———, *Worship,* New York, Harper & Row, 1936; paperback ed., 1957.

*Worship and Prayer in Judaism:*
Agnon, Samuel Joseph, *Days of Awe,* New York, Schocken, paperback ed., 1948.
*Daily Prayerbook,* ed. Ben Zion Bokser, New York, Hebrew Publishing Company, 1957.
Gaster, Theodore H., *Festivals of the Jewish Year,* New York, William Sloane Associates, 1953; paperback ed., New York, Apollo Editions, Inc.
Idelsohn, A. Z., *Jewish Liturgy and Its Development,* New York, Holt, Rinehart and Winston, 1932; paperback ed., New York, Schocken.
Schauss, Hayim, *The Jewish Festivals,* Cincinnati, Ohio, Union of American Hebrew Congregations, 1938.

Ecclesia Semper Est Reformanda


Bainton, Roland H., *The Age of Reformation,* New York, Van Nostrand, paperback ed., 1956.

Baron, Salo W., "The Modern Age," in Leo Schwarz, *Great Ages and Ideas of the Jewish People,* New York, Random House, 1956, pp. 315–484.

Berger, Peter L., *The Sacred Canopy,* Garden City, N.Y., Doubleday, 1967; paperback ed., 1969.

Blau, Joseph L., *Modern Varieties of Judaism,* New York, Columbia, 1966.

Burrell, Sidney A., ed., *The Role of Religion in Modern European History,* New York, Macmillan, paperback ed., 1964.

Butterfield, Herbert, *The Origins of Modern Science,* New York, Macmillan, 1951; rev., paperback ed., New York, Free Press.

Chadwick, Owen, *The Reformation,* Baltimore, Penguin, paperback ed., 1964.

Daniel-Rops, Henri, *The Catholic Reformation,* 2 vols., Garden City, N.Y., Doubleday, paperback ed., 1964.

Davidowicz, Lucy S., ed., *The Golden Tradition,* New York, Holt, Rinehart and Winston, 1967; paperback ed., Boston, Beacon Press.

Davis, Moshe, *The Emergence of Conservative Judaism,* Philadelphia, Jewish Publication Society of America, 1963.

Gay, Peter, *The Enlightenment,* 2 vols., New York, Knopf, 1966.

Glazer, Nathan, *American Judaism,* Chicago, The University of Chicago Press, hardcover and paperback eds., 1957.

Groethuysen, Bernard, *The Bourgeois: Catholicism Versus Capitalism in Eighteenth-Century France,* trans. Mary Ilford, New York, Holt, Rinehart, Winston, 1968.

O'Dea, Thomas F., *Alienation, Atheism and the Religious Crisis,* New York, Sheed, 1969.

Pauck, Wilhelm, *The Heritage of the Reformation,* rev. ed., New York, Free Press, 1961; paperback ed., New York, Oxford, 1969.

Philipson, David, *The Reform Movement in Judaism,* rev. ed., New York, Macmillan, 1931.

Tawney, R. H., *Religion and the Rise of Capitalism,* New York, New American Library, paperback ed., 1947.

Vidler, Alec R., *The Church in an Age of Revolution,* Baltimore, Penguin, paperback ed., 1961.

Ware, Timothy, *The Orthodox Church,* Baltimore, Penguin, paperback ed., 1967.

Weber, Max, *The Protestant Ethic and the Spirit of Capitalism,* trans. Talcott Parsons, New York, Scribner, hardcover and paperback eds., 1948.

Willey, Basil, *The Seventeenth Century Background,* New York, Columbia, 1942; paperback ed., Garden City, N.Y., Doubleday, 1953.

# PART TWO

# THE ISLAMIC RELIGIOUS TRADITION

CHARLES J. ADAMS

# THE BACKGROUND AND THE LIFE OF THE PROPHET

About the year A.D. 610 (the precise date is unknown) a hitherto obscure citizen of Makkah (Mecca) named Muhammad launched himself upon a public career as preacher and religious leader. As a member of one of the poorer clans constituting the tribe of Quraysh, who occupied the valley of Makkah, Muhammad had small claim to distinction among his fellows. For some time, however, he had cultivated a habit of seclusion and meditation in the barren hills surrounding the city. These solitary vigils came to a climax in a series of intense religious experiences in which Muhammad felt himself overborne by divine power and compelled to take up the burden of preaching a message to the people of his time. The message emerging from these experiences, which continued to be repeated until the end of Muhammad's life, proved at the same time to offer a new world view of great profundity and to contain the resolution of vexing social problems which then disturbed Arabian life. From it came the basis for the formation of a new community about Muhammad which in subsequent centuries evolved into the bearer of the most brilliant culture of the era. In our own day between one-seventh and one-sixth of the human race still acknowledge that message as divine truth and as the normative insight for human life in the world. In the beginning Muhammad was much disturbed by his experiences, even to the extent of doubting his own sanity and of suspecting that he had been possessed by an evil spirit. He endured a crisis of personality that was traumatic in the extreme, driving him almost to suicide. Finally, however, Muhammad won through to a clear conception of the meaning of what had happened to him and to acceptance of the role of prophet. He began thereupon to declare himself a prophet of the one God and to warn his fellow Arabs of the catastrophic consequences of their misguided way of life.

That to which Muhammad summoned his fellow citizens he called Islam. The summons was twofold, to recognize a sovereign divine power which fashions and controls human destiny, and to commit oneself in ever renewed obedience to following the pattern ordained by the divine will for men. Islam is, of course, an Arabic word, most often translated as submission, surrender, acceptance, or obedience. Each of these terms partially renders its sense if only it be remembered that the reference is to an inner attitude which should be continuous and always renewed, an attitude of willingness to place all of one's will and action under the divine control. Islam is the resignation of oneself into the hands of God, throughout life and in all respects. A man who holds this attitude is known as a Muslim, meaning literally that he commits himself to make the divine will the norm of his life.

Very little certain knowledge exists about Muhammad's early life before he rose to prominence as the Arabian prophet. Even the date of his birth, which must have occurred within a few years of 570, is unsure, though it is known that he was orphaned at a very early age by the death of his mother, his father having died before he was born. Muhammad was brought up in straitened circumstances in the household of a kindly uncle, Abu Talib, who, although he protected Muhammad against the hostile Makkans, never became a Muslim. We know also of his marriage to the wealthy widow, Khadijah, a union that seems to have been happy and which was blessed with several offspring. Khadijah played an important role in helping Muhammad to grasp and understand his prophetic calling, both by her personal support and by bringing him into contact with other men who were preoccupied with religious quests. For as long as his first wife lived, Muhammad took no other, his only serious disappointment in the marriage stemming from the failure of the male children to survive childhood. In later life, however, he contracted a number of marriages. Muhammad's life does not emerge into the full light of history until the point was reached that he had collected a number of followers who began to take a sharp interest in his activities. Thus, our information about the last ten years of his career in Madinah (Medina) is vastly fuller than for the period in Makkah, and the end of the Makkan period is better known than its beginning.

The immediate relevance of Muhammad's message of one sovereign God who demands men's obedience may be better appreciated against the background from which Muhammad himself emerged. As we have said, he was a citizen of Makkah, then a thriving city located on the coastal plain of the Red Sea at a point which commanded two important trade routes, one connecting the ports of Hadramawt and Yemen to Egypt, Palestine, and Syria, and the other joining the same ports with Mesopotamia across the Arabian deserts. Profiting from this favorable geographical situation and from the disruption of trade created by the hostility between Byzantine Rome and Sassanian Persia, the two great powers of the Middle Eastern region, the Makkans had become both wealthy and powerful. They were the middlemen in a rich commerce of luxury goods, producing nothing themselves but dealing in the products of others and supplying the transportation, the financial and diplomatic assistance, and other arrangements necessary for this commerce. At Muhammad's birth his tribesmen, the Quraysh, were the most prestigious and influential group in the whole of Arabia. The connection of Quraysh with Makkah, however, had been of only short duration. Less than one hundred years earlier this group of nomads, under the leadership of a ṣoldier of fortune named Qusayy, had captured the valley from a rival tribe and settled there. The transition from a wandering nomadic existence based upon the keeping of flocks and herds, to a settled life involving highly sophisticated arrangements for commerce over great distances, wrought profound changes in the outlook of Quraysh. Although they attempted to preserve the social organization appropriate to life in the desert and clung to its values, these prior attitudes proved inadequate to the new conditions of life in Makkah. Change in the economic basis of society brought in its train sweeping erosion of old ways of thinking and acting and produced new ones. Makkah was a society in a state of transition and, therefore, of social stress and disruption. Dissatisfaction was evident in many areas but especially centered around the breakdown of traditional tribal values which had protected the weak under the bond of kinship, around the emergence of a new merchant oligarchy whose power was based upon its wealth, and around the concentration of wealth in private hands. For any sensitive intelligence these conditions must have been a stimulus for reflection; in Muhammad's case an instinctive grasp of the realities of life about him was reflected in the revelation which pointed to a still different kind of social order based upon a comprehensive world view.

The older outlook which the Quraysh had preserved from their days of wandering in the desert was common to all of the Bedouin Arabs. At the time of Muhammad's appearance the majority of the Arabs, those who lived in the central highland known as the Najd, were nomads eking out a meager existence from flocks of camels, goats, and sheep. Their custom was to venture into the sand deserts separating the Najd from the surrounding regions during the months of spring when the annual rainfall brought a brief bloom of vegetation. When the feed and water for their animals were exhausted, they returned again to the central plateau, each tribe to a territory it claimed for its own. The competition among tribes for the sparse resources was fierce and constant, and the barren countryside was implacable in its demands of those who would survive. Stronger tribal groups would often overrun and drive out weaker ones, and in years when the rains failed or were inadequate, there was much hardship and even death. From time to time tribal groups were forced to migrate, always to the north since there was nowhere south for them to go. Life was harsh and normally quite short, affording but a few fleeting pleasures such as the wine cup, the glory of military conquest, or a couplet of poetry well-turned.

It is, perhaps, the experience of life's meanness which explains the character of extremeness that has often been noted in the life and actions of the pre-Islamic Arabs. They were a reckless, passionate, and vibrant people. Drinking and gambling, both of which they loved, they indulged in to excess. In their military exploits they showed utter disregard for personal danger and courted death for the glory which it might briefly bring to one who had met it as a hero. Even their prized virtues such as generosity and steadfastness, not to speak of courage, they evidenced in exaggerated and extreme form. Given but a short time to live and that in one of the cruelest environments known to man, they sought to wring life dry of its few rewards and pleasures. Theirs was literally a philosophy of "eat, drink, and be merry, for tomorrow we die."

The quality of pre-Islamic Arab life is also explained by the Arabs' lack of any religious conviction or mythology which gave life a meaning beyond the here and now. To be sure the pre-Islamic Arabs recognized certain deities, usually connected with the heavenly bodies, and also recognized and propitiated a host of demons and spirits who inhabited springs, groves, and other places. These, however, did not form a connected pantheon or coalesce into a religious outlook which gave the Bedouin assurance of their place in the order of things. On the contrary, these numerous supernatural powers which threatened men on every hand if they were ignored or trespassed upon constituted an additional element in the general insecurity and fearfulness of life. Some of the deities had shrines dedicated to them, and pilgrimages were made to these shrines for paying homage. Such was the case with the three goddesses al-Manat, al-Lat, and al-'Uzza, revered by Quraysh and called the "daughters of Allah." These three figured in an important incident early in Muhammad's career when for a time he seemed to waver in his devotion to the one God and to relapse into paganism. There was also an important shrine known as the Ka'bah (the word means "cube") in the center of a sacred area in Makkah. Pilgrimages were made to this shrine, whose principal god seems to have been Hubal, every year during the sacred month when fighting was forbidden. When Muhammad at last captured the city of Makkah, he destroyed the gods of the Ka'bah but incorporated the shrine itself and the pilgrimage connected with it into Islam. There is evidence of religious dissatisfaction and questing in Arabia in the existence of a vague group of men called Hanifs, of which Muhammad claimed to be one. The Hanifs appear to have come very near a belief in monotheism even before the advent of Muhammad's prophecy.

The closest approximation to a conception of an ultimate power controlling human destiny among the pre-Islamic Arabs was their notion of *dahr,* or time. In their poetry, the best source of information about them, *dahr* is spoken of as the destroyer against whom no man can stand, an inexorable force which eventually swallows up all things. As the one thing which no one could resist, it was the most powerful of the forces affecting man. Such a view is pessimistic in the extreme and must have reinforced the tendency to make the most of life while we have it. Also, however, it deprived life of all meaning or purpose beyond the effort to gain a reputation through deeds which would ensure one's being remembered for a time. The pre-Islamic view accepted the world for what it appears to be, a transient stage for a brief and difficult existence, totally under

*The Ka'bah, the holiest structure in all Islam. It contains the sacred Black Stone believed to have been sent down from Heaven by God in ancient times. Pilgrims circle the Ka'bah, in the great courtyard of the Sacred Mosque, seven times. (Courtesy of Aramco.)*

the control of capricious forces. It neither provided deep principles for ethics nor did it reveal any cosmic or eternal dimension to man's life.

The Arabs of that time, like those still living in Arabia today, were divided into tribal and clan groupings. The tie of kinship was the primary source of the individual's identity, and the Arabs took great pride in their descent. Enormous attention was paid to genealogy, each group claiming and believing its nobility to be superior to that of others. The bond of kinship also provided protection to the individual in the hazardous circumstances of desert life. A clan group considered itself a unit, and an offense against any of its members constituted a crime against the whole. If a clan member were killed or injured by an outsider, it was looked upon as a primary obligation to avenge the wrong suffered. Individuals who had lost relatives took the burden of revenge with awesome seriousness, swearing terrible oaths and refraining from the pleasures of life until their duty should have been fulfilled. The obligation of blood revenge was, perhaps, as close to a genuine religious and moral imperative as the Arabs recognized. Clan solidarity (*'asabiyah*) to some degree mitigated and policed the warlike tendencies of the Arabs for whom raiding was a sport—as well as a way of gaining prestige—and military prowess the greatest of virtues. In their raids designed to steal cattle, take captives for ransom, or simply to humiliate rival groups, the Arabs were careful to avoid the spilling of blood in order not to create a blood feud. When such feuds did erupt, they were often lengthy and devastating; in some instances entire tribes were wiped out.

In times of plenty all clansmen shared alike, as in times of want, and each rose to the protection of the other. Without the support of kinsmen no man could hope to survive, for he might become the victim of any whom he met. It was the withdrawal of his clan's protection after the death of Abu Talib that finally forced Muhammad to quit Makkah, just as it had been that very protection which had enabled him to endure against the fierce hatred of the Makkans during the previous years.

The mutual rivalry and hostility of clan entities was another factor of precariousness in desert life. Although solidarity formed some kind of shield against the more aggressive, weaker groups were at any time subject to depredations from their neighbors. Violence was, thus, an element in the unease which pervaded tribal society on the eve of Islam. The effect of Muhammad's message was to set aside loyalty to the tribe for loyalty to the newly formed religious community cutting across tribal lines, while at the same time preserving the values of solidarity, mutual protection, and mutual interest within the Islamic *ummah*. So far as the relations among its members were concerned, the Islamic community was a new and all-inclusive tribe in which all Muslims owed the duty of brothers to all others regardless of blood kinship. The coming of Islam also blunted the mutual hostility and aggressiveness of the Arab tribes by channeling their warlike energies into the service of a nobler cause. In this, as in many other areas, Islam preserved and built upon the pre-Islamic tradition while also subtly reorienting the pagan values by basing them upon a comprehensive world view whose fundamental element was a sovereign creative deity.

We do not know how long before he began his preaching it was that the first of the revelations collected in the Islamic Scripture, the *Qur'an,* came to Muhammad. Muhammad was far from an immediate success, being able in the beginning to attract only certain members of his family and a few other individuals to follow his call. In fact, during the entire ten or more years of his preaching in Makkah he never gathered more than a handful of the prominent men of the city into his following. Most of the believers were slaves or members of the lower classes. Even this small group was beset with problems. As time passed, opposition to Muhammad formed and intensified. Although his own clan could protect him from physical harm, nothing could stop the verbal abuse which the Quraysh poured upon him, and those followers who could not claim the protection of a prominent clan were often dealt with very harshly. At some point one group of his followers emigrated to Abyssinia. The reasons for the emigration are not altogether clear though Muslim tradition sees the move as an attempt to escape persecution. Recent scholarship, however, has tended to suggest that the move may reflect other motives, possibly a controversy and division within the young Muslim community.

The opposition to Muhammad in Makkah had several bases. At first there was a general refusal to take him seriously or a tendency to dismiss him as another of the soothsayers familiar to the pre-Islamic Arabs. This criticism had force, since the revelations were couched in the mode of speech used by these diviners. More important was the Makkans' response to Muhammad's attacks upon their forefathers for whom he predicted punishment in hell as a consequence of their misguided and contumacious lives. Among people to whom descent was the chief ground of nobility, suggestions that the way of the fathers was misguided and evil was not only an insult of a direct kind but, by questioning the authority of tradition, was a threat of destruction to the whole social fabric. Most frightening of all to the Makkans was Muhammad's very claim to be a prophet. If it were accepted that Muhammad truly spoke in the name of a divine power, there would have been no choice but to accept him as the chief man in the community. That the Makkans apprehended the implications of prophecy correctly is borne out by Muhammad's role as ruler when he had established himself in Madinah and later when he captured Makkah itself. The rich merchants were not likely willingly to see their place of primacy taken over by another. Muhammad also attacked the pagan gods of the Makkans, but these attacks as seen in the *Qur'an* were not frequent nor particularly virulent. At no point did he attack the cult of the Ka'bah. From all appearances the Makkans were not a strongly religious people, and they would have resented criticisms of customary beliefs and practices as much for the fact of their being departures from the hallowed tradition of the forefathers as for their religious implications. The Makkans tried a number of techniques short of outright violence to muzzle Muhammad, at one time enforcing a boycott against his entire clan, who despite the pressure refused to withdraw their protection. The breaking point was reached for the Makkans when Muhammad began to enter into relations with persons in other places, seeking alliances against his own people. In the end he was forced to flee for his life, having first sent away most of his followers to the oasis of Yathrib, some 200 miles to the north of Makkah, which in later times has been known as Madinat al-Nabi, the City of the Prophet. The departure from Makkah is the famous *hijrah* which not only marks a decisive turning in Muhammad's career but is also the date from which the Islamic calendar is reckoned to begin. The year was A.D. 622.

In Madinah Muhammad's situation was utterly different from that in Makkah. For one thing, Madinah was an agricultural community. Some time prior to the *hijrah* Muhammad had entered into negotiations with certain Madinese who came to Makkah for pilgrimage to the Ka'bah. These people became his followers and arranged that he should act as arbitrator in a bitter dispute about the ownership of land which had pitched the settled tribes of the oasis against one another in a destructive blood feud. Muhammad went to Madinah, therefore, with a recognized status, already having followers there, and bringing yet others with him, the *ansar* (helpers) and the *muhajirin* (emigrants) as they are known. In the oasis itself were several different tribal groups, some of them Jewish in religion though Arabic speaking. Muhammad's task was to consolidate his position into one of real strength and to weld these diverse elements into a unified community under his leadership. One of his first acts was to

*A sixteenth-century Turkish painting depicting Muhammad the Prophet preaching. Muhammad is rarely depicted in Islamic art; when he is shown, as here and in the miniature on p. 596, his face is almost always obscured.* (*Courtesy of the Metropolitan Museum of Art, Rogers Fund, 1955.*)

draw up a document, afterward called the Constitution of Madinah, declaring all the Madinese—Muslims, Jews, and pagans alike—to be one community under his leadership. As time passed the Prophet's conception of the community both narrowed and clarified until in the end it came to include only Muslims, those joined together by their common submission to the divine will.

The struggle to establish himself firmly in Madinah was difficult and long. Although all had agreed to the terms of the Constitution of Madinah, there were many who opposed Muhammad and feared his growing power. The *Qur'an* condemns these "hypocrites" for their deviousness. With the Jews Muhammad soon came to an open break, some of them being driven out and others killed or sold into slavery. In this case the cause of conflict was the steadfast Jewish refusal to accept Muhammad on his own terms as a genuine prophet; this religious intransigence produced a stream of ridicule against Muhammad for being uninformed or misinformed about the history of Jewish prophecy. Such attitudes must have stung the Prophet with great sharpness because of his expectation that the Jews (and Christians) would recognize and acknowledge him as a prophet like the others whom they revered.

Once he felt sufficiently secure in Madinah, Muhammad turned his attention to the countryside round about. A combination of shows of force and skillful diplomacy soon created a network of alliances with Bedouin tribes that rapidly expanded Muhammad's influence to the point where he was able to challenge even the power of the haughty Makkans. His objective was to disrupt the Makkan trade on which the life of the city depended. In 624 when he attempted to intercept a rich Makkan caravan, the Makkans sent a force against him and engaged the Muslims in battle at a place called Badr. This engagement, where a greatly outnumbered Muslim detachment won a resounding victory over superior forces, played a great role in confirming the community's sense of divine mission though, militarily, it was of little consequence. On two later occasions the Makkans attempted to deal with Muhammad by military force but without significant success. They actually won a victory over the Muslims at the Battle of Uhud, near Madinah, but were unable to follow it up. In the Battle of the Ditch, which saw the greatest army yet assembled in Arabia ranged against Muhammad, the Makkans proved utterly inept and allowed their effort to founder on bad leadership and tribal divisions. Military power was neither effective against Muhammad nor was it the method which he himself used to build his power. The secret of his success was a masterly diplomacy based upon an instinctive understanding of tribal relationships on the one hand and of the nature of Makkan power on the other. When Makkah fell to Muhammad in 630 and the Ka'bah was cleansed of its pagan symbols, this victory was achieved without a single sword stroke. The greatest military threat which Muhammad was compelled to face came in the Battle of Hunayn against the Bani Hawazin, after he had already won Makkah. The capitulation of Makkah broke whatever remaining resistance to Muhammad the tribesmen may have felt; they came flocking in thousands to accept Islam and to pledge their allegiance to the Prophet.

Muhammad died unexpectedly in 632 after a brief illness. In the short ten years between his arrival in Madinah and his death, he rose from the status of a hunted fugitive to become the most powerful man in Arabia. His life accomplishment was the double one of having propagated a new world view and of having founded a community. These two were to become the twin bearers of a brilliant civilization that may claim both past greatness and continuing contemporary relevance.

# THE RIGHTLY GUIDED KHALIFAHS AND THE EXPANSION OF ISLAM

The Muslims were not adequately prepared for Muhammad's death; and when it came, it was a shock that almost destroyed the infant community. There is some evidence that certain prominent men did not expect Muhammad to die at all and even refused to believe the reports of his death. Immediately upon hearing the news, the community plunged into a crisis. Personal and tribal rivalries posed such obstacles to the choice of a successor that there was genuine threat of civil war. Only a desperate act of acclaiming one of their number *khalifah* or successor to the Prophet on the part of his closest companions averted a disaster. The man chosen was Abu Bakr, an intimate associate of Muhammad and one of the early prominent converts in Makkah. He was already an old man however, and after a reign of two years, died, passing on his authority to the able and fiery 'Umar ibn al-Khattab, the most brilliant of the Rightly Guided Khalifahs, as the first four successors to Muhammad are known. 'Umar fell victim to the dagger of an assassin in 644 and was succeeded by 'Uthman ibn 'Affan with whom the decline of the pious caliphate had already begun. 'Uthman was murdered by a group of dissidents who accused him of corrupt rule, and his successor, the last of the four Rightly Guided Khalifahs, 'Ali ibn Abi Talib, the cousin and son-in-law of Muhammad, was never firmly established in power. From the beginning his claims to rule were contested by a powerful party who suspected him of complicity in the murder of 'Uthman, and after a protracted struggle he lost out to Mu'awiyah of the powerful Ummawi clan. Mu'awiyah's power derived from the support of Syrian tribesmen, and for this reason he established his capital in Damascus rather than Madinah, thus founding the Arab Kingdom which survived for a century until overthrown by the 'Abbasis in 750. In spite of the violence and unrest that characterized the period, Muslims have always looked back to the pious caliphate as the time of Islam's greatest purity and glory. The *khalifahs* themselves are among the most revered figures of Islamic history.

The accomplishments of the pious *khalifahs* were considerable. First of all they succeeded in maintaining the unity of the community in spite of break-away attempts by some Bedouin groups who considered their loyalty to have been to Muhammad and to have been dissolved with his death. Second, they laid the foundations of a polity which kept the Arab armies intact in their camp cities and which provided means of governing the new territories. Third, and perhaps most important of all, were the great conquests themselves. The outreach to other lands beyond the peninsula began under Abu Bakr but came to full flowering in the reign of 'Umar. In rapid succession the rich provinces of Syria, Iraq, Palestine, and Egypt came under Muslim control. As a result of the Battle of Nihavand (641) the entire Sassanian Empire was brought crashing down to disappear from the pages of history, and the whole of the Iranian plateau was added to the Muslim territories. By the end of the century North Africa had been overrun on the west, followed soon afterward by the establishment of an Ummawi state in Spain, and on the east the Muslims were penetrating the vast regions of Central Asia beyond the Oxus River. These initial conquests are notable not only for their rapidity but for their permanence. All of the land which the Muslims overran in their first great expansion, with the exception of Spain and portions of Central Asia, has remained under Islamic control until this day.

Today the greatest number and concentration of Muslims in the world live outside the regions taken in the earliest conquests. One of the later waves of Islamic expansion brought the faith to the Indian subcontinent in a decisive way, and although Muslims have never been the majority there, from the establishment of the Sultanate of Delhi by Muhammad Ghori in 1192 until 1857 they were rulers of a vast Indian Empire. At present something more than 160 million Muslims are found in India and Pakistan. A still later wave of growth introduced Islamic faith into the islands of the Indonesian archipelago, this time through the agency of traders and wandering mystics. The emergence of important Muslim influence there cannot be precisely dated, but it was a factor in the life of the islands by the twelfth century. In the fifteenth century the first important Muslim sultanate took form, and today the majority of Indonesians, more than 100 million in a rapidly growing population, are counted as Muslims. When the Bedouin Arab warriors under the Rightly Guided Khalifahs burst out of the Arabian peninsula, their arms quickly carried them to the borders of Anatolia but not beyond. It was left to the Turks, who began to enter Islamic territories and the service of rulers in large numbers in the tenth century, to subdue the vast region of Anatolia and Asia Minor for Islam. The Saljuq Turks were the first to establish themselves but eventually gave way to the Ottomans who at last overthrew Christian power in Constantinople (1453) and drove their armies far into Eastern Europe. At the height of their strength the Ottomans dominated the Balkan countries, sending a great army to the gates of Vienna as late as 1683. Thus was another important region added to the domain of Islam, and the permanent influence of Islam on European soil established.

# THE QUR'AN

The message which Muhammad preached to the Arabs came to him as a series of revelations, given in piecemeal fashion throughout his prophetic career until the very end of his life. After his death the various revelations were collected into a book called the *Qur'an,* which, as Scripture, is the fundamental authority for Muslims in all matters of religious belief or practice. The name comes from the pages of the book itself where some of the individual revelations are referred to as Qur'ans. This name is somewhat puzzling, but it is probably to be understood as meaning discourse or recitation. In reference to the Prophet's work it indicates Muhammad's function of reciting or discoursing a message that he had been chosen to deliver by a divine agency.

Both Muhammad himself and later Muslims have believed the *Qur'an* to derive from a heavenly original, a book that is with God, a "Well-Preserved Tablet that only the pure may touch." Also called the "Mother of the Book," this heavenly depository of truth, which may be taken as a symbolic embodiment of the Divine Will, has been partially revealed to men from time to time through a series of prophets. Throughout history the normal mode of divine communication with men has been the sending of books drawn from the heavenly prototype. Adam, the very first man created, was chosen a prophet and given a book so that he and his descendants might have guidance in the proper way to live and so be rescued from the aimless groping to which their creaturehood would otherwise have condemned them. When succeeding generations failed to appreciate the importance and sanctity of this guidance and began first to ignore it, then to distort it, the original act of divine mercy was repeated in the sending of another prophet who reestablished the race on the "right path." As seen in the light of the Islamic doctrine of prophecy, history is a process of mankind's having repeatedly fallen away from the path marked out by divine guidance and likewise having been continually restored to it again by renewed acts of mercy through the institution of prophecy.

The prophets who have appeared in the past are numerous, perhaps as many as one hundred thousand, one to each people, speaking in its own language. Among those whom the *Qur'an* mentions specifically are well-known figures from the Bible such as Moses whose book was the Torah, David who brought the *Zabur* or Psalms, and Jesus through whom was revealed the *Injil* or Gospel. Because these books were recognized as Scripture by Jews and Christians, the *Qur'an* grants these communities special recognition as Peoples of the Book or of Scripture. It was against this background that Muhammad's expectation of being favorably received by Jews and Christians grew up. Still other prophets, unknown to the biblical tradition, are spoken of also, for example, Salih and Hud. All prophets have spoken a message identical in content (if not form), and those who brought books as part of their missions were all delivering a revelation stemming from the Mother of the Book. Muhammad's prophecy and the book which he spoke or recited under the stimulus of inspiration were continuations of an already established divine method of communication with men as old as the world itself. The significance of Scripture was further underlined by theologians in the third Islamic century in the doctrine that the *Qur'an* is uncreated and coeternal with God; not, to be sure, the marks made with ink on paper and bound in covers, but the divine message itself.

The Muslim understanding of the *Qur'an* is shown clearly in the most common story of Muhammad's call to prophecy. According to tradition one night when Muhammad was keeping a lonely vigil of meditation and prayer in a cave on Mount Hira' near Makkah, an angelic being appeared to him and commanded, *Iqra'* ("Recite"). Muhammad's reply was a refusal, born perhaps of fear and confusion, or perhaps of misunderstanding. Thereupon the angel seized him by the throat and choked him while reiterating the command. Still a third time was the command repeated with such vigor that Muhammad's very life was threatened. Having been thus forced to give his consent, Muhammad received the first of the revelations, that which the majority of authorities identify with Surah 96:1–5:

> *In the Name of God, the Merciful, the Compassionate*
> *Recite: In the Name of thy Lord who created,*
> *created Man of a blood-clot.*
> *Recite: And thy Lord is the Most Generous,*
> *who taught by the Pen,*
> *taught Man that he knew not.*

This story makes indubitably clear that there was no initiative on Muhammad's part in seeking prophecy. Rather the revelation came to him against his will and in spite of his resistance through the compulsion of a force from outside himself. Nor was the message itself of Muhammad's own invention. The words which he spoke were given him by the angel, and his sole task was to repeat what was communicated to him. Muhammad claimed no special qualities for himself and assigned no significance to his person as such. Many verses in the *Qur'an* begin with the imperative, Say! (addressed to Muhammad), indicating in this unmistakable fashion the heavenly source of the words that follow. The intermediary who brought these revelations from heaven to speak them into Muhammad's ear was a "spirit" or a "holy spirit" which later Islamic tradition identified with the angel Gabriel. In the revelation experiences the thing of consummate importance is that God himself has spoken; both the content of the message and its form were "sent down" upon Muhammad. There was no element of conscious manipulation on his part and no factor of historical conditioning. Muhammad had been "chosen" as the instrument of a greater power who utilized him for transmitting a message of warning and guidance, a message which was eternal and which Muhammad neither originated nor formulated. The *Qur'an* is *Kalam Allah,* the word or speech of God.

The divine origin and character of the *Qur'an* are emphasized also by the common Muslim belief that Muhammad was illiterate and thus incapable of having composed a book of his own or of having copied, as some of his Makkan enemies charged, from the Scriptures of the Jews and Christians. Indeed, the *Qur'an* is miraculous in its quality, its revelation being the only miracle which the Prophet claimed in proof of his mission. Later Muslims interpreted this Qur'anic teaching of miraculousness in literary terms, claiming that the beauty and perfection of the *Qur'an,* incapable of duplication by mere men, are self-evident proofs of its heavenly origin.

The Muslim conviction that the *Qur'an* is the very words of God himself, preserved exactly to the last syllable as they were revealed, explains many things about religious attitudes and practice in Islam. First of all, it allows us to understand clearly why the *Qur'an* should rank as the foremost authority in all matters of religion or law. It is inconceivable to the pious mind that any other source of information or teaching should be placed above the expression of the divine will in its definitive and eternal formulation. From this fact also we gain insight into the basis for the characteristic Muslim method in solving religious problems or expounding normative belief and practice. Essentially, the method is deductive, one of unfolding or extracting from the revelation its implications for a host of particular situations. Religious thinking among Muslims is bound most closely to the text of the *Qur'an,* to which it constantly returns as the fountainhead of all guidance.

The devoted and tender reverence paid to the *Qur'an* on every occasion is also a reflection of the sacred character of the book. The *Qur'an* is never placed on the floor, allowed to come into contact with unclean substances, or otherwise dishonored. Perhaps the most eloquent expression of this regard is the widespread practice of memorizing the *Qur'an* text in its entirety. One who does so is a *Hafiz,* and his accomplishment is considered an act of great piety. Even in those parts of the Islamic world where Arabic is not spoken and understood, devoted men in the thousands labor to commit the divine words to memory. In almost every Muslim area there exist special schools for teaching young children to memorize and recite the text.

In size the *Qur'an* approximates the New Testament. It is divided into one hundred and fourteen chapters, each of which is known as

*An Arabic manuscript of the* Qur'an *from fourteenth-century Egypt.* (*Courtesy of the British Museum.*)

a Surah, and these are arranged roughly in the order of their length, with the longest coming first. Each chapter of the *Qur'an* has a name derived from something mentioned in it, though in recent times it has increasingly become the custom to cite Qur'anic passages by the number of the chapter. The Surah of the Believers (Surah 23), for example, gets its designation from the occurrence of the word "believers" in the very first verse, and the case is similar with other chapters. The division between chapters is marked by the formula *Bismillah al-Rahman, al-Rahim,* "In the Name of God, the Compassionate, the Merciful." With only one exception (Surah 9), every chapter of the *Qur'an* is introduced by this formula which also is repeated at many other points in the Muslim's life as a kind of invocation or blessing. The division into Surahs is very old and probably goes back to the time of Muhammad himself, but the further division of the Surahs into verses or *ayahs* is later and was done for the sake of convenience in locating passages easily. The word *ayah* means a "sign" or "indication," and the term is used numerous times in the *Qur'an* where the Prophet pointed to the wonders of nature about him as signs of the existence and sovereignty of the unique God. Its application to portions of the *Qur'an* is a reinforcement of the Muslim doctrine of revelation, for the "sending down" of this heavenly book is the most important and most convincing of all the evidences of God.

Unfortunately we do not know the exact state in which the materials composing the *Qur'an* were left at the death of Muhammad. There are indications in early Muslim histories that some of the text had been written down under the Prophet's personal supervision, but it is certain that he had decreed no definitive order for it. The *Qur'an* which we have today was collected and ordered under the initiative of the third Khalifah, 'Uthman, who feared conflict in the community over disagreements about the sacred book. He therefore appointed a certain Zayd ibn Thabit, who had been a kind of secretary to Muhammad, to prepare an official text based on a document in the possession of the daughter of the second Khalifah, 'Umar. At the time there were already other versions of the *Qur'an* in circulation among the Muslims, at least four of which are known from extensive references to them. Eventually, with pressure from the state authorities, the Uthmanic *Qur'an* came to displace these others, and today it is the sole text recognized and used by Muslims. The work of collecting, preserving, and writing down the revelations "sent down" upon the Prophet was begun in his lifetime and finished soon after his death. Furthermore, available information about the earliest versions of the *Qur'an* shows a great similarity of content between them and the official version. Thus, critical scholarship and Muslim faith both agree that the *Qur'an* is an authentic record of the message which Muhammad declared to the Arabs.

For the uninitiated person a first encounter with the *Qur'an* is likely to create some puzzlement. Those responsible for its collection appear to have paid scant attention either to the chronological sequence of the revelations or to the logical interconnection of subject matter. Further, the content ranges from vivid warnings of the punishment soon to befall the "ungrateful," to stories of former prophets, the exposition of detailed rules for different aspects of Islamic life, and passages of a sublime mystical content. The impression of the whole is likely to be that of disorganization. One should, however, remember the nature of the *Qur'an.* It was not composed as an ordinary book to be read; indeed, Muslim faith insists that it was not composed at all. Rather, it is a collection of inspired utterances delivered over a long period of time, each one couched in a rhetoric appropriate to the occasion when it was pronounced. The revelations were intended to be heard, not read, and only when one who understands Arabic hears the *Qur'an* recited can he begin fully to comprehend its unique force and attractive power. So compelling is the sonorous language of the sacred book that its skillful recitation will often reduce strong men to tears.

The *Qur'an* is perhaps the most widely read and studied book in all of human history. It is contemplated, recited, and commented upon daily in every land where Muslims dwell and in all of the numerous languages which they speak. In one sense the whole body of Islamic literature in theology, law, and mysticism may be considered as nothing more than an extended exposition of the sacred text. The most precious possession of Muslims is a body of truth, a definitive guidance for life and the hereafter, which God himself has vouchsafed in his own words.

# ISLAMIC THEOLOGY

Although the *Qur'an* lays down religious fundamentals for Muslims, including doctrines of the unity of God and the prophethood of Muhammad, it is not in any sense a book of theology. Nowhere in its pages will one discover religious doctrine presented in a systematic, comprehensive, or consistent manner. Everything about the *Qur'an* bespeaks its origin in the intensity of prophetic inspiration rather than in essentially intellectual motives. At many points the *Qur'an* is unclear in its teachings or incomplete, and in certain vital areas it even appears as inconsistent. With the passing of time Muslims found it imperative to be more precise in the intellectual statement of their religious faith. When after one hundred years or more they became acquainted with the modes of thought of Greek philosophy, a true Islamic theology was born. At the same time there was a parallel development of religious beliefs at the popular level. These popular beliefs were often in conflict with the opinions of the learned and sometimes depended heavily on doctrines of other religious groups, but they conveyed great meaning for the thousands who held them.

The stimulus to the development of a precise statement of religious doctrines was twofold: It arose on the one hand from tensions within the Islamic community and on the other from the confrontation with outsiders whom the Muslims encountered in the conquered territories after the great expansion. Internal problems, particularly those of political leadership, led to debate and the marking out of firm positions on such matters as predestination and free will, the nature of faith, and big and little sins. Predestination and free will, a problem that is especially confusing in its Qur'anic presentation, became of prime importance in the political controversies surrounding the Ummawi rulers after the establishment of the Arab kingdom in Damascus. There were many who accused the Ummawis of deserting the true faith and of gross worldliness as a result of their attempts to develop ways of ruling the vast territory which they controlled. For such pious people it became a religious duty to defy the Ummawi rulers and oppose them. To counter this pious criticism the rulers began to mount a religious propaganda, in which they employed a number of learned and respected men, arguing that all things happen in the world according to God's will by the principle of predestination. It followed, therefore, that Ummawi rule was legitimate and that to oppose it was to resist God's manifest will. Their pious opponents adopted the polar opposite stand, arguing that man has freedom to choose his actions and the duty to fight against tyranny and wrongdoing wherever they occur. Neither side faced difficulty in finding *Qur'an* verses to support its views. Although the issues were political and of life and death importance to the individuals concerned, the mode of argument was religious. From these early controversies arose several sectarian groups who have lent their names to the various positions on the problem of predestination and free will. The Qadariyah were those who accepted human freedom of choice and action, i.e., the anti-Ummawi faction; the Jabariyah were those who on the contrary believed in absolute divine compulsion in all things, i.e., the supporters of the rulers.

Early Muslim discussions about the nature of faith (*iman*) and about big and little sins also had to do with the political conflicts raging around the Ummawis. One party in the early days held that true faith is indistinguishable from pious works and the fulfillment of all a Muslim's religious duties. The commission of sin was nothing but apostasy from Islam, and according to the *Qur'an,* punishable by death. These fierce and puritanical fanatics, known as the Khawarij (the Seceders, because they withdrew from the majority of the community), bitterly opposed the Ummawis and made unrelenting war against them. For the whole of the first two centuries of Islamic history, before the sect was finally put down, the threat of Khawarij uprisings or assassins was a continuing nightmare to Muslim rulers.

Others, however, took a more moderate position. They drew a distinction between great sins (*kaba'ir*) and lesser ones (*sagha'ir*), holding that great sins, such as associating partners with God (*shirk,* or polytheism) or characterizing the revelations as lies (*takhdhib*), were unforgivable and plainly rendered a man outside the fold of Islam. Smaller offenses, however, were capable of finding pardon from a merciful and forgiving God and did not exclude one from membership in the community and all its rights. So long as the rulers were not guilty of great sins, it followed that the believers still had the duty to obey them.

Still others emphasized the difference between faith (*iman*) and works (*islam*) rather than their equivalence. According to their analysis, faith is an interior and personal matter, occurring within the heart of a man, and not visible to those about him, while one's actions do not necessarily indicate the state of the heart. From external evidence it is impossible to know whether or not faith abides in the heart. Such a stand did not escape the problem of why a man of faith would still commit sins, whether big or small, and some Muslim thinkers began to query whether faith might diminish or increase to account for lapses from piety in an individual's life. This issue like those above has been of continuing interest to Muslim religious thinkers through the centuries. The fourteenth-century theologian al-Taftazani, in a statement which represents the consensus of the greater part of Islamic opinion, defines faith as:

1) confession with the tongue; and,
2) assent in the heart.

Along with many others, al-Taftazani also holds that faith may increase and decrease. One sectarian group, the Murji'ah, took as their principle the suspension of judgment on the question whether a man is a Muslim in the true sense or not. In their view "who is a Muslim?" can be answered only by God, since he alone can see into the hearts of men. Their stand, in practical terms, was equivalent to supporting the Ummawis since they refused to judge the rulers, or anyone else who claimed to be Muslim, as falling outside the community.

The external stimulus to the growth of an Islamic theology arose when the Muslims became aware of the religious traditions of the peoples whom they overran in the great conquests. Both the Sassanian Persians and the hellenized peoples of the Mediterranean basin were inheritors of highly complex and sophisticated cultural traditions. These included well-articulated religious systems of much subtlety. In their first encounters with Zoroastrian, Buddhist, Christian, etc., thinkers, the Muslims, in spite of their ardor, were hard put to uphold the validity of their faith. Elements from these rival religious systems proved attractive to many Muslims, and pious men felt the need to defend the superiority of Islamic views against those of others. Formal debates between learned men of different persuasions were also a feature of the time, often sponsored by rulers at court for their own amusement or enlightenment. We know for example of the debates between St. John of Damascus and Muslim divines in the presence of the Ummawi prince. The challenge of rival religious systems produced a Muslim effort at self-expression and self-justification. The theology born under this impulse was largely apologetic, and Muslim theology retained that coloring throughout its subsequent development. Indeed, many Muslim thinkers, including the great al-Ghazali (d. 1111), have criticized the community's theological development as having been essentially negative, a reaction against unacceptable opinions rather than a positive outreach.

A sectarian group called the Mu'tazilah may be given the credit for having been the first among Muslims to develop a true theology. This group which appeared toward the end of the first Islamic century had gained fairly extensive acquaintance with Greek philosophy. Their leaders such as Wasil ibn 'Ata and al-Nazzam began to levy criticisms against the views of their more traditional contemporaries, using conceptual tools drawn from the Greeks. Their objections to traditional views were largely demands for more of rationality and consistency in the formulation of Islamic belief. For this reason they have sometimes been characterized as rationalists, but it should be clearly understood that they in no way sought to renounce or undercut their commitment to Islam. On the contrary, they saw their effort to build an intellectually more adequate system of belief as a move to rescue true Islam from those who were misrepresenting it in vulgar fashion. The Mu'tazilah were firm believers in revelation and prophecy and even in the authority of prophetic tradition.

The principal teachings of the Mu'tazilah are conveyed in their being called the "people of unity (*tawhid*) and justice (*'adl*)." Unity refers to the fundamental Islamic doctrine of the oneness of God. In the *Qur'an,* where God's uniqueness is much emphasized, the point is (1) to underline the exclusive sovereignty of God over the many powers recognized by the pagan Arabs, and (2) to call the Arabs' attention to the divine power which controlled their destinies. The Mu'tazilah, however, brought forward a more philosophical view of *tawhid* by interpreting God's unity in reference to the divine nature. They taught that God is one in the sense of being simple and uncompounded, not made up of parts, and incapable of any division in his constitution. Hence they would grant no independent and separate status to the divine attributes in spite of the *Qur'an*'s frequent mention of God's knowledge, will, power, etc. All of these qualities or attributes they held to be identical with the divine essence whose uncompromised unity was eternal. In similar fashion they denied all anthropomorphism in connection with God. The motivation in these doctrinal stands was primarily religious. Through their acquaintance with the Greeks the Mu'tazilah had gained a vision of a transcendental rational order, and they insisted that to speak of God in any other terms was untrue to his divine nature. Thus, they invoked rational criteria for assessing the validity of religious doctrines.

The same considerations apply in respect to their teachings about divine justice. The Mu'tazilah could not accept the predestinarian views of the majority of their traditionalist contemporaries. If God predestines men to do evil and then punishes them for it, he is guilty of injustice, which is inconceivable for the divine being. It follows that men must have free will and that reward or punishment must be in accord with the freely chosen actions of men. God by his nature always does what is best. Although this stand poses problems about the origin of evil in the world (does God create it, or is there another sovereign power alongside God responsible for evil?) the teaching of God's justice was one of the marks of the Mu'tazilah.

After some limited success that included the patronage of the 'Abbasi rulers, the Mu'tazilah were decisively rejected by the Muslims and the group passed out of existence. However, they made a permanent contribution to Islamic life by bringing the apparatus and approach of Greek philosophy into the service of Islam. They were the first to create a *kalam* (discussion) of Islamic doctrines, that is, the first to employ rational argumentation to express the community's faith. The subtlety and power of their methods obliged their opponents to adopt the same tools for self-defense. Thus was born the science of *kalam* (theology), i.e., the science of the rational defense of religious doctrine.

The individual who more than any other is responsible for the acceptance of *kalam* among traditionalist Muslims was Abu-al-Hasan al-Ash'ari (d. 873). In his early days al-Ash'ari had been a Mu'tazilah, but after a crisis of some sort he broke with his teacher, the famous al-Jubba'i, and renounced Mu'tazilah teachings in favor of more traditional views. To uphold his own stand, however, al-Ash'ari used the methods and vocabulary he had learned from his teacher. Whereas the Mu'tazilah had employed rational criteria in some degree as the judge and criterion of religious doctrine, al-Ash'ari made only an instrumental use of the reason. The doctrines which he espoused were derived from the authority of the revelation and the Prophet; the role of reasoned argument was only to defend and bolster what had been received as the truth. His purposes were, thus, primarily defensive, to ward off the attacks of those who questioned certain aspects of traditional Islam.

Al-Ash'ari was a literalist in his attitude toward the declarations of the *Qur'an,* insisting that they must be taken for what they say. Thus, he affirmed the reality of God's attributes (*sifat*) and upheld the Vision of God on the Last Day as a reality, both of which the Mu'tazilah denied as contrary to reason. His approach, however, was not naively anthropomorphic, and he was in the beginning subjected to bitter attacks from traditionalists who felt that any use of dialectical argument was heretical. Characteristic of al-Ash'ari was a kind of middle position on these controversial matters. While on the one hand affirming the reality of the divine attributes, on the other he refused to state precisely the nature of their relationship to the divine essence. He taught that God has attributes in reality, but "without saying how and without making comparisons." This convenient formula which was devised by al-Ash'ari's conservative predecessor, Ahmad ibn Hanbal (d. 780), was given even greater refinement by al-Taftazani who said of the divine *sifat* that "they are not He nor are they other than He." Al-Ash'ari believed with the *Qur'an* that God has hands and that he sits upon his throne, but the hands and the sitting are not like those of human beings.

Al-Ash'ari also took a strong stand in favor of predestination. He taught what is, perhaps, as strict an interpretation of the doctrine as can be found anywhere. Everything which happens is the result of divine initiative. When a man performs an action, it is God who creates in him the will, the power to act, the intention to do so, and the final impulse which precipitates the act itself. None of what happens is the cause of any of the rest; rather all comes about by the direct intervention of God. Al-Ash'ari's doctrine of predestination grew out of his vivid perception of the sovereignty of God which he would in no way compromise. He could not admit the existence of any power alongside God in the universe. In later years among al-Ash'ari's followers the implications of this doctrine were worked out in a metaphysical system of absolute consistency. Al-Baqillani, its chief author, taught that reality consists of a series of monads or atoms without connection among one another. The world may and does exist only as God re-creates it at each moment in time. Thus there is nothing which functions independently from God's direct stimulation, and what appear to men as "natural laws" or as "causes" are but God's habitual modes of behavior. Once more, however, in his doctrine of predestination al-Ash'ari exhibits the tendency to take a middle position. Although all things, including human action, are predestined, man is responsible for what he does. It is God who in reality acts, but man acquires (*kasb*) the action and accountability for it. This doctrine is of great subtlety and has been a puzzlement for Muslim thinkers through the ages.

In the course of Islamic development the theological position enunciated by al-Ash'ari has gained the assent of the great majority of Sunni Muslims, so much so that it is sometimes referred to as Islamic orthodoxy. His teachings were carried on and developed in a school of thinkers that includes some of the greatest names in Islamic history, al-Baqillani (above), ibn Furak, al-Juwayni, and the incomparable al-Ghazali who may be considered the climax of the development. With but small differences his views are accepted as normative by conservative Muslims to our own time.

# THE ISLAMIC LAW

Islam has often been called a religion of law, and this ascription of a central place to the law is more than justified. Perhaps the most fundamental of all words in the Muslim religious vocabulary is guidance (*hudan*), for it is guidance in all the manifold situations of life that the Muslim expects from his religion. Considered in one sense the law of Islam is nothing more than the effort to make divine guidance as explicit and detailed as possible so that at no point will the Muslim faithful be left in bewilderment about the course to be followed. In its broadest sense of general principles the law is spoken of as the *shari'ah,* a word meaning pathway or roadway, the course along which God intends that men should walk. What came to Muhammad in the revelations was the *shari'ah,* a guidance, a road map to successful life in the world and to communion with God in the hereafter. The *shari'ah* is thus a transcendental expression of the eternal divine will for men. The Islam or commitment which God demands is commitment to following the *shari'ah,* for in no other way can men be pleasing to God and escape his wrath.

The first and most important thing about the *shari'ah* is the fact that it is a divine law. In the history of mankind many different sanctions for legality have emerged, some having derived the authority of law from the traditions of old, others from the decree of rulers, others from the consent of the governed, etc. Islamic law accepts none of these but claims its origin, and authority, from the very words of God himself. According to the Islamic understanding, man, a mere creature, with his unaided faculties is incapable of distinguishing between right and wrong or of determining how he should live. God has decreed a way of life for men, and this decree is the sole and determinative norm. All obligations as well as all rights arise because God in his wisdom has decreed them; their character

*Left, enameled glass mosque lamp, early fourteenth-century Syrian.* (*Courtesy of the Metropolitan Museum of Art, Bequest of Edward C. Moore, 1891*); *right, brass bowl inlaid with gold and silver, mid to late fourteenth-century Persian.* (*Courtesy of the Metropolitan Museum of Art, Rogers Fund, 1941.*)

is juridical. There is no question of human rights or of other "natural" bases of moral judgment. What is right is right because God has decreed it and not the other way around. If he had so chosen, there would have been nothing to prevent God in his freedom from making what he decreed as right to be wrong, for there is no moral order apart from his eternal decree. A law which thus represents the eternal will of the universe's Creator is infallible, and man's attitude toward it should be one of humble submission.

Furthermore, the divine *shari'ah* is comprehensive in that it offers all of the guidance necessary to humankind and, indeed, touches every sphere of life. Islamic law along with the usual areas of legal concern also regulates a great number of things which in the modern understanding fall outside the scope of law altogether. Not only contracts, criminal matters, marriage and divorce, etc., but also dress, foodstuffs, ritual, and even the forms of greeting and courtesy are decreed by the law. The subject matter of the law is traditionally divided into (1) obligations owing to God (*'ibadat*), such things as the profession of faith, performance of prayer and other religious duties, and (2) obligations owing to other men (*mu'amalat*) or all those things which affect individual and social morality, the conduct of state, etc. Among the obligations to God proper belief is one of the foremost. Technically speaking, therefore, theology is an aspect of law though the science of *kalam* has tended to assume an independent status in the course of Islamic history. In later Islamic times the jurists have emphasized the comprehensiveness of the *shari'ah* by classifying all human activity without exception under one of five headings, thus showing that the *shari'ah* is indifferent to nothing. Actions are either *fard* (obligatory, like confessing the unity of God and the prophethood of Muhammad), *mandub* (recommended), *mubah* (permitted), *makruh* (disapproved but not outright forbidden, like divorce), or *haram* (absolutely forbidden, like eating pork). In another simpler scheme things are characterized as being *halal* (permitted) or *haram* (forbidden). All of the obligations under the *shari'ah* arise from an identical source and have ultimately an identical sanction. None can be more or less important than the others, for all represent the will of God which it is man's duty to fulfill.

Another characteristic of the *shari'ah* is the fact that most obligations arising under it fall upon individuals. Each man stands in an immediate relationship of accountability with God, and none can substitute for another. Although there are some aspects of the *shari'ah* that may be called public law, for the most part it does not imply enforcement by the state through police power or a system of courts, nor does it recognize many obligations that fall upon a collectivity as such. Even criminal offenses are considered as injuries to individuals, and it is the individual's responsibility, not the state's, to seek redress from the judge of the religious court (the *qadi*). In certain respects therefore the *shari'ah* is not really law at all as we understand it and should perhaps be designated by another term.

Every functioning legal system must have, in addition to ultimate sanctions, some trustworthy method of applying its broad principles to specific situations in life in the form of rules of law. This is no less true of Islamic law than of others. The process of finding definite rules from the broad principles is what we know as jurisprudence, in the Islamic case as *fiqh*. The word *fiqh* means understanding, and in connection with the law it refers to two things. On the one hand it is the name accorded the process of deriving explicit rules of law from the transcendental *shari'ah,* and on the other it is used for the result of that process, that is, for the books of rules compiled through the jurists' efforts. One customarily speaks, not of the books of *shari'ah,* but of the books of *fiqh.* A person who is skilled in the science of jurisprudence is called a *faqih* (pl. *fuqaha'*).

The impulse toward developing a science of jurisprudence came from the brevity and frequent unclarity of the revelations in the *Qur'an.* The book is, after all, relatively small in size, and as the Muslims spread out from the Arabian peninsula over the vast territories which they conquered, they began to confront a multitude of problems and situations for which the *Qur'an* had no specific provisions. It was necessary both to find additional sources of authority and to achieve a more precise statement of the Muslim's religious duties. For more than two centuries there was uncertainty and some controversy among the learned men of the community about the way in which Muslims might arrive at normative decisions on matters not specifically treated in the *Qur'an.*

The discussion about the sources of legal authority came to a climax in the work of a brilliant lawyer and polemicist of the late second and third centuries, al-Shafi'i (b. 767). Through an extensive series of writings in which he analyzed and discussed the rival opinions of jurists he worked out a concise and clear theory of the sources or roots of Islamic law. Although it was some time before his view was generally accepted, in due course it won universal assent among Sunni Muslims.

Al-Shafi'i held that there are four roots (*usul*) of the law, which stand in a definite order of precedence. The first and most authoritative is the *Qur'an,* the words of God, which no other authority may supersede. If on a given subject there are clear Qur'anic commandments, these are unqualifiedly to prevail above everything else. The scope of such clear Qur'anic dictums, however, is very small, and it was precisely this fact that gave rise to the science of jurisprudence and the search for other authorities.

The second source of norms in order of importance was the customary usage or *sunnah* of the Prophet. Where it could be established on the basis of reliable reports that the Prophet had acted or judged matters in a particular way, such a precedent was not only trustworthy but constituted an obligation upon the Muslims to follow it. It cannot be too strongly emphasized that the Muslim tendency to look to the past as a storehouse of valid and normative guidance is of the very essence of the Islamic mentality. The pre-Islamic Arabs were a strongly tradition-bound people, taking it as their duty to revere the generations gone by, as in the case of their pride in genealogy, and to preserve the time-honored ways of their fathers. The early Islamic community preserved this familiar Arab attitude but changed its focus to concentrate upon the Prophet and his companions. Instead of emulating the heroes of the glorious "Days of the Arabs," the Muslims found their tradition in the exploits, sayings, and actions of Muhammad and those around him. These they endlessly repeated, sometimes embroidered, and always respected. The content of the Islamic understanding of the world was different from that of pagan Arabia, but the attitude toward the importance of the past was identical.

Al-Shafi'i's contribution to the elaboration of the prophetic *sunnah* as a norm was particularly significant. Although almost all Muslims had resort to tradition as one basis of legal judgment, there was widespread disagreement about precisely what constituted tradition. Some held that anything coming from the companions of Muhammad was authoritative, while others preferred the practice of the people of Madinah where Muhammad had passed the latter and most successful part of his career. Still others based their legal thinking on customary usage in the particular region where they happened to reside or upon the teachings of a learned man whom they respected. Al-Shafi'i cut through this confusion by maintaining against many opponents that the normative *sunnah* was that of the Prophet and the Prophet alone. What must be sought is Muhammad's example, and those of all others are irrelevant.

The content of the Prophet's *sunnah* is known to Muslims through a series of oral reports about him which record his sayings, doings, and implicit approbations. Such an oral report is called a *hadith*, and it consists of two parts, the *matn* or text and the *isnad* (lit. "foundation") or chain of authorities through which it has come down. Virtually all the information we have about early Islamic history, the life of Muhammad, etc., has reached us in the form of such oral reports, gathered, written down, and preserved by men of later times.

In view of their consuming desire to remain true to the traditions of those before them, when they confronted a difficulty or a novel situation, the Muslims would, almost instinctively, search for a report which would supply guidance by way of precedent. The normal form of religious and/or political disputation among Muslims has been the citation of *Qur'an* verses and of oral reports of the earliest and most respected generation, but especially those relating to the Prophet. In the early centuries when no such report was found readily to hand, Muslims often supplied one of their own devising that served to make the desired point, that is, they deliberately put into circulation reports about the Prophet which had no basis in fact. Sometimes the motives for such fabricated *hadith* were cynical, but more often they were an expression of pious belief resting upon the conviction that the Prophet would have adopted the position taken in the fabricated report were he still alive. Such people thought that they understood the mind of the Prophet, and instead of stating what he might have said, chose simply to put words into his mouth.

By the end of the second Islamic century there was in common circulation a vast body of traditional material purporting to come from the earliest generations, but a major portion of which was fabricated to answer the changing needs of a growing society. Inevitably this situation provoked a reaction from more pious and conservative people who apprehended that the genuine prophetic example would be lost among the multitude of reports. In consequence there emerged a science for the criticism and authentication of *hadith* which has remained until today one of the central preoccupations of Islamic learning. The noteworthy feature of this science is that it concerns itself only with the *isnads* of the *hadith* and not with their subject matter. The purpose is to investigate the process of transmission to determine whether or not it is sound and uninterrupted. The students of *hadith* (*muhaddithun*) paid great attention to the personal histories and characters of the individuals constituting the chains of transmission, and under the stimulus of this inquiry, called "impugning and justifying," there grew up a large biographical literature dealing with the companions of Muhammad and the learned men of the early generations. This information allowed one to discover whether the relater of a *hadith* had actually known the man from whom he claimed to have heard it, whether he was generally trustworthy and honest, etc. There also emerged an elaborate system for the classification of **hadith** according to the number of channels through which they were transmitted and according to the characteristics of their *isnads*. In the most general terms the investigation of a *hadith* by applying the principles of this science permits one to judge it as *sahih* (sound), *hasan* (good), or *da'if* (weak).

In the late second Islamic century the criticism of *hadith* and the effort to separate the true from the false came to fruition in certain carefully sifted collections that have an authority for all Sunni Muslims second only to the *Qur'an*. These collections are the so-called Six Sound Books of tradition of which the most respected and best known are those by al-Bukhari (b. 810) and Muslim ibn al-Hajjaj (b. 821). Al-Bukhari is said to have sifted more than 600,000 separate *hadith* in order to arrive at his collection of 2,762 which he considered authentically to have come from the Prophet. The organization of al-Bukhari's famous book under headings drawn from legal discussions of the time shows clearly that the endeavor to achieve authoritative collections of *hadith* was stimulated by considerations of jurisprudence.

In spite of the special recognition given to the Six Sound Books, Muslims do not hesitate to make use of a great number of other works on *hadith.* The literature in the field is extensive, and the *faqih* or learned man ranges freely through it to find the *hadith* that help him to solve whatever problem may be under consideration.

In modern times there has been an attack on the authenticity of *hadith* from both without and within the Islamic camp. Some Western scholars, having noted that the Six Sound Books contain *hadith* that are contradictory, tendentious, and anachronistic, look upon even these authoritative collections as being composed largely of fabricated materials. In their view the *hadith* collections, though they tell us little that is trustworthy about Muhammad and his sayings, are very important as an index of the religious and legal doctrines most widely held in the Islamic community at the time of their collection. Taking their point of departure from this critical approach, some Muslim reformers in the twentieth century have declared their freedom from the authority of *hadith* altogether. Rejection of the *hadith* has liberated these thinkers from the rigid confines of the medieval Islamic schools of law that based their systems for the most part on tradition.

We may return now to take up the thread of al-Shafi'i's theory of the roots of law. After the *Qur'an* and the *sunnah* of the Prophet, the third source of legal guidance which he recognized was the consensus or *ijma'* of the community. If in looking at the past one discovers that the community at large or its most learned men have generally agreed upon a doctrine or a practice, he may take this consensus as sanction, provided always that the consensus does not go against *Qur'an* or *sunnah.* It is to be emphasized that the consensus is always that of past generations; in al-Shafi'i's terms it is, thus, not a power of legislation given to the contemporary community though some modernist Muslims take it to be precisely that. The appeal to *ijma'* underlines the Islamic attitude toward the past, for in the final analysis it is nothing more than another name for tradition, in this case the well-known and firmly established way of doing things in the community as a whole. The principle involved is nowhere more clearly expressed than in the saying attributed to Muhammad: "My community will never agree in an error." If one reflects deeply on the implications of this saying, he will perhaps be able to understand the agonized crisis of soul of many present-day Muslims as they contemplate the military, political, and economic subordination of Muslim peoples to outside powers.

The last of al-Shafi'i's four *usul al-fiqh* (roots or sources of the law), to be resorted to only when the preceding ones have not produced the required guidance, is *qiyas* or analogical reasoning. This technique, however, may be used only under the strictest control. In certain circumstances it is legitimate to extend the implications of an explicit rule of law arrived at on the basis of one of the three preceding *usul* to cover a different but analogous situation that is

*The seventeenth-century Sultan Ahmad Mosque in Istanbul, known as the Blue Mosque. In the foreground is the obelisk constructed by Emperor Constantine Porphyrogenius, grandson of Emperor Basil, the Macedonian. (Courtesy of the Turkish Tourism and Information Office.)*

not specifically provided for. For instance, the Qur'anic prohibition of wine on the basis of its being an intoxicant allows the *faqih* to judge that other intoxicants are also to be forbidden. Analogical thinking must always proceed from a previously established rule and can never in any way be innovative or serve to overturn or supersede judgments based on one of the other *usul*. The principle of *qiyas* is, therefore, by no means a license for speculation or the exercise of personal opinion in legal matters. In fact, it is clear from al-Shafi'i's entire stance that the thing which he most abhorred was the intrusion of arbitrary, unsubstantiated personal preference or whim into the formation of legal judgments. His criticism on this point was most severe, especially against the 'Iraqi jurist, Abu Hanifah (d. 767), whose use of *qiyas* was much less restrained.

Al-Shafi'i was but one of several prominent and creative jurists who did their work in the first and second Islamic centuries. The first important figure was Malik ibn Anas (d. 795) who passed most of his life in Madinah where he sought to uphold the usage and custom of that place as a norm for Muslim conduct. To him goes the credit for having compiled the oldest surviving book on Islamic law, his famous *Kitab al-Muwatta'* (*The Book of the Paved Path*). By the third Islamic century several distinct schools of law had emerged under the influence of prominent men who had passed down their teachings through a series of disciples. Many of these schools passed away or were displaced by others in the course of time, such as those founded by the Syrian al-Awza'i (d. 722) and the famous historian al-Tabari (b. 839), but four of them have survived to the present. A school of jurisprudence or legal interpretation is called a *madhhab* (a path). The four great *madhahib* (Arabic plural of *madhhab*) of Islamic history are the Maliki, after Malik ibn Anas; the Hanbali, after Ahmad ibn Hanbal; the Hanafi, after Abu Hanifah; and the Shafi'i after al-Shafi'i.

Among Sunni Muslims it is the custom to adhere to one of these schools which each man is free to choose for himself. In the content of their teachings there is very little difference among them, differences being confined for the most part to certain items of detail. All the four are considered to represent true Islam and to offer acceptable teachings. Important centers of Islamic learning such as the al-Azhar University in Cairo give instruction in the doctrines of all four schools, and in many Muslim countries it was formerly the custom to maintain religious courts with judges drawn from different schools so that each man's cause might be heard according to the legal doctrine which he accepted.

Each school is also associated with a certain region of the Islamic world where its acceptance has become customary for the majority of people. The teachings of Malik ibn Anas, for example, are the norm in North Africa and in much of the rest of Africa where Islam has penetrated, excepting Egypt. Probably the most widespread school is that of Abu Hanifah which prevailed in the Ottoman Turkish Empire and in Central Asia from where it was taken to India by the Turkish Muslim conquerors of the subcontinent. The strictest school in doctrine and that having the smallest number of followers today is the Hanbali *madhhab.* In the past this school was widespread throughout Iraq and Greater Syria, but at present its adherents are concentrated in the Arabian peninsula where the puritanical Wahhabi sect has opted for its strict view of Islamic teaching. The legal opinions of al-Shafi'i prevail in the largest of the Islamic nations, Indonesia, and in Egypt, Syria, and East Africa. Although in certain areas two or more of these schools exist side by side in the same society, there is an attitude of mutual acceptance so that relations among them are peaceful.

As in much else in their history the Muslims have shown a decidedly traditionalistic attitude toward the science of jurisprudence. The early great jurists and their followers for several generations after were engaged in a systematic unfolding of the *shari'ah* in all its implications for human activity. By applying themselves to understanding the source materials of the law, they built up elaborate systems of rules of conduct in every sphere of life. The process of striving to understand the sources of the law and to derive the rules of law from them is called by the technical term *ijtihad,* meaning to make a personal intellectual effort. Through their personal effort the founders of the *madhahib* had worked out the broad principles of *fiqh* while their followers in subsequent generations strove to elucidate the details. A time came, however, when the generality of Muslims began to consider that the fundamental work of expounding the law in both its principles and details had been completed. From that time the "Door of Ijtihad," to use the classical expression, was closed, and the duty of men was no longer to return to the sources of the law to make their own judgments but rather to accept as authoritative the opinions of the doctors of the *madhhab* to which they adhered. From that point the study of the law became exclusively the perusal of the works of the founders of the schools and their most important disciples rather than of the sources themselves. One who thus binds himself to the teachings of a particular legal school, as virtually all Muslims in medieval and early modern times have done, is said to be *muqallad* (tied) to that school. Although men learned in the law (*faqihs*) have always had freedom to offer legal opinions (*fatwas*) on questions put to them, their task has not been to seek new directions or principles in the law but only to discover from the writings of the authoritative teachers of their respective schools what resources may be brought to bear on the question at hand. The result of the attitude of *taqlid* (i.e., the attitude of a *muqallad faqih*) has been to make all later writing on Islamic law take the form of commentaries on earlier works and so effectively to cut Muslims off from fresh insights into the basic sources of Islamic piety.

Throughout Islamic history there have been isolated individuals who rejected *taqlid* and who claimed the right of studying and expounding the fundamental Islamic sources for themselves. In recent times an insistence that the "Door of Ijtihad" is still open has become one of the pillars of Islamic modernism. Many modernists see *taqlid* as perhaps the chief cause for the failure of their community to keep pace with the rival civilization that has come to dominate it. So long as Muslim religious leaders remain *muqallad,* just so long will they be caught up in a static understanding of law and society and so be unable to adapt to the changed conditions of modernity. For modernists Islam is dynamic and progressive, incorporating in such principles as *ijtihad* the means for its own perpetual self-regeneration and self-adaption to new circumstances. For these men *taqlid* is a grave misunderstanding of Islam which denies its very spirit.

The strenuous efforts of many countries in the Islamic world to modernize their societies has also affected Islamic law in recent times. While in the Arabian peninsula things have remained much as they were, in other places the trend has been to restrict the functioning of the traditional *fiqh* in an ever-increasing variety of ways. A majority of contemporary Muslim states has adopted constitutions patterned after Western models, and many of the same states have enacted legal codes that are virtually identical with the French or Swiss civil law. Criminal law also is now for the most part built upon bases that have little to do with the *shari'ah.* The religious courts of a few years back have also generally been abolished. Where the Islamic *fiqh* continues to have certain influence in the modern world is in the sphere of family and personal law. To the extent possible, many Muslim states attempt to regulate inheritance, marriage, divorce, patrimony, etc., in the ways traditional to the Islamic community. Even here, however, there have been profound changes. In Tunisia and Pakistan, for example, recent legislation has regulated both marriage and divorce in ways unknown to the Islamic *fuqaha'* of the past. The dual tendency to displace Islamic law by other systems and to change its provisions in ways more pleasing to modern minds has brought about a crisis of conscience for many pious people. If, as we have said, Islam is primarily a religion of law, it could not be otherwise. There is no question more fraught with significance or more hotly debated than that concerning the role which the *shari'ah* should play in the emergent national states of the Islamic world.

# ISLAMIC WORSHIP AND RELIGIOUS PRACTICES

The most basic religious duties of Muslims, those usually described in the sections on *'ibadat* (obligations owing to God) in books of *fiqh,* are known as the Five Pillars of Islam. These five essential obligations are witnessing (*shahadah*), ritual prayer (*salat*), fasting in the month of Ramadan (*sawm*), almsgiving (*zakat*), and the pilgrimage to Makkah (*hajj*). They are accompanied by a great series of other religious celebrations, occasions, and practices of varying degrees of merit in Muslim eyes.

It is obligatory upon every Muslim to give public testimony of his faith in the unity of God and the prophethood of Muhammad by verbal declaration. The customary formula reads, "I testify that there is no God but the one God, and Muhammad is his prophet." The willingness solemnly to affirm this statement in the presence of witnesses is the mark of a man's being a Muslim for purposes of membership in the community and sharing in its rights and duties. Other articles of belief deemed essential but not included in the witnessing formula are belief in angels, in the books of God, in all the apostles, and in the coming Judgment Day.

Perhaps the most visible mark of Islamic piety is the ritual prayer which adult Muslims of sound mind and body everywhere are expected to perform as an absolute obligation five times each day. Any who have visited the Islamic world will have seen this simple but impressive ceremony performed in streets and public places as well as mosques. The prayer consists of a set ritual that differs slightly for the different times of day. The worshiper begins in a standing position facing toward Makkah with his hands crossed before him, and as the prayer proceeds, he assumes positions of kneeling and then of bowing in prostration with the forehead touching the ground. These acts are accompanied by the recitation,

*Pilgrims rest and worship at the Sacred Mosque at Mecca* (*Makkah*). (*Courtesy of Aramco.*)

mostly silently, of portions from the *Qur'an,* of the witnessing formula, of praises to God, and of prayers. *Salat* may be validly performed only when the worshiper is in a state of ritual purity; therefore, it is always preceded by a washing, or a full bath, depending upon the degree of impurity that has been incurred. Because of this requirement it is customary that mosques include the facilities for purification when they are constructed. In general it is considered preferable that *salat* be performed in the company of others, but it is perfectly permissible to observe the ritual alone. On Fridays, however, there is a special value given to the performance of *salat* along with a congregation. On these occasions the prayers are led by one called simply the leader (*imam*) who stands in front of the ranks of worshipers, facing as they do toward the niche in the wall of the mosque (*mihrab*) that marks the direction of Makkah (the *qiblah*). This congregational prayer is normally followed by a sermon

*A mosaic mihrab, or prayer niche. Fourteenth-century Iranian; glazed earthenware set in plaster. (Courtesy of the Metropolitan Museum of Art, Harris Brisbane Dick Fund, 1939.)*

(*khutbah*) preached from the pulpit which in many mosques is the only furniture to be found. The times of prayer (before sunrise, dawn, noon, afternoon, after sunset) are today, as throughout the whole of Islamic history, announced to the faithful from the minaret of the mosque by a *mu'adhdhin* (one who calls to prayer). The common observance of this time-honored ritual throughout the Muslim lands constitutes a great bond of unity for Islamic peoples everywhere.

In addition to the obligatory *salat,* Muslims know and observe many other kinds of prayer. Special prayers are often added at the end of the *salat* itself by pious worshipers, while others are reserved for special vigils and meditations. There is, in fact, an entire catalogue of prayers to accompany each act and undertaking of life. This aspect of Islamic religious life is often overlooked by observers, with the consequence that its devotional richness is missed.

Fasting during the entire month of Ramadan, the sacred month "when the *Qur'an* came down," is another of the duties incumbent upon every adult Muslim in possession of his faculties. The fast continues for the entire day, beginning from the first light when it becomes possible to distinguish a white thread from a black one and ending only when the sun has set. During these hours it is forbidden to take anything into the body, food, drink, tobacco smoke, etc., even to a prohibition of swallowing one's own saliva where it is avoidable. Since Muslims follow a lunar calendar for religious purposes, the month of Ramadan moves successively through all the seasons of the year. In the more arid and hot regions of the earth the fast can become a great burden when it falls during the months of summer; nonetheless, faithful Muslims subject themselves to its discipline scrupulously. Throughout the month much of each night is passed in the mosques where the *Qur'an* is recited in divisions that allow it to be completed within the span of thirty nights. The end of the month of fasting is marked by the greatest festival of the Islamic year, the 'Id al-Fitr or festival of the breaking of the fast. The occasion is one of great joy. After congregational prayers, which are the most universally attended of the entire year, there is feasting, for on this day fasting is categorically forbidden. In many countries it is the custom to wear new clothing, to visit friends, and to exchange gifts. As with most of the other pillars of Islam there are some exceptions to the requirement for fasting in special instances. The ill and infirm, travelers who have begun their journey before sunrise, those who must perform strenuous physical labor, and some others may be excused, though the *shari'ah* provides in many instances that the days of fast shall be made up at a later time.

*North Persian (probably Tabriz) nineteenth-century wool prayer rug. (Courtesy of the Metropolitan Museum of Art, Mr. and Mrs. Isaac D. Fletcher Collection, Bequest of Isaac D. Fletcher, 1917.)*

Fasting at times other than the month of Ramadan is also widely practiced by Muslims as an act of self-discipline and dedication to God. Such fasting is voluntary though religious authorities have advocated it especially in connection with days of religious importance, with certain days of the month or the week, or with religious festivals. The famous al-Ghazali, for example, recommended in particular that the first, middle, and last days of each month be marked by fasting and especially during the months of the year that are considered sacred. Islam, however, generally counsels moderation in fasting as in other things, and most authorities forbid fasting more than four days continuously outside Ramadan. Fasting also serves as a form of penance for Muslims when they have neglected or broken certain aspects of *shari'ah.*

In the early days of Islam the payment of alms, along with the performance of *salat,* was particularly emphasized as the sign of submission to the authority of the Prophet. The basis for this religious tax is the Islamic emphasis on the virtue of charity which runs through the *Qur'an* as a continuing and important theme. Muslims are obligated to pay fixed amounts on various types of property, and the revenue so collected may be employed only for specified purposes of which the most important are help to the poor and needy and to the wayfarer, and support for the cause of God, i.e., to finance the holy war against infidelity. Through much of Islamic history rulers and states have provided arrangements for the collection of *zakat,* but the individual has also been free to pay his *zakat* directly to those who may legitimately receive it. There has been great irregularity, however, in the state-organized systems of collecting the tax, both in the manner of its collection and in the uses to which the revenue has been put. With the growth of other taxes and the assumption of a considerable financial burden by peasants, it becomes increasingly difficult to realize *zakat* revenue. In modern times the adoption of legal codes based on Western models and the use of a great variety of secular taxes has created new problems for the state administration of *zakat.* Nevertheless, the payment of this annual sum remains a firm obligation of religion for every adult Muslim possessed of property beyond the minimum designated in *shari'ah,* and the devout are scrupulous in fulfilling it.

The last of the Five Pillars is the duty to perform the pilgrimage to Makkah at least once during a lifetime. Every healthy adult Muslim of either sex who can command the means should make this journey of piety. Each year during the month of pilgrimage thousands upon thousands of devoted Muslims pour into the sacred city by every conceivable mode of transport to participate in the complex rites. The great majority, when they have finished the obligatory ceremonies in Makkah and its vicinity, complete their journey of faith by also visiting Madinah to pray at the tomb of the Prophet and perform other ceremonies. For countless Muslims the pilgrimage to Makkah is the dream and goal of a lifetime, and many labor and struggle for years to save the sums necessary to accomplish it. Most of the ceremony of the *hajj,* which requires several days for its fulfillment, dates back to pre-Islamic times, and the rite is an outstanding example of the manner in which Muhammad adapted certain of the practices of his ancestors to the new world view of Islam, both maintaining continuity with the past and promoting a new perspective on life at one and the same time. The principal parts of the ceremony are the assumption of pilgrim dress upon entering the sacred area, circumambulation of the Ka'bah, climaxed by kissing the black stone set in one of its corners, running back and forth between the hills of Safa and Marwah, standing (*wuquf*) at the hill of 'Arafat, and casting stones at Mina. The latter is a ceremony whose meaning is far from clear; it consists in throwing seven stones onto one of three piles of stone. Muslim commentators have explained it as "stoning the devil." With the completion of these rites the pilgrimage proper is finished, but it is customary to observe yet other ceremonies, the most important of which is the sacrifice of an animal. This occasion at the end of the *hajj* provides the Islamic world with its second great festival of the year, the 'Id al-Adha, or festival of sacrifice. Not only the pilgrims but all Mus-

*Pilgrims in the courtyard of the Khaif Mosque at Mina, near Mecca. (Courtesy of Aramco.)*

lims who can afford it make sacrifice on that day. Much of the meat from sacrificial animals goes to the poor, and in recent times it is customary for religious associations to collect the animal hides from whose proceeds they support a variety of charitable and religious activities.

It must never be thought that the range of Islamic ceremony and religious celebration is limited to the Five Pillars, although they are the fundamentals of Muslim worship. Many other times in the year also take on special significance and are marked by rites and celebrations. For example, it is customary throughout the Islamic world to celebrate the birthday of the Prophet though this festival has no *shari'ah* status. Among all the Shi'ah the most important day of the year is the tenth of the month of Muharram, on which the martyrdom of Imam Husayn is remembered and lamented. For the millions of Muslims drawn to Sufi forms of piety, each Thursday night is a time of particular importance, when the Sufi circles meet to "remember" the name of God, for on that night God is believed to draw close to the earth to hear the petitions of the faithful.

# MYSTICISM

During the same period when the *kalam* and the *fiqh* were being formed and given their classical expressions another element made its appearance in Islamic religious life. From small beginnings in the ascetic practices of a few isolated but influential individuals there emerged a mystical movement that rapidly swelled until it dominated the religious horizon. The rise of the movement had many causes, but important among them was the increasing distance between ordinary Muslims and their religious leaders. As *kalam* and *fiqh* became established sciences, they also grew more specialized and made greater demands upon their practitioners. For the majority of people it was impossible to follow the involved arguments and reasoning of the learned who became always more technical; in consequence, there was little of personal inspiration or religious guidance to be gained from them. With mystical leaders, however, the situation was entirely different. These men offered not only personal association and guidance at the level of the common man's spiritual needs, but as well, their piety was highly charged with emotional content that provided warmth of religious experience otherwise lacking for many. By the sixth Islamic century mysticism had such a hold in the life of the community that it touched virtually everyone; even the learned custodians of the legal tradition were caught up by it. For more than five hundred years, and continuing well into our own century, some form of mystical piety has been the effective religion of most people in the Islamic world. The hold of mysticism has somewhat lessened in recent times under the impact of criticisms from Muslim reformers and modernists, but in such areas as Sindh, the Frontier Province of Pakistan, Afghanistan, and Iran, especially among rural people, it is still the reality of Islam for the majority.

In Islamic dress mysticism is known as Sufism or more properly as *tasawwuf,* and one who practices it as a Sufi or *mutasawwif.* Many etymologies have been suggested for the word by Sufi writers themselves, but it is most commonly agreed to derive from *Suf,* Arabic for "wool." It was the practice of ascetics in the early days to wear a rough garment of white wool which then became the trademark of their peculiar religious practice. Definitions of Sufism are almost as numerous as Sufi writers, but the following may be taken as characteristic. Abu al-Hasan al-Nuri is reported to have said: "The Sufis are they whose spirits have been freed from the pollution of humanity, purified from carnal taint, and released from concupiscence, so that they have found rest with God in the first rank and the highest degree, and have fled from all save Him." [1] Another Sufi saint put it in this way: "He that is purified by love is pure (*saf*), and he that is absorbed in the Beloved and has abandoned all else is a Sufi." [2]

There are many elements in the *Qur'an* and the life of Muhammad which have given spiritual nourishment to persons of mystical temperament. Such verses as "Whether ye turn to the East or the West, there is the Face of God," and "God is nearer to thee than thy jugular vein," bear a mystical import that is evident at first reading. Perhaps the most significant *Qur'an* passage for the mystics is the famous "Light Verse" of Surah 24:35 ff.:

*God is the Light of the heavens and the earth;*
*the likeness of His Light is as a niche*
*wherein is a lamp*
*(the lamp in a glass,*
*the glass as it were a glittering star)*
*kindled from a Blessed Tree,*
*an olive that is neither of the East nor of the West*
*whose oil well nigh would shine, even if no fire touched it;*
*Light upon Light.*[3]

These words have been contemplated and commented upon by thousands of Sufis who see them as an unambiguous teaching of God's ubiquitous presence in all things, places, and times. Even the mode of the *Qur'an*'s coming to the Prophet has a mystical significance, for it was accompanied by visions of a spiritual being, and consisted of direct communication with an order of reality above and beyond the mundane. The Sufis, however, have not contented themselves with contemplating only straightforwardly mystical verses but have seen the entire *Qur'an* as a great allegory of the soul's quest for union with God. Beyond the outward and evident sense of the words lies a hidden and more profound meaning which is uncovered in the tradition of esoteric knowledge which God has bestowed upon his saints.

The Prophet's life is equally rich in material for Sufi contemplation. Whether or not Muhammad could be called a mystic in the technical sense is debatable, but he had cultivated the habit of meditation, fasting, and prayer in his lonely night vigils; and his mode of life, even during the time of his greatest success, had been

1. Al-Hujwīrī, *Kashf al-Maḥjūb,* trans. Reynold Nicholson, London, Luzac and Company, 1936, p. 37.

2. Ibid., p. 34.

3. A. J. Arberry, *The Koran Interpreted,* New York, Macmillan, 1955, vol. 2, pp. 50–51.

modest and self-denying in the extreme, almost to the point of asceticism. Thus, the Prophet could be seen as a model of Sufi discipline to be followed and emulated. Most important, however, was the legend of Muhammad's miraculous Night Journey from Makkah to Jerusalem, thence ascending through the Seven Heavens to meet face to face with God before the Throne. Based on a verse in the *Qur'an* (Surah 17:1), this legend has given rise to many interpretations. For some it has portrayed the soul's rise from earthly involvement to divine truth, and for others it has generated a cult of imitation of the Prophet whose access to the Divine Presence is seen as the unique key opening the way for other men to attain that high prize. Thus, there was no lack of elements of a mystical nature in the early period of Islam. Although at a later point the mystical thought and practice of others, especially Christians and Neoplatonists, and perhaps even Buddhists, to some extent influenced the Muslims, there is no reason to seek further than the fundamental Islamic experience itself to explain the rise of Sufism. Sufism is a thoroughly Islamic phenomenon that sprang from the prime sources of the community's faith.

The first stage in the growth of a specifically mystical movement was the appearance of ascetics (*zuhada'*) among the Muslims as early as the first Islamic century. The most famous of them was a certain al-Hasan al-Basri (d. 728) whose name is also associated with the beginnings of the Mu'tazilah sect. Al-Hasan was noted for his piety and his courage in outspoken criticism of the Ummawi rulers. His ascetic ways appear, as also for others showing the same tendencies, to have been an expression of protest against the increasing worldliness of the state. To keep themselves and their faith pure the ascetics found it necessary to withdraw from the world. In the beginning they were interested only in physical self-denial and purity, but in time they also developed an elaborate practice of inner or spiritual asceticism as well. Just as the first was intended to break the seductive hold of the world upon the ascetic, the latter sought to destroy even the hold of his thoughts, emotions, and desires and to discipline the inner life so that he might be free entirely to seek God.

Asceticism, however, is not necessarily in itself mystical. The self-denying disciplinary practices of the *zuhada'* soon took on a different coloring as they began to see the culmination of their flight from the world in the contemplation and love of God. Rabi'ah al-'Adawiyah (d. 801), a renowned woman who is looked upon as a kind of ideal mystic, gave eloquent expression to this all-consuming love in her prayers: "O God, if I worship Thee for fear of Hell, burn me in Hell, and if I worship Thee in hope of Paradise, exclude me from Paradise; but if I worship Thee for Thy own sake, grudge me not Thy everlasting beauty." Or again: "O God, whatsoever Thou hast apportioned to me of worldly things, do Thou give that to Thy enemies; and whatsoever Thou hast apportioned to me in the world to come, give that to Thy friends; for Thou sufficest me." [4]

4. A. J. Arberry, *Muslim Saints and Mystics,* London, Routledge, 1966, p. 51.

*Sixteenth-century Iranian miniature from the Safawi period depicting Muhammad's ascent to Heaven. (Courtesy of the Seattle Art Museum.)*

From these beginnings emerged a complex Sufi system of thought. It is perhaps paradoxical to call attention to mystical philosophies as an important aspect of mystical life in Islam, for to the Sufis it is not intellectual teaching but the actual experience of immediate intimacy with God that is the goal desired. The mystical reality is ineffable, utterly beyond the possibility to be expressed in words. Nevertheless, as part of their instruction to followers and disciples, Sufi masters found it necessary to give verbal expression to their goals and the means leading to them. The details differ with individual Sufis and schools, but in general all agree upon a spiritual pilgrimage that leads the devotee through ascending spiritual stages (*maqamat*) that are attainable by sheer human effort until the limit of man's self-perfectibility is reached. Thereafter the pilgrimage traverses a variety of states (*ahwal*) which are the gift of God's grace to those who seek him. The spiritual journey reaches its culmination and climax in *tawhid* or unification with God, an experience in which the mystic in some sense merges with the Divine Reality in the most intimate way. As one of the Sufis' favorite expressions states, the goal of the mystic quest is a "taste" of God's being. *Tawhid,* however, has a double aspect. On the one hand it is a passing away or disappearance of the devotee's personality and identity into that of God so that nothing remains of distinction between the two. For the mystic there is only God. Such snuffing out of the personality bears the name *fana',* a word used for extinguishing a fire, and it represents the absolute loss of the mystic's own identity, even to the renunciation of the desire for union with God itself. The goal, however, is not simply to attain *tawhid* but to sustain that state of ineffable blessedness; thus, on the other hand the peak experience of *fana'* is followed by *baqa',* remaining or subsisting in God as a permanent condition even though one may continue to be physically present in the world and attending to its mundane affairs. It is given to but few to make this arduous journey in full, but they, who are saints, live in unutterable bliss.

Sufi thought has exhibited differences of view at many points. For example, there are variant interpretations of the exact nature of unification, thinkers being divided in their opinion of how it takes place and whether and to what extent there remains any possibility of distinction between the mystic and God. Sufis also disagree on the metaphysical systems which they teach. Followers of Muhiy al-Din ibn al-'Arabi, a highly influential Andalusian mystic of the twelfth century, teach outright pantheism, that there is only one reality, God, who is the sum of all things. This view is echoed in the most famous of the Persian mystic poets, Jalal al-Din al-Rumi (d. 1273). Such a view was highly offensive to numerous Muslims otherwise sympathetic to Sufism, and there have been many to condemn it. Another polar question in discussions among Sufi theorists has been the mystic's attitude toward the observance of the *shari'ah.* While the great majority have held unswervingly to the need for observing all its injunctions as the first step on the mystic path, others have taught that the Sufi adept, having attained unification with God, is beyond good and evil and the need to bestow attention on the law. One prominent group has gone so far as deliberately to flaunt the *shari'ah* in order to incur the blame and censure of men as part of their renunciation of the world.

The earliest Sufis encountered considerable opposition from traditionalist Muslims, and the reasons are not far to seek. Not only were Sufi teachings innovations, departures from tradition, and equivalent, therefore, to heresy; but in their public utterances the Sufis were often guilty of radical statements that outraged traditionalist sensibilities. The best-known instances are those of Abu Yazid al-Bistami who reportedly said, "Glory be to me! How great is my glory!" and of al-Hallaj whose passionate utterance, "I am the Truth," brought about his crucifixion in 922. The reconciliation of Sufism with traditionalist Islam is commonly said to be the work of the great al-Ghazali. This man, who was a brilliant jurist, theologian, and philosopher, became a teacher in one of the religious schools established by the Saljuq rulers of Baghdad in the late eleventh century to combat the Isma'ili and other heresies. Although he found much success in his profession, al-Ghazali underwent a profound spiritual crisis that debilitated him both spiritually and physically. After several years of wandering and searching, the reintegration of his personality was achieved with his conversion to Sufism. His monumental work, *Ihya' 'Ulum al-Din* (*The Revivification of the Religious Sciences*), which embraces the full scope of the Islamic sciences, is thoroughly mystical in its basic orientation.

In the twelfth century still another dimension was added to Sufism with the introduction of organized Sufi brotherhoods. The first of those still surviving is reputed to have been found by 'Abd al-Qadir al-Jilani (d. 1166), and the so-called Qadariyah order continues to have many thousands of followers in different parts of the Islamic world even today. Other major orders also bear the names of the great mystics responsible for their foundation. A brotherhood is known as a *tariqah* (another word meaning road, path, way, or method, in this case to true knowledge of God) and is characterized by several distinguishing features, such as the belief in saints, possession of a peculiar ritual all its own, and a communal life.

The doctrine of the saints or friends of God (*walis*) is essential to later Sufism. Each *tariqah* takes its authority from a *silsilah* or chain of saints, every one of whom has received from his predecessor a store of esoteric knowledge which alone illuminates the means of attaining unity with God. Great importance is given to the chain of authority, and the orders are virtually unanimous in tracing their beginnings back to 'Ali ibn Abi Talib, though, of course, they diverge from this beginning. Because of his intimacy with the Prophet, 'Ali received instruction in the most profound mysteries not made known to others. The fundamental conception is that of a store of secret insight, a spiritual truth lying behind the externals of religion, spread through the world by a network of divinely chosen pious men. The bliss of union with the Divine Reality and the means toward it could never have been known but for God's grace in revealing them to his specially chosen "friends." For all others guidance in the exercises and spiritual discipline that lead to union with God must be had by association with the *wali* and subjecting oneself in obedience to his direction. A *wali* is a person who is himself of the highest spiritual attainment, and this penetration to the very Divine Being has conferred on him miraculous powers (*karamat*), by which he may be recognized. Even after death many of the *walis* are believed to retain their miracle-working ability. One of the most common expressions of popular Sufi piety is visitation at the tombs of great saints to bring gifts and to benefit from their blessedness (*barakah*) or to ask their miraculous help in solving some of the problems and difficulties of life. Tombs of Sufi saints are scattered throughout the Islamic lands, and some of them, like that of Mu'in al-Din Chishti at Ajmer in India, annually attract hundreds of thousands of pilgrims at celebrations in the saint's honor.

The doctrine of the saints has also taken the form of cosmological and metaphysical schemes among Sufi theorists. It is thought that there exists in the world at any given time a comprehensive hierarchy of saints whose many degrees and stages culminate in the highest spiritual authority who is called the *Qutb,* the pole or pivot. Whenever some member of the hierarchy passes away, he is replaced by another, so that the invisible spiritual structure of the universe remains always intact. These saints represent the means of the mediation of Divine Truth (*haqq*) in the world; they are literally the essential being and reality of things, the principle of wisdom and order without which there could be no existence at all. In this manner the cult of the saints is closely tied with the teachings of philosophy.

Just as the teaching of each Sufi brotherhood is in some degree different from that of others, so each also has its unique form of worship. The mystics refer to their worship as *dhikr,* remembering the Name of God, in obedience to a verse of the *Qur'an* that commands: "Remember God always." Typically the members of a brotherhood in a particular locality meet once each week for the celebration of the *dhikr,* which is the richest ceremonial known to the Islamic tradition. The ritual is based upon the continued repetition of a verbal formula that is different for each brotherhood. In some cases only the name of God, *"Allah,"* is spoken while others may chant, *"Allahu akbar"* ("God is most great!"), *"Subhan Allah"* ("Praise be to God!"), etc. Often the *dhikr* is accompanied by swaying movements of the Sufis who stand with arms linked, and its tempo tends to increase with the length of the repetition. The object of this form of devotion is to fix the mystic's mind on the unique reality of God so that all else is driven from the consciousness. Its climax is an ecstacy which to a greater or lesser degree for individuals approximates the desired union with the Divine Nature. Probably the best known *dhikr* in the Western world is that of the Mawlawiyah or so-called Whirling Dervishes of Turkey, the order founded by Jalal al-Din al-Rumi in the thirteenth century. Wearing a peculiar costume, the Mawlawi brothers perform a spectacular whirling dance, often around a pillar of the building where the *dhikr* is held. Another unusual aspect of this order's devotion is that the dance is accompanied by music, something that is normally considered against the tenets of religion by Muslims. The authentic Mawlawi *dhikr* can no longer be seen, however, for the order, like all others in Turkey, was abolished by law at the time of the Turkish Revolution in the 1920s.

Although Muslims have generally resisted anything resembling monasticism, the Sufi brotherhoods are marked by a strong communal life. Sufi adepts gather about themselves disciples and inquirers and establish a center from which the work of instruction and propagation and other activities of the order may be conducted. The resultant institution (Arabic *zawiyah;* Turkish *tekke;* Persian *khanqah*) somewhat resembles a monastery, though the Sufis may not always be resident there but rather engaged in the life of wandering mendicants. A Sufi leader of this kind is called a *pir, shaykh, murshid,* or *rahbar* while those who have been fully initiated into the lore of the order are known as *darwishes.* At the lowest level stand those who are only beginning the Sufi quest as inquirers, the *murids,* or seekers after knowledge. Life together affords the Sufis opportunity for association with the *shaykh* who is their source of guidance and allows him in turn to supervise their meditation and spiritual development. Each head of an order customarily chooses from among the most advanced *darwishes* one who shall be his *khalifah* to maintain the spiritual tradition of the brotherhood after the *shaykh*'s death. The Sufi *khanqahs* have historically also served important social functions. They have been places of resort for men in difficulty and in need of help. Not only advice and spiritual comfort but also food, shelter, medical attention, and sometimes even money were available to the needy under Sufi auspices. These centers were supported in part by contributions from lay people but more often by pious endowments which guaranteed a fixed income from agricultural land or some other such capital asset. In several notable instances the *shaykh* of an order has acted as a virtual ruler of the surrounding territory, being responsible for the maintenance of law and order and the well-being of the inhabitants. Such is the case with the well-known Sanusiyah order of North Africa which led the struggle for independence from Italian colonialism in the first part of this century. The Safawi dynasty, probably the most brilliant of the Islamic rulers in Iran, had its origin in a Sufi order of Ardabil in northwestern Iran, where the brothers organized themselves into a military fraternity about their *shaykh.* A close relationship is also to be discerned between the communal aspects of Sufism and the craft guilds and chivalrous organizations (*futuwah*) which were such vital institutions in the life of the medieval world.

At the present Sufism is passing through a period of decline, though it is still very much alive. The modernization of Islamic society has weakened virtually every one of its traditional institutions in a more or less radical way, and the Sufi brotherhoods are no exception. To many of those who are leaders of the struggle toward development and modernization Sufism has appeared as a villain in the recent history of the community. They see the Sufi cult of the saints, the visitation to tombs, and the belief in miracles as departures from true Islam and as reasons for the loss of spiritual vitality.

Furthermore, they consider Sufi cosmological and philosophical teachings to be obscurantist and to act as an impediment to the acceptance of progressive and scientific ways of understanding. Thus, there is virtual unanimity among the leadership, both intellectual and religious, in turning away from Sufi practice and condemning it.

# THE SHI'AH AND THE SUNNIS

In a tradition popularly ascribed to the Prophet, Muhammad is alleged to have said, "My community will divide into seventy-three sects of which only one is correct." In fact, Islamic history has produced vastly more sectarian groupings than the traditional number of seventy-three. Muslims have been no less fruitful than other religious communities in multiplying their internal divisions. We have spoken above of some of the early sects, such as the Khawarij and the Murji'ah, but a catalogue of the whole is impossible because it would occupy us far beyond the space available.

One schism, however, is of such importance that particular attention must be paid to it. The Islamic community falls into two great divisions, the Sunnis (sometimes, and in our opinion erroneously, called "orthodox") and the Shi'ah. Sunni Muslims speak of themselves as *ahl al-sunnah wa al-jama'at,* the people of established custom and of the (genuine) community. Plainly this terminology carries a connotation of positive judgment; it amounts to a claim to be the living representatives and bearers of true Islam, of the practices, beliefs, and expressions that have consistently characterized the majority of the community throughout its history. Another way of explaining the Sunnis is to say that they see themselves as the traditionalists of the community, for their claim is to maintain the ways established by pious men of old. This notion of a living community which embodies and unfolds the divine guidance in its practice in continuingly relevant form is basic to the Islamic understanding of religious authority. In addition to continuity with the past, such a concept of the community provides a means for expanding the guidance to meet changed needs and conditions without compromising the fundamental belief in revelation.

The other great division of Muslims, the Shi'ah, date their origins from, at latest, the death of Muhammad and perhaps even earlier. The word *shi'ah* means party, and the group got its name from its partisanship for 'Ali, the cousin and son-in-law of Muhammad, in the early struggles for leadership in the community. Those who favored 'Ali believed that succession to Muhammad's role as ruler should remain within his family, the *ahl al-bayt* (people of the house) of whom the most qualified was clearly 'Ali. They justified their stand by citing traditions from Muhammad and even *Qur'an* verses where the Prophet is said to have designated 'Ali as his successor. Thus, they opposed the election of the first three *khalifahs,* whom to this day the Shi'ah consider as usurpers; and after the short and unsettled reign of 'Ali, which was brought to an end by a Khawarij assassin in 661, they took up the cause of his sons, Hasan and Husayn, as legitimate claimants to the leadership. In Arabic the word for leadership is *imamah,* and the exclusive claim to the *imamah* for Muhammad's family has been a cardinal Shi'i doctrine through history. Although at various times there have been Shi'i states in the Islamic world, the descendants of 'Ali were never successful in establishing their rule for any length of time.

From the very beginning, however, the political interests and claims of the Shi'ah were tinged by religious elements. Even during Muhammad's lifetime there were individuals who paid a degree of respect to 'Ali that was nothing short of pious. With time the religious concern of the Shi'ah strengthened and diversified, producing many sects and exhibiting great richness, particularly in theology and philosophy, but also in religious practice and piety. Gradually these more religious elements took the foremost place as the political ambitions of the Shi'ah were frustrated.

Among the religious elements peculiar to the Shi'ah the most important are the passion motif and the doctrine of the *imamah,* which are closely interrelated. The passion motif came into prominence around the history of 'Ali's younger son, Husayn. After 'Ali's murder, the Shi'ah looked to the elder son, Hasan, to take up his father's cause, but Hasan had no spirit for the struggle and resigned his claims to the caliphate. Thereupon, Husayn, the younger brother, launched into a campaign against the Ummawis in which he was pitted against hopelessly superior forces. Ultimately he and his family were trapped by Ummawi troops and killed in pitiable circumstances on the battlefield of Karbala' in southern 'Iraq. This tragic event occurred on the tenth day of the month of Muharram in A.H. 61 (A.D. 680), and the annual celebration of this tragedy is the most important festival of the year for Shi'ah Muslims. Husayn's martyrdom and the great role it has played in Shi'ah thought have introduced the elements of sorrow, suffering, of the just man unjustly killed, and of pious sacrifice into the Shi'i strain of Muslim religiosity. There is, thus, a warmth and emotional fervour in Shi'i religious life that is one of its most noteworthy characteristics. During the Muharram celebrations each year the story of Husayn is repeated by preachers and storytellers and dramatized in passion plays called *ta'ziyahs.* The Shi'ah march in processions where they exhibit symbols of the slain martyr while beating their breasts and wailing or engaging in self-inflicted flagellation. The occasion is one of great grief that purges the souls of the worshipers while at the same time it is cause for rejoicing in the salvation and guidance which Husayn's noble self-sacrifice has bestowed on the faithful. The passion motif is not tied exclusively to the events surrounding Husayn, however; rather the Shi'ah believe that all of their *imams* (see below) and other members of the holy family, including the Prophet himself, have suffered martyrdom at the hands of unjust men. In the passion plays, which often last for days, the history of these martyrdoms is traced in a recurring pattern while the worshipers mourn and weep. According to the Shi'ah most of the *imams* have died by poison, usually administered at the instigation of the *khalifahs* who usurped the *imam*'s rightful place of rule.

The word *imam* means simply a leader, and it is used for several purposes. The one who stands before the congregation to lead the prayer is called an *imam;* an especially learned man may also gain the title, as in the case of the founders of the four Sunni schools of law, or certain other distinguished individuals. Among the Shi'ah the word is invested with a meaning that goes far beyond the usual one, however. Upon Muhammad's death the Shi'ah believe that not only his function as ruler but also his role as religious guide devolved upon his descendants beginning with 'Ali. The divine guidance did not stop with the decease of the Prophet but continued to be shed in the world through his family, each of whom under divine direction, designated his successor in the *imamah* just as Muhammad had designated 'Ali. The series of visible *imams,* living openly in the world, however, came to an end with the mysterious disappearance of the last *imam.* For a time the *imam* retained contact with his followers through representatives who had direct access to him, but soon even this was broken off. The *imam* remains in the world but is hidden until he will come again at the end of time as the *Imam Mahdi* to establish the kingdom of God. Meanwhile the learned men of the Shi'i community act as interpreters of the divine will through their exercise of *ijtihad.* This doctrine gives a distinctive character to Shi'i religiosity, for the *imam* constitutes a living source of guidance in the world at all times. The importance of the doctrine is shown in the saying: "He who dies without knowing the *imam* of the age dies in unbelief."

The precise nature of the *imam* is understood differently by the numerous Shi'i sects, but the belief in the *imamah* is common to them all and is, indeed, their distinguishing characteristic. For the more extreme Shi'ah (the *ghulat*) the *imam* is considered as virtually an incarnation of God. There is a veritable indwelling of the divine spirit in the *imam* so that in knowing him one experiences the full reality of divine presence in the world. The *imam* is the localization of the supreme mystery and creative force that has brought the universe into being and that continues to sustain it. Should the *imam* ever be withdrawn, the entire order of reality would literally collapse because of the absence of its essential principle. Such a view of the *imam* is almost precisely parallel to the Sufi understanding of the *Qutb,* or great saint around whom the whole order of reality turns. At the other extreme of Shi'ah opinion, as for example among the Zaydi sect of the Yemen, the *imam* is considered only to be inspired or divinely led, much as the Prophet himself was. Between the two extremes stand the great majority of Shi'ah who hold a kind of doctrine of metempsychosis with respect to the *imams.* According to their understanding a spark of the eternal divine wisdom was implanted in Muhammad and upon his death was transplanted into 'Ali and from thence into the series of his descendants whom God has chosen. Although there is, thus, an element of the divine in each of the *imams,* there is not the complete indwelling in which the *ghulat* believe. In every case the importance accorded the *imam* in Shi'i thinking has radical implications for the understanding of religious authority, for so long as the *imam* is accessible either personally or through his representatives in the form of learned men, there is a living source of guidance always at hand.

There have been some differences among the Shi'ah also about the number of *imams* and their identity. The major distinction is between those who accept a series of seven and those who accept a series of twelve. They are called respectively the Seveners and the Twelvers or the Isma'ilis (after the last *imam* they recognize) and the Ithna 'Ashariyah (Arabic for "Twelvers"). Generally speaking, the Isma'ilis have been more radical in their views than the Twelvers. For a great part of Islamic history the Isma'ilis existed as secret societies which, in the effort to spread their creed among Muslims, engaged in revolutionary activities against established rulers and states, often, as in the case of the famous Assassins, using terrorism as one of their methods. Isma'ili propaganda gained impetus and support with the rise of the Fatimi dynasty of Egypt (969–1174) whose rulers reckoned themselves in the line of descent from Muhammad ibn Isma'il, the last *imam* of the Isma'ilis. The Fatimi state was, thus, self-consciously Isma'ili in its constitution, and the period of its ascendancy must be reckoned as among the most brilliant eras of Islamic history. The founding of modern Cairo, the establishment of the famous al-Azhar University in that city, and many other feats testify to the greatness of the Fatimis. Numerous subgroups of Isma'ilis continue to flourish at the present time, among which are included the Druze and Nusayris of Syria, and perhaps best known of all, the followers of the Agha Khan, the majority of whom are found in India and the areas around the Indian Ocean where Indians have immigrated. Isma'ilis are also sometimes known as Batiniyah (from *batin,* hidden) because they profess an esoteric teaching accessible only to those who have gained initiation to this secret knowledge. This esoteric teaching is an elaborate philosophy, strongly influenced by Neoplatonic and gnostic ideas, whose basis is a doctrine that everything in the external and visible world represents or prefigures on a small scale the realities (*haqa'iq*) of a spiritual and invisible world. Penetration beyond the external to knowledge of the spiritual realities is the aim of the teaching.

The Twelver Shi'ah are much more numerous than the Isma'ilis. At present they may be found spread over a great area with the majority concentrated in Iraq, where they are more than half the popu-

*Koutoubya Minaret in Marrakesh, Morocco, as it looks today. The 220-foot minaret, built by the Andalusians, was completed in 1195.* (*Courtesy of Mr. and Mrs. S. C. Isler.*)

lation, in Iran, and in the Indian subcontinent. Twelver Shi'ism received a great boost to its fortunes in the sixteenth century when the founders of the Safawi dynasty in Iran chose to make it the official religion of the state. It has continued to enjoy that favored status, and Iran is now the stronghold of the group. Although the principal Shi'i shrines are located at Najaf and Karbala in Iraq (the burial places of 'Ali and Husayn), Iran also has holy places and centers of pilgrimage in Mashhad and Qum where great theological schools maintain the tradition of Shi'i learning and teaching.

Apart from the doctrine of the *imamah,* the Shi'ah are also distinguished from the Sunnis in several other ways. There is a separate and distinct Shi'i *fiqh* which recognizes completely different authorities from those of the four "orthodox" Sunni schools. In actual content the rules of law differentiating Shi'ah and Sunni are small, being limited for the most part to minor details. The greatest variation arises in jurisprudential theory because of the preponderating role of the *imam* in Shi'i thinking and the continued Shi'i espousal of *ijtihad.* The Shi'ah also have their own distinctive collections of traditions such as the book entitled *Al-Kafi* (The Sufficient One) by al-Kulayni (d. 939) and others. One must not be misled by the word "Sunni" into thinking that the Shi'ah have any less reliance on the authority of tradition than their fellow Muslims; if anything, the contrary is the case, for the Shi'ah pay full respect to the sayings and reports of the men of old, though, to be sure, the authorities they recognize are not the same as for Sunnis. Another important area of difference between the two major groups lies in the area of theology. On the whole the Shi'ah have inclined in a far more rationalistic direction than has Sunni Islam. Much of the doctrine of the Mu'tazilah has survived among the Shi'ah, and in their theological method they show a preference for rational argument above traditionalist views. No doubt, the inclination to rationalism accounts in large part for the great richness in philosophy, theology and speculative science generally among the Shi'ah.

At various times in Islamic history there has been sharp conflict between Shi'ah and Sunni over both political and religious issues. Even today in Lebanon, India, and Pakistan, for example, civil tranquillity is sometimes marred by altercations between the groups, especially at the time of the Muharram celebrations when Shi'i fervor is at its highest. These unfortunate conflicts should be seen, however, against the background of the strong Islamic sense of community and the feeling of kinship among all who belong to it, no matter what their differences. As great as the disagreements may be between Sunnis and Shi'ah, they have not shattered the *ummah*'s sense of its own distinctiveness and unity. In modern times in particular, because of the pressures of outside forces and ideologies, there has been a determined effort to play down the divisive effect of religious differences and to recapture the community's sense of oneness.

# ISLAM IN MODERN TIMES

The modern period of Islamic history has been marked by a reawakening of the Muslim peoples that has touched their lives in virtually every sphere of activity, including the religious. Underlying this new dynamic are a pervasive and profoundly disturbing sense that something has gone wrong with the community's life and a determination to rectify it. Preceding the reawakening was a long period of relative decline which saw the Muslim nations outstripped and then dominated by the rising civilization of Western Europe, and it is this fact, together with some elements internal to the community, that has created the sense of crisis and malaise. A once proud and brilliant people whose religious faith assured them of worldly success in addition to future reward had become the pawns of others. How was this disaster to be explained, and what was to be done about it? Contemplating these questions has produced a ferment among Muslims that has led to searching examination of traditional modes of life, to reforms, and to political revitalization.

In the seventeenth century there were three great Islamic empires in existence, each exercising an important influence in the world. In comparison with the small states of divided Europe, still in the early stages of their modern evolution, Islamic power represented a massive force that seemed secure in the control of its own destiny and which for a time threatened even to engulf Eastern Europe. As late as 1683 a great Ottoman army stood before the gates of beseiged Vienna, and it required the combined powers of a number of East European princes to turn it away. These three empires, the Ottoman in Turkey and the Mediterranean Basin, the Safawi in Persia, and the Mughal in India, were each culturally creative as well as militarily strong.

By the nineteenth century, however, the situation had changed radically for the worse in the Muslim lands. The great Safawi dynasty, whose era saw the flowering of some of the finest elements in Persian culture, art, and thought, had succumbed to fissiparous tendencies and to the attacks of wild Afghan tribesmen. The Ottoman Turks who only shortly before had been the masters of the Eastern Mediterranean were now recognized as the "Sick Man of Europe," overpowered by the diplomacy or the outright military might of the rising Western powers. Throughout the nineteenth century and climaxing in the revolution of the 1920s, Turkey struggled desperately with a series of reforms and political experiments designed to restore her power and to insure her growth as a modern nation. With the death in 1707 of its last great ruler, Awrangzeb, the Mughal Empire began the long slide toward its eventual destruction. Bitter wars of succession shattered its unity and fostered the growing influence of the empire's Maratha and Sikh rivals. By 1800 the British were the strongest power in the subcontinent, and they put an end to even the fiction of Mughal sovereignty in 1858 after the great Indian Mutiny by incorporating India directly into the British Empire and declaring Queen Victoria to be her sovereign.

This decline in imperial strength coincided with the emergence of European colonialism that resulted in outright European rule over vast regions of the Islamic world. In the 1860s and 70s the armies of the Tsars overran Islamic Central Asia and brought the region permanently within the Russian sphere. The peoples of the area were able briefly again to reassert their independence after the Russian Revolution of 1917, but the Bolsheviks soon broke the Khanates and brought them within the Soviet system. The Dutch who had gained a commercial foothold in Indonesia from an early time ruled the islands of the archipelago with a firm hand. The British were established in Egypt, in addition to India, after 1882, and they exercised control as well in Adan at the southern entrance to the Red Sea, in the Persian Gulf, along the southern coasts of Arabia, and in Malaya. In an elaborate diplomacy aimed at keeping the borders of their Indian Empire safe from Russian encroachment, the British also wielded considerable influence, involving coercion at times, upon the rulers of Persia and of Afghanistan. French military activity in North Africa had given them control of Morocco after 1830, and their intense rivalry with the British for the upper hand in Egypt led them eventually to extend their sphere in the Maghrib until it included also Algeria and Tunisia. As a result of Turkey's decisive defeat in World War I, the eastern Arab regions also fell under European hegemony. The system established by the Sykes-Picot Agreement (1916) divided Greater Syria between the French and the British and allowed to Britain a kind of tutelage over Iraq. In short, there was no important region of the Islamic world that was untouched by European power or safe from European colonialism. To even the most uninstructed observer, Muslim political, military, and economic weakness was abundantly evident. The decline in worldly power was accompanied also by disruption of traditional institutions and social forms as a result of reform measures, by a dependence upon authority in the religious sphere, and by a degree of cultural stagnation. As Muslims became increasingly aware of the state to which they had fallen, partially through the efforts of a series of brilliant leaders who emerged in the last quarter of the nineteenth century, there was a gradual reawakening that first centered in efforts at religious reform but in its later phases turned increasingly to political and secularist alternatives.

The earliest efforts at religious reforms in the modern period were not, however, a response to the impact of the West as an external force but seem rather to have been the result of Islamic awareness of internal decay. The outstanding instances are the Wahhabi movement of Arabia and the activities of Shah Waliyullah of Delhi and his disciples. The Wahhabis are so called after Muhammad ibn 'Abd al-Wahhab (1703–1792), who launched the movement. This man traveled widely in the Near East and devoted himself to religious studies at several leading Islamic centers of learning, including those in Iraq and Iran where Shi'i views were propagated. Eventually he came to hold a very strict view of Islam that most closely resembled the position of the classical traditionist, Ahmad ibn Hanbal. 'Abd al-Wahhab was outraged by what seemed to him the great corruption of pure Islamic teaching that had come about in the course of time, and he set out to purify the body politic of these foreign and debilitating elements. His particular wrath fell upon practices associated with Sufi worship, especially the cult of the saints. He condemned the building of mausoleums, the visitations to saints' tombs, the bringing of gifts, the invocation of saints' names in prayer, the belief that saints might intercede for their devotees or otherwise assist them, and the doctrine that the saints possess special means of communication with the divine. Coupled with this attempt to return to a more pristine Islam was a strong puritanism that would use the power of the authorities to enforce performance of the prayer and to forbid such un-Islamic practices as drinking and smoking tobacco. To 'Abd al-Wahhab it seemed that the Muslims had forsaken the path of true religion; his was, thus, not a reform movement but an effort to restore or revive the genuine Islam of the earliest generation, the faith that had brought success, strength, and spiritual blessing to the early community.

The movement, whose strict teachings in themselves attracted many who were concerned about the state of the community's life, took on added significance when a cooperative relationship was contracted between the founder and the Su'ud family of Arabia. Under the leadership of the Su'udis the sect came into armed conflict with other tribesmen in Arabia, and the military strength of the Wahhabis grew steadily until by the turn of the nineteenth century they were in actual control of large areas of Arabia proper, of Syria, and Iraq. The revivalist zeal was given a military and political expression. Apprehending a danger to their suzerainty, the Ottomans took vigorous steps to suppress the sect; an expedition was despatched under Muhammad 'Ali Pasha, the ruler of Egypt, to recapture the holy cities of Islam and subdue the Wahhabis. There were important victories in 1812 and 1813 for the Egyptians, and in 1818 a second Egyptian expedition under Ibrahim Pasha put an end to the first phase of the Wahhabi empire by capturing their headquarters at Dar'iyah. The sect did not disappear, however, but by slow degrees reestablished its rule over the regions around the Persian

Gulf and some of the interior parts of Arabia. It gained a new lease on life in 1901 when 'Abd al-'Aziz ibn Su'ud captured the city of Riyadh and reestablished the Su'udi dynasty, which rules Arabia to this day. The dynasty has officially espoused Wahhabism and the strict teachings of the school of Ahmad ibn Hanbal, but in the years since World War II it has evidenced considerable flexibility in encouraging the modernization of the country and its intercourse with foreign states. The major factor in this change is the economic upswing following the discovery and exploitation of enormous petroleum resources in the eastern portion of the country. Nevertheless Wahhabism is the foremost attempt at Islamic revival that the modern world has witnessed, and it has had repercussions in every Islamic land.

The life of Shah Waliyullah (1703–1762) of Delhi coincided with the beginning of the Mughal decline. As a child he witnessed the fratricidal wars of succession among the sons and heirs of Awrangzeb and saw the power of the emperor eroded until the ruler scarcely exercised authority over the capital city, Delhi, itself. Shah Waliyullah has been called the "thinker of crisis," for it was in his day that the Muslims of India had for the first time to face the fact that they could no longer live in the subcontinent as its rulers. With the rise of indigenous Indian powers on one hand and Western colonialism on the other, the former custodians of Islamic greatness in India were doomed to play a lesser role. Waliyullah responded to the challenge of the time by launching a campaign of Islamic revival. In its negative aspects, like Wahhabism, it was concerned with purifying Islamic practice of historical accretions that had robbed the Muslims of their vitality and obscured the genuine faith. For an Indian Muslim the principal target of concern was a great variety of Hindu customs that Muslims had inevitably adopted through their centuries long association with their Hindu fellow countrymen. Waliyullah was also opposed to the excesses of Sufi thought and practice, but his attitude was less rigorous than that of the Wahhabis, and he himself was a Sufi adept who used certain Sufi institutions to forward his cause. The principal means of realizing his program of revitalizing Indian Islam was teaching. He gathered about himself in a *madrasah,* or theological school, founded by his father in Delhi a variety of disciples and imparted his views on Islam to them. A list of impressive works came from his pen, wherein he set out an interpretation of Islamic doctrine that was dynamic and which sought to resolve many of the religious issues that had spawned disunity among the Indian Muslims. Through a series of letters he also strove to awaken in the decadent Mughal nobility some sense of responsibility toward salvation of the Islamic cause in the subcontinent. In his view the matter of primary concern was to restore Muslim hegemony in a deteriorating situation, and to this end he initiated correspondence with Muslim rulers in Afghanistan and Iran, whom he besought to intervene in India on behalf of the Islamic cause. Both politically and religiously the vision of society he labored to realize was that of a restored and strengthened medieval Islam.

The result of his effort was a greatly increased consciousness among Muslims of their Islamicness and of its implications. A continuing stream of disciples propagated and worked out his ideas in the years that followed his death. His four sons in particular were instrumental in passing on his influence, and one of them, Shah 'Abd al-'Aziz, provided the religious and intellectual stimulus to a major movement in the Frontier area in the first decades of the nineteenth century. The movement, sometimes called Indian Wahhabism because of its similarity to the program of revival of 'Abd al-Wahhab but more properly known as the Mujahidin, recruited Muslims and collected funds all over India for the conduct of an armed struggle in the Frontier and Panjab to reestablish Muslim power against the Sikhs. Eventually the Mujahidin came into conflict with the British, and their principal leaders were killed at the Battle of Balakot in 1831. Remnants of the movement persisted and continued to have influence, however, throughout the century. The many Islamic movements of the Indian subcontinent in the nineteenth and twentieth centuries all owe some debt to Shah Waliyullah, who first called forth a new burst of interest in what it means to be a Muslim. The thrust of his efforts was toward the purification and reestablishment of the ancient ideal that had guided the community in the past, but at the same time his teachings offered a dynamic and provided principles that others have used to build a more modern interpretation of Islam.

Of greater relevance to recent times are those religious reformers whose thought appears to be a direct response to the threatening impact of Western Europe upon Islamic society. They are called Muslim modernists, in contrast to Muslim revivalists or fundamentalists such as 'Abd al-Wahhab and Shah Waliyullah, because their principal purpose has been to demonstrate the viability and relevance of Islam in the modern world. Islamic modernism has been a powerful force that has affected governing and intellectual classes in every Islamic country and that continues today as one of the important alternatives for Muslims who face the problems of modernity.

We may gain some understanding of Islamic modernism by looking at one of its most important and influential representatives, the Egyptian savant Muhammad 'Abduh (1849–1905). 'Abduh came from humble beginnings in a lower Egyptian village and showed an early bent toward mysticism. His life, however, was oriented in a radically new direction from the year 1872, when he came into contact with the fiery Jamal al-Din al-Afghani (1839–1897), whom he quickly espoused as his master. Al-Afghani is one of the towering individuals of modern Islamic history, an indefatigable worker for the liberation of Muslims from European dominance, who traveled extensively throughout the Islamic world and Europe preaching the need for Islamic unity and the requirement of a revived Islam as the key to renewed Muslim strength. Al-Afghani's powerful personality left a legacy of ferment throughout the Islamic regions, but he did not possess the qualities of a systematic thinker and wrote but little outside the journalistic field. It was 'Abduh who gave intellectual expression to the bases of a modern Islamic religious reform in a series of lectures, articles, and books. In his later life 'Abduh held a number of important posts in Egypt, as Chief Mufti (consultant on Islamic law), as member of the Superior Council of the leading institution of religious learning, the Azhar University, and as member of the Legislative Council which was Egypt's first step toward representative political institutions. These places of influence allowed him the opportunity to put many of his ideas and theories into practice. Even after his death his ideas continued to be vigorously propagated—with some new interpretation, to be sure—by his disciple Rashid Rida in the journal *Al-Manar.*

Like al-Afghani, 'Abduh was interested primarily in the liberation of the Muslims and the regaining of their vitality and strength. The desired end, he felt, could be achieved through Islam's own resources by restoring it to its original purity. Thus the solution to the modern dilemna of Muslims was to be found in a return to religion and its purification. Since in his opinion no civilization could flourish whose moral foundations were not firm, the central place in the rehabilitation of Muslim fortunes had to be given to religion. Unlike some conservative Muslims who opposed him bitterly, 'Abduh welcomed the changes which European influence had wrought in Egyptian society, as, for example, in the revolutionary reforms of Muhammad 'Ali Pasha at the beginning of the nineteenth century. He considered such developments to be an inevitable part of modernity, and the problem for one concerned in preserving the Islamic spiritual heritage was to bring such changes within an Islamic framework. This 'Abduh did by demonstrating that the essential element of Islam is its rationality and its faithfulness to the reality of things. Thus, he held that science, which, in common with all the modernists, he identified as the secret of European success, was a genuinely Islamic activity, the extension into practical affairs of the very spirit that lay at the heart of Islamic commitment. The generation of modernists who had preceded him had argued negatively, that science is not incompatible with Islamic faith; 'Abduh passed from this defensive stance vis-à-vis European thought to take the offensive by proclaiming that Islam is the very origin and inspiration of science, even of the science of Westerners, who had made their first steps in its direction under the influence and tutelage of Arab thinkers from classical Islamic times. In similar fashion he proclaimed the progressiveness of Islam and its inherent flexibility which permitted accommodation even of its law to the changing circumstances of human life. 'Abduh conducted an uncompromising polemic against the doctrine of *taqlid,* or of the obligation to follow blindly the teachings of one of the four accepted schools of law, calling instead for the reopening of the gates of *ijtihad,* for the right of exercise of personal judgment, and for a new *ijma'* in the community that would approximate the function of legislation in modern society. In the latter teaching 'Abduh exhibits a general characteristic of Islamic modernism to equate traditional Islamic concepts with institutions or values of modern times. 'Abduh also joined battle with Christianity in a sharp polemic aimed at upholding the superiority of Islam and putting down, once and for all, any suggestion that Europe's dominance might be attributable to Christianity or the weakness of Muslims due to faults in their fundamental conception of the world. His views on such traditional theological doctrines as free-will and the concept of prophecy reflect his bias toward a rationalistic interpretation of Islam. In many respects his foremost theological treatise, *Risalat al-Tawhid* may be seen as an attempt to rehabilitate the status of the long despised Mu'tazilah of a previous time. Conscious always of the European threat to Islam looming somewhere over the horizon, 'Abduh wrote, spoke, and worked for the betterment of Muslim fortunes through a revival of the true and genuine Islam. What is notable about his stance, and that of virtually every other modernist, is the steadfast refusal, however, to grant any shortcoming or deficiency in original and genuine Islam, whose truth he held to be enduringly valid. Although he admitted change in the social sphere and, indeed, welcomed it from an Islamic perspective, neither he nor his disciples saw any need for reconstruction or reformulation in the fundamentals of Islamic faith.

Many of 'Abduh's ideas were echoed in other parts of the Islamic world by men acting either independently or under his or similar influence. Very like notions may be read, for example, in the writings of Sir Sayyid Ahmad Khan (1817–1898), the founder of the 'Aligarh Muslim University in India, or in stronger and more exaggerated expression in the famous book of Sayyid Amir 'Ali (1849–1928), *The Spirit of Islam,* which has been called the Bible of Islamic modernism. In greater or lesser degree modernist Islam, in all its many contexts, has a unity in showing the following characteristics: (1) a strong sense of dynamism, i.e., that the meaning of Islam in modern times is a call to action; (2) a need to counter explicit or implicit criticism of Islam arising out of the Western impact; (3) a preference for rational methods in the interpretation of religious doctrine with a tendency to deny supernatural, legendary, or miraculous elements in the tradition; (4) a romantic interpretation of Islamic history, particularly of the earliest generations, that is part of the general defense of Islam; (5) an insistence upon the agreement between Islamic teachings and those of science; (6) a preoccupation with the personality of the Prophet and a tendency to exalt his moral and intellectual qualities; (7) the identification of Islamic teaching with liberal and humanitarian values compatible to the present age; (8) an anti-Sufi attitude which looks upon later Islamic mysticism as obscurantist and the partial cause of Muslim weakness; and (9) a rejection of the authority of the medieval legal schools and a refusal to adhere to their methods. In this body of teachings the modernists offer massive reassurance to the contemporary Muslim who in this light finds his spiritual heritage to be more than capable of meeting his needs as a modern man.

Far from dissolving in the acids of modernity, Islam has gained a new grasp on life; indeed, the resurgence of the Muslim peoples in every sphere, not the religious alone, is one of the principal facts of the twentieth century. In the period since the close of World War II one Islamic country after the other has thrown off foreign domination and gained its independence. The only major region still controlled by non-Muslim power is Soviet Central Asia where Islam is rapidly disappearing among the younger generation under the relentless pressure brought to bear upon it. In other countries, however, such as Pakistan, which emerged as a separate state for Muslims after the British departure from India and the partition of the subcontinent in 1947, there have been sustained attempts to work out the implications of Islamic commitment for social and political life. Islam is entering upon a new stage in its history, one in which its expression is taking new forms and where it faces novel problems, but as the spiritual cradle of a major portion of mankind it continues to provide a satisfying answer to men's deepest needs.

## BIBLIOGRAPHY

### General Works

The most important reference work for students of Islam is the *Encyclopædia of Islam* in its various editions. The original edition, consisting of four volumes and a supplement, was edited by M. T. Houtsma (Leyden, E. J. Brill, 1913–1938). The encyclopedia is in process of republication in a completely revised and expanded form under the title *Encyclopædia of Islam, New Edition,* edited by H. A. R. Gibb and J. H. Kramers (Leyden, E. J. Brill, 1960– ). Two volumes and most of the fascicles for the third have appeared by the time of this writing. There also exists a *Shorter Encyclopædia of Islam* (Leyden, E. J. Brill, 1953), edited by H. A. R. Gibb and J. H. Kramers. This volume contains articles on religion taken from the new edition of the larger encyclopedia.

The best guides to periodical literature on Islam are:

Pearson, J. D., and Julia F. Ashton, eds., *Index Islamicus, 1906–1955,* Cambridge, Heffer, 1958.

Pearson, J. D., ed., *Index Islamicus Supplement, 1956–1960,* Cambridge, Heffer, 1962.

The best currently available general work on Islam is H. A. R. Gibb's *Mohammedanism* (New York, Oxford, 1949, reprinted 1950; now also available in paperback). For general reading the following are also recommended:

Lammens, Henri, *Islam Beliefs and Institutions,* trans. E. D. Ross, London, Methuen, 1929.

Levy, Reuben, *The Social Structure of Islam,* New York, Cambridge, 2nd rev. ed., 1957; also available in paperback.

Von Grunebaum, G. E., *Mediæval Islam,* Chicago, The University of Chicago Press, 1953; also available in paperback.

The following anthologies of Islamic writers are useful:

Jeffrey, Arthur, ed., *Islam: Muhammad and His Religion,* New York, Liberal Arts, paperback ed., 1958.

———, ed., *A Reader on Islam,* New York, Humanities Press, 1962.

Schroeder, Eric, ed., *Muhammad's People,* Freeport, Me., Bond Wheelwright, 1955.

Williams, John A., *Islam,* New York, George Braziller, Inc., 1961; paperback ed., New York, Washington Square Press, 1961.

**Pre-Islamic Arabia**

Much of the writing in this field is highly specialized, but the student of Islam can gain information on things important for his purposes from the following:

Izutsu, Toshihiko, *The Structure of the Ethical Terms in the Koran,* Tokyo, Keio Institute of Philological Studies, 1959.

Lewis, Bernard, *The Arabs in History,* London, Hutchinson, 1950; paperback ed., New York, Harper & Row, 1966. A short but splendid volume.

Nicholson, Reynold A., *A Literary History of the Arabs,* New York, Cambridge, 1953; also available in paperback.

**Muhammad the Prophet**

The most important sourcebook in English is *The Life of Muhammad* translated by Alfred Guillaume (London, Oxford, 1955; also available in paperback). This volume is a translation of the most important Arabic biography of the Prophet; the original is the work on which all biographical studies of Muhammad depend.

The best modern biography and study of Muhammad is to be had in the works of W. Montgomery Watt, *Muhammad at Mecca* and *Muhammad at Medina,* both published by the Clarendon Press at Oxford, in 1953 and 1956 respectively.

**The Qur'an**

The translation of the *Qur'an* that best renders the traditional Muslim understanding of the text is Marmaduke Pickthall's *The Meaning of the Glorious Koran* (Hyderabad, Dakkan, 1938; paperback ed., New York, New American Library, 1953). Those interested in a translation of high literary quality and in the interpretations of modern scholarship should consult A. J. Arberry's two-volume work *The Koran Interpreted* (London, G. Allen, 1955; paperback ed., New York, Macmillan).

The foremost critical study of the *Qur'an* in English is R. E. Bell's *Introduction to the Qur'ān* (Edinburgh, Edinburgh University Press, 1953.)

For an exacting study of the *Qur'an*'s teaching two books by Toshihiko Izutsu are recommended: *Ethico-Religious Terms in the Qur'ān* (Montreal, Institute of Islamic Studies, 1967) and *God and Man in the Koran* (Tokyo, Keio Institute of Cultural and Linguistic Studies, 1964).

**The Prophetic Tradition**

The only complete translation of one of the *sahih* books is in French:

Houdas, O., and W. Marçais, *Les traditions islamiques,* 3 vols., Paris, Imprimerie Nationale, 1903–1914.

Selections from the *hadith* can be found in the second edition of Muhammad Ali's *A Manual of Hadith* (Lahore, Ahmadiyyah Anjuman Isha'at Islam, n.d.).

The best critical work in English on the *hadith* is Alfred Guillaume's *The Traditions of Islam* (Oxford, Clarendon Press, 1924).

**Kalam, or Theology**

The writing in this field is not as far advanced as one might like, but the following can be recommended as introductions to a vast and complex subject:

MacDonald, Duncan Black, *Development of Muslim Theology, Jurisprudence, and Constitutional Theory,* New York, Scribner, 1903.

Watt, W. Montgomery, *Islamic Philosophy and Theology,* Islamic Surveys Vol. 1, Edinburgh, Edinburgh University Press, 1962.

Wensinck, A. J., *The Muslim Creed,* New York, Cambridge, 1932.

Those who are interested in studying an original piece of Islamic theological writing in detail should peruse Walter Klein's translation of Al-Ash'ari's *Al-Ibānah 'an Usūl al-Diyānah* (New Haven, American Oriental Society, 1940).

**The Law**

The following are the best introductory works for this highly technical subject:

Coulson, Noel J., *A History of Islamic Law,* Islamic Surveys Vol. 2, Edinburgh, Edinburgh University Press, 1964.

Schacht, Joseph, *An Introduction to Islamic Law,* Oxford, Clarendon Press, 1964.

**The Shi'ah**

Books by missionaries constitute the best introductory sources for information on the Shi'ah. The two books by the following are especially good:

Donaldson, Dwight M., *The Shi'ite Religion,* London, Luzac and Co., 1933.

Hollister, John N., *The Shi'a of India,* London, Luzac and Co., 1953.

**Sufism**

The best general work in English on this subject is *Sufism* by A. J. Arberry (London, G. Allen, 1950). There is a fine anthology of Sufi ideas and writing in Margaret Smith's *The Sūfī Path of Love* (London, Luzac and Co., 1954). Those who wish first-hand acquaintance with a basic Sufi work should consult Reynold A. Nicholson's translation of *Kashf al-Maḥjūb* by Al-Hujwiri (London, Luzac and Co., 1911).

**The Modern Period**

The literature on this subject is vast and grows with each passing day. A good introduction to the nature of modern Islamic development may be had from the following:

Berkes, Niyazi, *The Development of Secularism in Turkey,* Montreal, McGill University Press, 1964.

Gibb, H. A. R., *Modern Trends in Islam,* Chicago, The University of Chicago Press, 1947.

Hourani, Albert, *Arabic Thought in the Liberal Age, 1798–1939,* New York, Oxford, 1962.

Smith, Wilfred Cantwell, *Islam in Modern History,* Princeton, N.J., Princeton University Press, 1957.

**Additional Bibliography**

See the chapter "Islam" in Charles J. Adams, ed., *A Reader's Guide to the Great Religions,* New York, Free Press, 1965.

# GLOSSARY

*A NOTE ON TRANSLITERATION*
*The simplest English transliterations of Arabic terms, without diacritical marks, have been used in the text to make reading easier for the student unfamiliar with the language. The more linguistically correct forms, with diacritics, can be found in the Glossary.*

**Pronunciation of Arabic**

*Consonants:*

**b, d, f, h, j, k, l, m, n, r, s, t, z,** and **sh** are pronounced roughly as in English.

**w** This letter is either a consonant or a vowel according to its use. When it is a consonant it is transliterated as w and when a vowel as ū.

**y** This letter is either a consonant or a vowel according to its use. When it is a consonant it is transliterated as y and when a vowel as ī.

**'** Called hamzah, the Arabic sign rendered in this fashion represents a glottal stop or gentle closing of the throat. Such a throat closure is necessary, for example, in the pronunciation of any English word that begins with a vowel. In the middle of a word the hamzah is in effect a slight pause.

**th** Like the th in *th*ink.

**ḥ** A guttural h pronounced with a strong emission of breath from an open throat.

**kh** A guttural fricative as in Scottish "lo*ch*" or German "a*ch*tung."

**ṣ, ḍ, ṭ, ẓ** Veliorized consonants corresponding with s, d, t, and z. These are all emphatic sounds achieved by pressing the tongue strongly against the upper teeth and releasing it suddenly. These letters also affect the following vowel, as may be seen in the contrast between sā (sa as in English *sag*) and ṣā (so as in English *sol*emn).

**dh** Like the th in *th*is.

Transliteration of the Arabic letter ayn, which has no equivalent in English. It is a strong guttural sound pronounced deep in the throat with a strong emission of breath.

**gh** A sound like that made in gargling. It is very close in pronunciation to the r in Parisian French.

**q** A hard k produced in the back of the throat.

*Vowels* (Arabic has three short vowels, three long vowels, and two dipthongs):

Short vowels (these are normally not written in an Arabic text):

**a** Called fatḥah, it is pronounced like English a in m*a*n, English u in n*u*n, or English e in m*e*lody, according to the consonant on which it is borne. The variety of sounds for all the short vowels is considerable.

**i** Called kasrah, it is pronounced as in English d*i*m.

**u** Called ḍammah, it is pronounced as in English p*u*ll.

Long vowels (these are always written by separate characters in an Arabic text. The long vowels are formed by drawing out the sound of the short vowels):

**ā** Called 'alif, this letter is pronounced with

a lengthening of the English a sounds, as in saw or sag.

ī Called yā', this letter is pronounced like the English doubled e, as in eel.

ū Called waw, this letter is pronounced like the English doubled o as in booth.

Diphthongs:

**ay** Like English pay.

**aw** Like English ow, as in cow.

There are no rules for stress in Arabic; the length of syllables causes some to appear stronger than others.

In the Arabic definite article al-, the initial a is a connective that may be pronounced as a, i, or u, according to the conditions determined by the rules of grammar. A student who does not know Arabic should pronounce it simply a as in alfresco. When the definite article is followed by any one of the following letters; the l assimilates to that letter and is given the same pronunciation: t, th, d, dh, r, z, s, sh, ḍ, ṣ, ṭ, ẓ, l, n. For example, the Arabic expression meaning "the man," al-rajūl, is pronounced ar-rajūl (arrajool). If the definite article is followed by any other letter, the l is pronounced as l.

**'Abbasi** (*'Abbāsī*). An adjectival form referring to the dynasty that succeeded the Ummawīs and that established its capital in Baghdad. The name is derived from that of Ibn 'Abbās, an uncle of the Prophet, who was the ancestor of the 'Abbāsī rulers.

**'Abd al-'Aziz ibn Su'ud** (*'Abd al-'Azīz ibn Su'ūd*). King of Arabia and founder of the Su'ūdī dynasty. His dates were 1880–1953.

**'Abd al-Qadir al-Jilani** (*'Abd al-Qādir al-Jīlānī*). A famous Ṣūfī and founder of the Qadarīyah order of mystics. His dates were A.D. 1077–1166.

**Abu Bakr** (*Abū Bakr*). A companion of Muḥammad, one of the first converts to Islām, and the first Khalīfah of the community.

**Abu Hanifah** (*Abū Ḥanīfah*). An 'Irāqī jurist of the second Islamic century and the founder of one of the four accepted Sunnī schools of law. He lived between A.D. 700 and 767.

**Abu al-Hasan al-Ash'ari** (*Abū al-Ḥasan al-Ash 'arī*). An early Islamic theologian of great importance. He was the first to use Greek dialectic in the exposition and defense of traditionalist religious doctrines. He was, thus, the father of kalām among Sunnī Muslims. The great majority of Sunnī thinkers have considered themselves to belong to the school of al-Ash'arī. He died in A.D. 935.

**Abu al-Husayn al-Nuri** (*Abū al-Ḥusayn al-Nūrī*). A well known Islamic mystical poet and companion of al-Junayd. He died in A.D. 908.

**Abu Talib** (*Abū Ṭālib*). The uncle of Muḥammad and the father of 'Alī. After Muḥammad was orphaned, he was raised in this uncle's home.

**Abu Yazid al-Bistami** (*Abū Yazīd al-Bisṭāmī*). A celebrated mystic of the third Islamic century who is well known for his preference of the doctrine of mystical intoxication over the doctrine of mystical sobriety and for his ecstatic utterances (shaṭaḥāt). He died in A.D. 874.

**Adan** (*'Adan*). The port city at the southwest tip of the Arabian peninsula.

**Adl** (*'adl*). Justice; in theology, the doctrine of God's justice.

**Agha Khan** (*Aghā Khān*). The title of the leader of one group of Ismā'īlī Muslims. The Aghā Khān's followers are concentrated principally in India, Pakistan, and East Africa. The present Aghā Khān is considered to be the forty-ninth imām of the group.

**Ahl al-bayt.** Lit. the people of the house, meaning the descendants of the Prophet. The political claim of the Shī'ah was that the khilāfah belonged exclusively to the ahl al-bayt.

**Ahl al-sunnah wa al-jama'at** (*ahl al-sunnah wa al-jamā'at*). Lit. the people of established custom and of the community. This is the self designation of the majority group of the Muslim community, those who are commonly called Sunnī.

**Ahmad ibn Hanbal** (*Aḥmad ibn Ḥanbal*). An early Islamic traditionalist famous for the strictness and conservatism of his views, also the founder of one of the four accepted Sunnī schools of law. He lived between A.D. 780 and 855.

**Ahwal** (*aḥwāl*). The spiritual states through which a Ṣūfī passes on the path to mystic union with God.

**Aligarh** (*'Alīgaṛh*). A town in Uttar Pradesh, India, which is the site of the 'Alīgaṛh Muslim University founded by Sir Sayyid Aḥmad Khān in 1875.

**'Ali ibn Abi Talib** (*'Alī ibn Abī Ṭālib*). The son of Muḥammad's uncle, Abū Ṭālib, and the husband of Muḥammad's daughter, Fāṭimah. 'Alī is the first of the imāms recognized by the Shī'ah.

**Allah** (*Allāh*). God. The word is composed of two elements, the Arabic article (al) and a contraction of the term meaning deity (ilāh). It is, thus, not a name for God but simply means "the God," the only God who exists.

**Allahu akbar** (*Allāhu akbar*). Lit. "God is greater," an expression of praise used in the call to prayer, in the prayer itself, and on many other occasions in the Muslim's life.

**Ansar** (*anṣār*). Lit. "helpers," the title bestowed on the followers of Muḥammad in Madīnah. It is contrasted with muhājirīn, or the followers who emigrated with Muḥammad from Makkah.

**Arafat** (*'Arafah*). A large plain near Makkah where pilgrims carry out the ceremony of wuqūf, or standing in the presence of God, which is the heart of the pilgrimage rites.

**Ardabil** (*Ardābīl*). A town in Azarbaijan, now in the northwestern section of Iran. The town was the headquarters of the Ṣūfī order, headed by Shaykh Ṣafīy al-Dīn, which gave rise to the Ṣafawī dynasty of Iran. The despoiled tomb of Shaykh Ṣafīy al-Dīn may still be seen there.

**'Asabiyah** (*'aṣabīyah*). The tie of solidarity among the members of an Arab tribe.

**Al-Awza'i** (*al-Awzā'ī*). An early Syrian jurist whose opinions are representative of the primitive stage of development of Islamic law. He died at approximately age 70 in A.D. 774.

**Ayahs** (*āyah*, pl. *āyāt*). Lit., "sign." In the *Qur'ān* the word means one of the evidences of God's existence and power. It is also used as the name for a Qur'anic verse which constitutes such an evidence.

**Al-Azhar University.** A famous center for Islamic learning established by the Fāṭimī rulers in Cairo in the tenth century. The school attached to the mosque of al-Azhar is perhaps the most famous and most respected such center in the entire Islamic world.

**Badr.** The site of the first and most important military engagement between Muḥammad and the Makkans.

**Balakot** (*Bālākōṭ*). A place in the foothills of the Himalaya where the Mujāhidīn suffered a decisive defeat in 1831 at the hands of the Sikhs.

**Bani Hawazin** (*Banī Hawāzin*). An Arab tribe against whom Muḥammad fought a major military engagement at the Battle of Ḥunayn.

**Baqa'** (*baqā'*). Lit. "remaining," the Ṣūfī expression for a state of mystical attainment beyond even extinction (fanā') in which the soul indwells continually in God.

**Al-Baqillani** (*al-Baqillānī*). A well known Muslim theologian adhering to the school of al-Ash'arī. He is reputed as a foremost exponent of the doctrine of occasionalism, which characterized the Ash'arī school in its later phases. He died in A.D. 1013.

**Barakah.** Blessedness, or even holiness, a quality possessed by the mystic saints (awliyā') through which they exert their governance of the universe.

**Batin** (*bāṭin*). Lit. "hidden" or "concealed," the esoteric aspect of a doctrine or teaching that can be understood only through instruction from an authoritative teacher. The bāṭin is to be contrasted with the ẓāhir or the obvious, evident and, exoteric meaning of a doctrine or practice.

**Batiniyah** (*Bāṭinīyah*). Lit. "esotericists," the name given those of the Shī'ah who emphasize the importance of esoteric teaching in their doctrines. This designation implies extremism in the mouths of the opponents of the Bāṭinīyah. The name derives from the word bāṭin (q.v.).

**Bismillah al-Rahman, al-Rahim** (*Bismillāh al-Raḥmān, al-Raḥīm*). In the Name of God, the Compassionate, the Merciful. This formula occurs at the beginning of each chapter of the *Qur'ān* except one and is repeated for devotional purposes at many points in the Muslim's life.

**Bourgiba** (*Ḥabīb Bourgiba*). The president of the Republic of Tunisia. Prior to the independence of Tunisia he was a nationalist leader and head of the Destour Party. President Bourgiba was born in 1903.

**Al-Bukhari** (*Muḥammad ibn Ismā'īl al-Bukhārī*). Famous Arab traditionist whose ḥadīth collection is the most respected of the Six Sound Books. He lived between A.D. 810 and 880.

**Caliphs.** Khalīfahs (q.v.).

**Dahr.** Time; in the poetry of the pre-Islamic Arabs, considered to be the most powerful of the forces affecting human destiny.

**Da'if** (*ḍa'īf*). Weak. In the classification of traditions, this word refers to those which are least acceptable. In general it designates any tradition having a serious defect in the isnād.

**Dar'iyah.** A town in Arabia which was the headquarters of the Wahhābī Empire in the first phase of its existence. The town was captured by the Egyptians in 1818, and the Wahhābī power went into temporary eclipse.

**Darwishes** (*darwīsh*, pl. *darāwīsh*). A member of a Ṣūfī order, a Ṣūfī adept. The word is sometimes used in special reference to wandering Ṣūfī mendicants.

**Dhikr.** Lit "remembrance," the Ṣūfī ceremony of worship, of a different nature in each order. The principal element in such worship is the repetition of the name of God.

**Druze** (*Durūz*). A religious sect holding Ismā'īlī doctrines now to be found in the mountains of Lebanon and Israel. The group had its origin in religious controversies dating to the time of the Fāṭimīyah in Egypt.

**Fana'** (*fanā'*). Lit. "extinction," the Ṣūfī expression for the loss of personality and identity in the mystic's union with God.

**Faqih** (*faqīh*, pl. *fuqahā'*). An Islamic lawyer or one learned in the science of jurisprudence (fiqh).

**Fard** (*farḍ*). Under Islamic law that which is strictly obligatory, a religious duty whose performance is rewarded and whose neglect is punished. This is one of the five categories into which Islamic law divides all actions.

**Fatimi** (*Fāṭimī*). An adjectival form referring to the Fāṭimīyah, a North African Ismā'īlī dynasty with its capital in Cairo. The dynasty flourished between A.D. 909 and 1171; the period of its reign was one of the most brilliant in the history of Egypt.

**Fatwa** (*fatwā*, pl. *fatāwā*). The opinion of a juriconsult (Muftī) in response to a legal question (istiftā') referred to him. Such opinions do not constitute precedents, and the questions may be put by anyone whether part of the judicial system and the state machinery or not.

**fiqh.** Lit. "understanding." (1) In its oldest Islamic usage a word for theology. It is no longer used in this way. (2) Jurisprudence, the science of finding specific rules of law from the sources. This is the precise use of the word. (3) The body of law, written in books, resulting from the application of jurisprudential science. This is an imprecise and loose use of the word but a common one.

**Fuqaha'.** Pl. of faqīh (q.v.).

**Ibn Furak** (*ibn Fūrak*). Muslim theologian and author of a book entitled *Bayān Mushkil al-Aḥādīth,* which discusses problems in the ḥadīth, especially the problem of conflicting aḥādīth.

**Futuwah** (*futūwah*). (1) Fraternal corporations common in medieval Islām. The members of these corporations normally followed the same trade and lived together a communal existence. (2) The virtues of chivalry. The cultivation of these virtues played an important role in the Islamic guild organizations and in Ṣūfism.

**Al-Ghazali** (*al-Ghazālī;* sometimes *al-Ghazzālī*). An important Muslim philosopher, mystic, theologian, and jurist who died in 1111.

**Ghulat** (*ghulāt*). Lit. "extremists," an epithet applied to certain radical Shī'ah groups who believe that the imām is an incarnation of deity or in similar doctrines.

**Hadith** (*ḥadīth,* pl. *āḥādīth*). Something related or told, an oral report, something said; therefore, oral tradition. In religion ḥadīth refers especially to the reports of the sayings, actions, and approbations of the Prophet Muḥammad handed down from the earliest generations.

**Hadramawt** (*Ḥaḍramawt*). The southernmost section of the Arabian peninsula which borders the Indian Ocean.

**Hafiz** (*Ḥāfiẓ*). One who memorizes the text of the *Qur'ān.*

**Hajj** (*ḥajj*). The pilgrimage to Makkah.

**Halal** (*ḥalāl*). Lit. "untied" or "unbound," i.e., permissible. In Islamic law actions are broadly classified as either forbidden (ḥarām) or as permissible (ḥalāl).

**Al-Hallai** (*al-Ḥallāj*). An important mystic, best remembered for the extremeness of his ecstatic utterances. He was executed in a particularly horrible way in Baghdād in A.D. 922 with the assent of some of the leading mystics of the day. In consequence he has become the great martyr of the Ṣūfī tradition. He is often referred to in mystical literature by the name Manṣūr. al-Ḥallāj lived between 858 and 922.

**Hanbali madhhab** (*Ḥanbalī madhhab*). The school of law founded by the famous traditionist, Aḥmad ibn Ḥanbal.

**Hanafi** (*Ḥanafī*). An adjectival form referring to the legal school founded by the Irāqī jurist, Abū Ḥanīfah.

**Hanifs** (*Ḥanīf,* pl. *Ḥunafā'*). A member of a group of religious seekers contemporary with Muḥammad. The Ḥunafā' appear to have been monotheists.

**Haqa'iq** (*ḥaqīqah,* pl. *ḥaqā'iq*). Lit. "realities." (1) Among Ṣūfīs a term for the attributes of God which are to be distinguished from his essence (dhāt or ḥaqq). (2) Among the Ismā'īlīs a term for the spiritual truths of their philosophical and religious system.

**Haqq** (*ḥaqq*). Lit. "truth" or "reality." This word is used as a designation of God or ultimate reality, especially by the Ṣūfīs.

**Haram** (*ḥarām*). Forbidden, one of the five categories into which all human actions are classified in Islamic law. Acts that are ḥarām are absolutely forbidden under pain of punishment.

**Hasan** (*Ḥasan*). The eldest son of 'Alī ibn Abī Ṭālib by Fāṭimah, the daughter of Muḥammad. He was, therefore, the elder brother of Imām Ḥusayn, the martyr of Karbalā'.

**Hasan** (*ḥasan*). Good or beautiful. In the classification of traditions from the prophet, this word refers to those of the middle category which are acceptable but not perfectly sound.

**Al-Hasan al-Basri** (*al-Ḥasan al-Baṣrī*). An important early Muslim ascetic, mystic, and theologian. His name is associated with the origins of taṣawwuf and with the sects known as the Qadarīyah and the Mu'tazilah. He lived between A.D. 642 and 728, largely in Baṣrah, where he was perhaps the best known religious figure of his day.

**Hijrah.** Flight, the name given to Muḥammad's emigration from Makkah to Madīnah. The Islamic calendar begins from this event.

**Hubal.** A pre-Islamic deity who was the principal god of the Ka'bah in Makkah before Muḥammad's conquest of the city.

**Hud** (*Hūd*). A pre-Islamic prophet mentioned in the *Qur'ān.*

**Hudan.** Guidance, one of the most important words in the Islamic religious vocabulary. The revelations in the *Qur'ān* claim themselves to be hudan for the God-fearing. See Sūrah II.1.

**Al-Hujwiri** (*Abū al-Ḥasan 'Alī al-Hujwīrī*). An Iranian mystic who wrote one of the earliest and most important descriptive works on Ṣūfism, *Kashf al-Maḥjūb* (*The Uncovering of That Which is Veiled*). He lived the latter part of his life in Lahore, where he is buried. He died sometime between 1072 and 1079.

**Hunayn** (*Ḥunayn*). A place near Makkah to the south where Muḥammad fought the greatest and most dangerous battle of his career against the Banī Hawāzin.

**Husayn** (*Ḥusayn*). The younger son of 'Alī ibn Abī Ṭālib by Fāṭimah, the daughter of Muḥammad. When his elder brother renounced claims to the leadership of the community, Ḥusayn took up the cause. He was martyred with his family at Karbalā' by Ummawī troops.

**'Ibadat** (*'ibādāt*). Those religious duties which man owes to God, such as fasting and pilgrimage.

**Ibrahim Pasha** (*Ibrahīm Bāshā*). The son of Muhammad 'Alī Bāshā. Ibrahīm commanded the 1818 Egyptian military expedition to put down the Wahhābīs.

**'Id al-Adha** (*'Īd al-Aḍḥā*). The festival of sacrifice, part of the concluding ceremonies in the rites of the pilgrimage. Pilgrims make their sacrifice at Minā while Muslims who have not made the pilgrimage sacrifice in their respective places. The sacrifice is made in commemoration of Ibrahīm's (Abraham's) willingness to offer his son.

**'Id al-Fitr** (*'Īd al-Fiṭr*). The festival of the breaking of the fast which is celebrated on the first day of the month following Ramaḍān. The festival is an obligatory religious duty, just as the fast which precedes it is also obligatory.

**Ihya' 'Ulum al-Din** (*Iḥyā' 'Ulūm al-Dīn*). The *Revivification of the Religious Sciences,* the most important of the many writings of Abū Ḥāmid al-Ghazālī. The book is encyclopedic in scope and is notable especially for its attempt to weave Ṣūfī ideas and Sunnī doctrine into an integrated whole.

**Ijma'** (*ijmā'*). Consensus or agreement. In the science of jurisprudence ijmā' ranks as one of the roots of the law subordinate in importance to the *Qur'ān* and the sunnah.

**Ijtihad** (*ijtihād*). Exertion or effort, a legal term signifying personal intellectual endeavor toward the solution of a legal problem. The effort meant is that directed to the interpretation of the sources of the law and not free speculation.

**Imam** (*imām,* pl. *ā'immah*). Leader. (1) The leader in prayer. (2) The khalīfah or head of the community. (3) A title given to learned and respected men such as the founders of the schools of law and certain theologians. (4) Among the Shī'ah the word refers to the group of descendants of 'Alī through whom the spark of divine wisdom has been transmitted from father to son.

**Imamah** (*imāmah*). Lit. "leadership." Each of the major Islamic groups and sects has held a view of how and from what group the leader of the community should be chosen. Sunnī Muslims believe that the imām (leader) must be chosen from Quraysh while Shī'ah believe that he must be from the ahl al-bayt. The doctrine of imāmah acquired a special religious coloring among the Shī'ah, who believe the series of imāms to have been chosen by God and each of them to have been the locus of a divine spark of wisdom passed down through the chain of 'Alī's descendants.

**Imam Husayn ibn 'Ali** (*Imām Ḥusayn ibn 'Alī*). The younger son of 'Alī ibn Abī Ṭālib by Fāṭimah, the daughter of Muḥammad. It is he who was martyred by Ummawī troops at Karbalā'. He is given the title Imām as one in the series of persons in 'Alī's line in whom the spark of divine wisdom has come to reside.

**Imam Mahdi** (*Imām Mahdī*). (1) Among the Shī'ah the title given to the hidden Imām whose return is expected. The Imām Mahdī will restore true religion as one of the events of the last days. (2) Among Sunnī Muslims the one who is expected as the restorer of religion in the last days is sometimes called the Mahdī, though not always. The belief in the Mahdī is not essential for Sunnī Muslims as it is for the Shī'ah.

**Iman** (*īmān*). Most often translated "faith," the word refers to the inner attitude of religious commitment and to the resulting certainty of heart.

**Injil** (*Injīl*). An Arabic transcription of the Greek word Gospel. The Islamic name for the Scripture that, according to Muslim belief, was revealed to Jesus.

**Iqra** (*Iqra'*). Read! or Recite! The angel's command to Muḥammad at the time of first revelation.

**'Iraqi** (*'Irāqī*). Referring to the geographical region known as 'Irāq.

**Islam** (*Islām*). (1) The name that Muslims give to their religious commitment as a whole. (2) In theology, the word means works as opposed to faith (īmān).

**Isma'ili** (*Ismā'īlī*). An adjectival form referring to the Ismā'īlīyah, one of the subgroups of Shī'ī Islām. They are in turn divided into several other subsects. They are famous for their belief that exoteric doctrine always has an esoteric counterpart (bāṭin).

**Isnad** (*isnād*). Lit. "foundation" or "support," the list of names of the transmitters of an ḥadīth which constitutes its authority.

**Ithna 'Ashariyah** (*Ithnā 'Asharīyah*). Lit. "twelvers," the largest of the subgroups of Shī'ī Muslims, those who accept a series of twelve imāms.

**Jabariyah** (*Jabarīyah*). An early Islamic sect who believed that all things happen as the result of the direct exercise of the divine compulsive power (Jabr). They were, in other words, determinists.

**Jalal al-Din al-Rumi** (*Jalāl al-Dīn al-Rūmī*. Mystical poet and founder of the Mawlawīyah order, or the order of the Whirling Dervishes. He has been called the greatest of the Persian poets for the beauty of his numerous verses. Born in Balkh in Khūrasān, he lived most of his life in Konyā in Anatolia. His dates were A.D., 1207–1273.

**Jamal al-Din al-Afghani** (*Jamāl al-Dīn al-Afghā-*

*nī*). Muslim politician, agitator and reformer of the nineteenth century. Al-Afghānī played an important role in the contemporary Islamic renaissance. His name indicates that he was of Afghān origin, but the matter is disputed. His dates were 1839–1897.

**Al-Jubba'i** (*al-Jubbā'ī*). An early theologian of the Mu'tazilī school, the teacher of al-Ash'arī, against whom the latter revolted. He lived between A.H. 235 and 303.

**Al-Juwayni** (*al-Juwaynī*). A renowned Muslim jurist and theologian, most often known by the title, Imām al-Ḥaramayn (Imām of the Two Holy Places). He was born in A.D. 1028 and died in 1085.

**Ka'bah** (*Ka'bah*). The cubical stone building in the center of the sacred area of Makkah, called by Muslims the House of God. In pre-Islamic times the Ka'bah was a pagan shrine until Muḥammad cleansed it.

**Kaba'ir** (*kabā'ir*). Lit. "large ones." In Islamic theology the word refers to great sins whose consequences are the severance of the sinner's membership in the community.

**Al-Kafi** (*al-Kāfī*). The most important and respected book of traditions among the Shī'ah. Compiled by al-Kulaynī (d. A.D. 939), it is one of the "four books" that constitute the Shī'ī canon of ḥadīth literature.

**Kalam** (*Kalām*). Speech or word. Both the *Qur'ān* and Jesus are referred to as Kalām Allāh, the Word of God. In the expression 'ilm al-kalām, the science of discussion, the word refers to the activity of producing reasoned arguments for the elucidation and support of religious doctrines. In this sense it can best be translated as "theology." Whenever the word appears alone, it can normally be understood in the sense of "theology." Kalām may also often be translated as "dialectic."

**Kalam Allah** (*Kalām Allāh*). Lit. "the Word of God." Both the *Qur'ān* and Jesus are so designated.

**Karamat** (*karamāt*). The miracles of the Ṣūfī saints.

**Karbala'** (*Karbalā'*). A place in southwestern 'Irāq where Ḥusayn, the younger son of 'Alī ibn Abī Ṭālib and Fāṭimah, the daughter of Muḥammad, was martyred on the tenth day of the month of Muḥarram in A.H. 61 by Ummawī troops. The city is now a place of pilgrimage for Shī'ī Muslims.

**Kasb.** Lit. "acquisition," the doctrine taught by al-Ash'arī with regard to the problem of man's responsibility for his acts. Al-Ash'arī taught that all acts are performed by God's immediate initiative but once performed man acquires (kasb) them. Thus, men are responsible for their acts, and it is in accord with the justice of God that they should be punished or rewarded for what they do.

**Kashf al-Mahjub** (*Kashf al-Maḥjūb*). A treatise on Sufism by Al-Hujwiri (q.v.).

**Khadijah** (*Khadījah*). The widow whom Muḥammad married as his first wife.

**Khalifahs** (*Khalīfah*, pl. *Khulafā'*). Successor, the title of the men who succeeded Muḥammad in the rule of the Islamic community. The word is also used for the favorite disciple of a Ṣūfī shaykh, the one who will succeed to the shaykh's spiritual authority as head of the order upon the shaykh's death.

**Khanqah** (*khānqāh*). The Persian term for the headquarters of a Ṣūfī order. In Turkey and North Africa the corresponding terms are tekke and zāwiyah, respectively.

**Khawarij** (pl. *Khawārij*). Lit. "those who go out," an early Islamic sect with strict puritanical views. The Khawārij believed that the leadership of the community must be determined by the principle of unrestricted election, and the more extreme among them believed the commission of sin to be equivalent to apostasy.

**Khutbah** (*khuṭbah*). The address or sermon following Friday prayers in the mosque.

**Kitab al-Muwatta'** (*Kitāb al-Muwaṭṭa'*). The earliest surviving book of Islamic law, written by the Madīnah jurist, Mālik ibn Anas, who was the founder of one of the four accepted Sunnī schools of law. The book deals with matters of law and religion according to the practice of the people of Madīnah.

**Al-Kulayni** (*Muhammad ibn Ya'kūb al-Rāzī al-Kulaynī*). A highly respected Shī'ī scholar considered by many to be the renewer (mujaddid) of the fourth Islamic century. He was the compiler of the collection of traditions known as al-Kāfī (The Sufficient One).

**Al-Lat** (*al-Lāt*). A pagan goddess of pre-Islamic Arabia.

**Madhhab** (*madhhab*, pl. *madhāhib*). The generic term for the accepted Sunnī schools of law. Literally the word means "way," but it is usually translated as "school."

**Madinah** (*Madīnat-al-Nabī*). The City of the Prophet; the name given by Muslims to the oasis settlement on the Red Sea coastal plain of Arabia to which Muḥammad and his followers emigrated from Makkah. It was known as Yathrib prior to the emigration.

**Makkah.** The city on the Red Sea coastal plain of Arabia where the Prophet, Muḥammad was born and where Islām had its rise.

**Makruh** (*makrūh*). Lit. "hated, disapproved"; in Islamic law one of the five categories into which all human actions are classified. This category includes acts which should be avoided, though they are not subject to punishment.

**Malik ibn Anas** (*Mālik ibn Anas*). A famous traditionist and jurist of Madīnah and founder of one of the four accepted Sunnī schools of law. He lived between approximately 722 and 795 A.D.

**Maliki** (*Mālikī*). An adjectival form referring to

the legal school founded by Mālik ibn Anas, the Madīnah jurist.

**Al-Manat** (*al-Manāt*). A pagan goddess of pre-Islamic Arabia.

**Al-Manar** (*al-Manār*). An Egyptian journal published by Muhammad Rashīd Riḍā from 1897. This publication was the principal vehicle for the spread of the teachings of Muḥammad 'Abduh. The name means "the minaret."

**Mandub** (*mandūb*). Recommended or approved, an action which is not strictly obligatory but which is worthy. This is one of the five categories into which Islamic law classifies human actions.

**Maqamat** (*maqamāt*). The stages or stations on the mystic path to unity with God.

**Marwah** (*al-Marwah*). A small hill or eminence of ground in Makkah which plays a role in the rites of the pilgrimage. Pilgrims run back and forth seven times between al-Marwah and al-Ṣafā, a second hill, to commemorate Hājar's (Haggar's) search for water for her thirsty son. Formerly the hill was the site of a pagan shrine.

**Mashhad,** sometimes **Meshed.** A city in Khurāsān, now included in the northeastern portion of modern Iran, and the capital of the Persian province of Khurāsān. In the year A.D. 818 'Alī al-Riḍā, the eighth imām of the Ithnā 'Asharīyah, died and was buried in this place. An enormous and impressively beautiful shrine has been erected about his grave, and it is the most revered place of pilgrimage for the Shī'ah of Iran.

**Matn.** The text or content of an ḥadīth or oral report about the Prophet. The matn is distinguished from the isnād, or list of supporting authorities.

**Mawlawiyah** (*Mawlawīyah*). The Ṣūfī order founded by Jalāl al-Dīn al-Rūmī with its headquarters at Konyā in Turkey. Members of the order are distinguished by a peculiar costume and a whirling dance to the accompaniment of music. The name derives from the title given to the founder Mawlānā (Our Master). The Turkish form of the word is Mevlevi.

**Mihrab** (*miḥrāb*). The niche in the wall of a mosque that indicates the direction of Makkah.

**Mina** (*Minā*). A town in a narrow valley east of Makkah where the concluding rites of the pilgrimage are performed. These include sacrificing an animal, throwing stones at three small pillars set at intervals in the main street of the town, and clipping the pilgrim's hair and nails.

**Mount Hira'** (*Mount Hirā'*). A hill on the outskirts of Makkah where Muḥammad retired for meditation and nocturnal vigils, also the site of the first revelation to Muḥammad.

**Mu'adhdhin.** The one who calls to prayer, usually from the minaret of the mosque. This word is most often imprecisely transliterated as muezzin and is familiar in that form.

**Mu'amalat** (*mu'āmalāt*). The religious obligations which a man has toward other men.

**Mu'awiyah** (*Mu'āwiyah*). The first Ummawī khalīfah and the founder of the Ummawī dynasty.

**mubah** (*mubāḥ*). Permissible or allowed, in Islamic law one of the five categories into which all human actions are classified. This category includes a wide range of acts that are morally neutral.

**Muhaddithun** (*muḥaddithūn*). Persons learned in the science of ḥadīth, as the traditions of the Prophet are called.

**Muhajirin** (*muhājirīn*). Lit. "emigrants," the title by which are called the Makkan followers of Muḥammad who emigrated with him to Madīnah.

**Muhammad** (*Muḥammad ibn 'Abdullāh*). The prophet of Islām. Muḥammad means "the praised one."

**Muhammad Abduh** (*Muḥammad 'Abduh*). A modern Egyptian reformer, theologian, and jurist of enormous influence. 'Abduh may be considered the founder of Islamic modernism in the Arab world. He was an associate and disciple of Jamāl al-Dīn al Afghānī and held important posts in Egypt that allowed him to effect major reforms in education. The main thrust of his teaching was toward a purified Islam that would be in accord with reason and science. He was born in 1849 and died in 1905.

**Muhammad Ali Jinnah** (*Muḥammad 'Alī Jinnāh*). A Muslim political leader in undivided India who lead the movement for Pākistān. After the partition of India and the creation of Pākistān, he became the first Governor General of Pākistān. His dates were 1876–1948.

**Muhammad 'Ali Pasha** (*Muḥammad 'Alī Bāshā*). An Albanian Muslim who, as Khedive of Egypt under Turkish suzerainty, initiated in the first decades of the nineteenth century a series of educational, economic, and military reforms of far-reaching consequences. He lived between 1769 and 1849.

**Muhammad ibn 'Abd al-Wahhab** (*Muḥammad ibn 'Abd al-Wahhāb*). An eighteenth century Islamic reformer who led a movement to restore and purify Islam. His principal concern was to purge Islām of all innovations (bid'āt), especially those introduced by the Ṣūfīs, such as the reverence for saints. The school of his followers is called Wahhābīyah, and the sect is prevalent today in Sa'ūdī Arabia where it has connection with the ruling house. His dates are 1703–1787.

**Muhammad Ghori** (*Muḥammed Ghōrī*). The ruler of a kingdom in what is now Western Afghanistan. In the middle of the twelfth century this man conquered North India and founded the Sultanate of Delhi.

**Muhammad Rashid Rida** (*Muḥammad Rashīd

*Riḍā*). A Syrian disciple of Muḥammad 'Abduh and the publisher of the journal *Al-Manār*. Riḍā was largely responsible for the widespread dissemination of 'Abduh's ideas and for the interpretation of them that led to the Salafīyah movement.

**Muharram** (*Muḥarram*). The name of one of the months in the Islamic lunar calendar. It is of religious importance because the Shī'ah celebrate the passion and martyrdom of Imām Ḥusayn during the early part of the month, culminating on the tenth day, the anniversary of his tragic death.

**Muhiy al-Din ibn al-'Arabi** (*Muḥīy al-Dīn ibn al-'Arabī*). An Andalusian mystic whose teachings of pantheism have wielded an enormous influence on the history of later Sufism. He lived between A.D. 1165 and 1240, the first part of his life in Spain and the latter in the Eastern Islamic regions.

**Mu'in al-Din Chishti** (*Mu'īn al-Dīn Chishtī*). A famous mystic saint of the Chishti order who was a contemporary of the Emperor Akbar and through whose intercession a son was born to the Emperor. The Chishti order is among the most important in India where it is widely spread.

**Mujahidin** (*Mujāhidīn*). Lit. those who strive or make jihād, the holy war in the cause of Islām; a title adopted by the members of an Islamic revivalist movement in the Frontier region of India in the early nineteenth century.

**Muqallad.** One who accepts the opinions of a founder of one of the four accepted Sunnī schools of law as absolutely authoritative, or one who acts in obedience to blind authority in legal matters.

**Murids** (*murīd*, pl. *murīdūn*). Lit. "desirer," the Ṣūfī neophyte, seeker, or student who attaches himself to a shaykh in order to gain instruction and guidance in the Ṣūfī path (ṭarīqah).

**Murji'ah.** An early Islamic sect who held the position that commission of sin does not place one outside the community; rather, the decision is left to God.

**Murshid.** Lit. "guide," the title given to a Ṣūfī master, teacher, or shaykh by his disciples.

**Muslim ibn al-Hajjaj** (*Muslim ibn al-Ḥajjāj*). A famous collector of traditions from the Prophet. His ḥadīth collection along with that of al-Bukhārī are the two most respected of the Six Sound Books.

**Mutasawwif** (*mutaṣawwif*). A Muslim mystic or Ṣūfī, one who is an adept in taṣawwuf.

**Mu'tazilah** (*Mu'tazilah*). The name of the great theological school, also called the People of Unity and Justice, who were the true founders of Muslim dialectical theology. The school originated in Ummawī times and for some period enjoyed the patronage of the 'Abbāsī rulers before it disappeared.

**Najaf** (al-Najaf). A town in southwestern 'Irāq near Kūfah that is believed to be the burial place of 'Alī ibn Abī Ṭālib. It is, in consequence, a place of sanctity and pilgrimage for Shī'ī Muslims.

**Najd.** The high central plateau of the Arabian peninsula.

**Al-Nazzam** (*al-Naẓẓām*). An early Islamic thinker of the Mu'tazilī school. He was a poet and dialectician but above all a theologian. He died between A.D. 735 and 745 at an unknown date.

**Nihavand** (*Nihāvand*). A place near modern Hamadān in Iran where the Arab Muslim armies won a decisive victory over the Sassanians. The Battle of Nihāvand brought the Iranian plateau under Muslim control.

**Nusayris** (*Nuṣayrī*). An extreme Shī'ī sect of Syria.

**Pir** (*pīr*). The title given to a Ṣūfī master or shaykh, especially in the Indian subcontinent.

**Qadariyah** (*Qadarīyah*). (1) The name of an early Muslim sect which upheld the doctrine of free-will believing that man has the power (qadar) to control his own actions. (2) The name of a mystic order (ṭarīqah) founded by the saint 'Abd al-Qādir al-Jīlānī.

**Qadi** (*al-qāḍī*). The judge in one type of Islamic court.

**Qiblah.** The direction which the Muslim faces for prayer, i.e., the direction of Makkah.

**Qiyas** (*qiyās*). Analogy. In jurisprudence qiyās is considered one of the roots of the law, though it is subordinate to all of the remaining three.

**Qum.** A city in central Iran where is located the tomb and shrine of Fāṭimah al-Ma'ṣūmah, the sister of Imām 'Alī al-Riḍā, the eighth imām of the Ithnā 'Asharīyah. After Mashhad, it is the second most important place of pilgrimage for the Shī'ah of Iran.

**Qur'an** (*Qur'ān*). The Islamic Scripture.

**Quraysh.** The tribe into which Muḥammad was born.

**Qusayy** (*Quṣayy*). An ancestor of Muḥammad who was responsible for the Quraysh gaining possession of Makkah.

**Qutb** (*Quṭb*). The Pole or Axis, the great mystic saint who stands at the apex of the heirarchy of Ṣūfī saints that is always present in the world.

**Rabi'ah al-'Adawiyah** (*Rābi'ah al-'Adawīyah*). An early woman mystic of Baṣrah who was famous for her ascetic life and her teachings on mystic love. She lived between A.D. 714 and 801, chiefly in Baṣrah.

**Rahbar.** Leader, a title given to a Ṣūfī teacher, master, or saint.

**Ramadan** (*Ramaḍān*). The month of the Islamic lunar calendar in which fasting is obligatory during daylight hours.

**Risalat al-Tawhid** (*Risālat al-Tawḥīd*). *Treatise*

*on the Unity of God,* the title of the principal work on theology of Muḥammad 'Abduh.

**Riyadh** (*Riyāḍ*). A city in east central Arabia, the capital of the Kingdom of Sa'ūdī Arabia.

**Saf** (*ṣāf*). Pure, one of the words which scholars have cited as the possible origin of the term, Ṣūfī. Were this etymology accepted, which by and large it is not, then the word Ṣūfī would mean "seeker after purity."

**Safa** (*al-Ṣafā*). A small hill or eminence of ground in Makkah which plays a role in the rites of the pilgrimage. Pilgrims run back and forth seven times between al-Ṣafā and al-Marwah, a second hill, to commemorate Hājar's (Haggar's) search for water for her thirsty son. Formerly the hill was the site of a pagan shrine.

**Safawi** (*Ṣafawī*). An adjectival form referring to the Persian dynasty of the sixteenth and seventeenth centuries. Under this dynasty Iran enjoyed one of the most brilliant periods of its cultural expression, especially under the greatest of Ṣafawī rulers, Shāh 'Abbās.

**Sagha'ir** (*saghā'ir*). Lit. "little ones." In theology the word refers to minor sins that may be forgiven and which do not affect one's membership in the community.

**Sahih** (ṣaḥīḥ). Sound, healthy, right. In the classification of traditions from the Prophet the category "ṣaḥīḥ" designates the strongest and most reliable traditions. For this reason the word is applied to the six most respected collections of traditions known as the Six Sound Books. Ṣaḥīḥ is also frequently used as the title of each of the two collections of ḥadith by Muslim and al-Bukhārī. Together they are called by the dual form, Ṣaḥīḥayn.

**Salat** (*ṣalāt*). The ritual prayer which each believing Muslim is obligated to perform five times daily.

**Salih** (*Ṣāliḥ*). One of the pre-Islamic prophets mentioned in the *Qur'ān.*

**Saljuq Turks** (*Saljūq Turks*). A people of Central Asian origin who entered the 'Abbasī territories in the eleventh century and rapidly rose to become the ruling group in the 'Abbasī empire.

**Sanusiyah** (*Sanūsīyah*). One of the most important mystic orders of North Africa founded by Sīdī Muḥammad ibn 'Alī al-Sanūsī (born A.D. 1791). This widespread order was the spearhead of resistance to Italian imperialism in North Africa in the first part of the twentieth century.

**Sawm** (*ṣawm*). Fasting.

**Sayyid Ahmad Khan** (*Sayyid Aḥmad Khān*). An Indian Muslim thinker and leader of the nineteenth century. He was the founder of the college at 'Alīgaṛh in the United Provinces which later became the 'Alīgaṛh Muslim University. He was born in 1817 and died in 1898.

**Sayyid Amir 'Ali** (*Sayyid Amīr 'Alī*). Indian Muslim modernist and polemicist of the late nineteenth and twentieth centuries. He was a member of the Ismā'īlī community and a judge in the Indian High Court. His book, *The Spirit of Islam,* is perhaps the most widely read of all Islamic modernist writings. He lived between 1849 and 1928.

**Sayyid Jamal al-Din al-Afghani** (*Sayyid Jamāl al-Dīn al-Afghānī*). A nineteenth century Muslim pamphleteer and politician who led a vigorous movement against European imperial domination of the Islamic world. He traveled widely, attracted many disciples, and had a part in important political events in several different Islamic countries. He was born in 1839 and died in 1897.

**Shafi'i** (*Shāfi'ī*). An adjectival form referring to the legal school founded by the jurist, al-Shāfi'ī.

**Al-Shafi'i** (*Abū 'Abdullāh Muḥammad ibn Idrīs al-Shāfi'ī*). The famous jurist who was the founder of the Shāfi'ī school of law, one of the four accepted Sunnī schools. It is he who formulated and promulgated the theory of the four uṣūl al-fiqh. He lived between A.D. 767 and 820.

**Shahadah** (*shahādah*). Witness; the short testimony of faith that reads, "There is no God but the one God, and Muḥammad is His Prophet."

**Shah 'Abd al-'Aziz** (*Shāh 'Abd al-'Azīz*). One of the sons of Shāh Walīy Ullāh Dihlawī who promulgated the teachings of his father to others after him. He played a key role in the early nineteenth century in the development of Muslim consciousness, especially through his famous decision declaring India to be Dār al-Ḥarb, the Abode of War.

**Shah Wali Ullah** (*Shāh Walīy Ullāh*). Called the traditionist (muḥaddith) of Delhi (Dihlawī), an eighteenth century Indian Muslim reformer who led a movement for the restoration of Islam and the recouping of Muslim political fortunes in India during the time of decline of the Mughul Empire. His dates were A.D. 1703–1762/3.

**Shari'ah** (*sharī'ah*). Lit. "pathway," the normative pathway in which God wills that men should walk; therefore, a general name for the Islamic law.

**Shaykh.** Lit. "elder." (1) The title given to the man recognized as the leader of an Arab tribe. (2) A title of respect bestowed upon any learned or accomplished man. (3) A title given to a Ṣūfī master, teacher, or saint.

**Shi'ah** (*Shī'ah*). Lit. "party," one the major groups into which the Muslim community is divided. The original Shī'ah were distinguished by their view that leadership of the community after Muḥammad belonged by right to 'Alī. In later times the Shī'ah developed a distinctive religious point of view in which the principal element is the doctrine of the imamate.

**Shirk.** Polytheism, or the act of associating partners with God. Shirk is the most heinous sin in the Islamic catalogue.

**Sifat** (*ṣifah,* pl. *ṣifāt*). Qualities or attributes; in theology, the attributes of God.

**Silsilah.** Lit. "chain." (1) The chain of authorities making up the isnād of an ḥadīth. (2) The chain of spiritual authorities through whom the esoteric teaching of a Ṣūfī order has been transmitted.

**Subhan Allāh** (*subḥān Allāh*). "Praise be to God," an expression of adoration employed in Muslim worship and other times in Muslim life.

**Sufi** (*Ṣūfī*). A Muslim mystic. Originally the word referred to an ascetic practice of wearing rough robes of wool (ṣūf) but has come to be a designation of the Islamic mystical tradition altogether.

**Sufism.** The usual Western word for Islamic mysticism. Clearly, it is derived from Ṣūfī.

**Sunnah.** Established practice or custom; the recognized, accepted, and time-honored way of doing things. For all Muslims the word sunnah has a normative connotation, especially in matters of religion.

**Sunni** (*Sunnī*). A term applied to the majority group of Muslims, those who claim for themselves the title ahl al-sunnah wa al-jama-'at. It is sometimes translated orthodox, but this rendition is inaccurate. Sunnī is to be contrasted with Shī'ah.

**Surah** (*Sūrah*). A chapter in the *Qur'ān*.

**Al-Tabari** (*Abū Ja'far Muḥammad ibn Jarīr al-Ṭabarī*). Arab historian, jurist, and theologian. He is best known for two monumental works, his *History of Prophets and Kings* and his great commentary on the *Qur'ān*. He lived between A.D. 839 and 923.

**Al-Taftazani** (*Sa'd al-Dīn al-Taftāzānī*). An important Muslim thinker who lived between A.H. 722 and 791. Author of a well known commentary on the creed of al-Naṣafī

**Takhdhib** (*takhdhīb*). Giving the lie to someone or accusing someone of being a liar. In the *Qur'ān* the act of giving the lie to God in the sense of considering His revealed words to be a lie is among the most reprehensible of sins.

**Taqlid** (*taqlīd*). Blind acceptance of authority; the doctrine that one must follow absolutely the teachings of one of the accepted four schools of law without resort to the roots of law and without exercising personal interpretation.

**Tariqah** (*ṭarīqah*). Lit. "pathway," the word used to designate one of the mystic orders or brotherhoods. The pathway is that leading to union with God, and it can be known only through the instruction given by a saint (walī) who has trod it.

**Tasawwuf** (*taṣawwuf*). Mysticism in its Islamic expression.

**Tawhid** (*tawḥīd*). Lit. "Unity," the doctrine of the unity of God which is the cardinal principle of Islamic theology.

**Ta'ziyahs.** (1) Popular dramatizations of the passion and martyrdom of the Shī'ī imāms. (2) Model buildings, often very elaborate, carried by Indian Shī'ī Muslims in processions on the tenth day of Muḥarram to symbolize the tomb of Imām Ḥusayn at Karbalā'. These models are destroyed at the conclusion of the procession and rebuilt the following year.

**Tekke.** The Turkish term for the headquarters of a Ṣūfī brotherhood. In North Africa and Iran the corresponding terms are zāwiyah and khānqāh, respectively.

**Uhud** (*Uḥud*). A hill on the outskirts of Madīnah where the Makkans won an indecisive victory over Muḥammad and his followers. The battle of Uḥud was potentially disastrous for Muḥammad, and though he was wounded, the Makkans did not follow up their advantage.

**'Umar ibn al-Khattab** (*'Umar ibn al-Khattāb*). A companion of Muḥammad, one of the first converts to Islām, and the second Khalīfah of the community. During the reign of 'Umar the first wave of the great conquests was carried out.

**Ummah.** Community or sometimes nation. The Islamic community is called an ummah in the *Qur'ān*, and the term is applied to other groups as well.

**Ummawi** (Ummawī). An adjectival form referring to the Banī Ummayah, a clan of Quraysh, from whom all the khalīfahs of the Ummawī dynasty were drawn.

**Usul** (*uṣūl*). Roots or principles. (1) The principles of any science or branch of learning. (2) In law, used in the phrase uṣūl al-fiqh, the reference is to the four roots or sources of the law.

**Usul al-fiqh** (*uṣūl al-fiqh*). The roots or sources of the law, a technical term in jurisprudence. The roots of the law are four: *Qur'ān;* sunnah; ijmā'; and qiyās.

**'Uthman ibn 'Affan** (*'Uthmān ibn 'Affān*). A companion of Muḥammad and third Khalīfah of the community. 'Uthmān was murdered by a group of dissidents.

**Al-'Uzza** (al-'Uzzā). A pagan goddess of pre-Islamic Arabia. She had a shrine not far from Makkah.

**Wahhabi** (*Wahhābī*). An adjectival form referring to the sect constituted by the followers of Muḥammad ibn 'Abd al-Wahhāb, the eighteenth century Arabian reformer; also, a member of that sect. The sect is noted for its puritanism and its zeal. The sect is now prevalent in Sa'ūdī Arabia because of its association with the ruling dynasty.

**Walis** (*Walī* pl. *awliyā'*). A mystic saint, one to whom the esoteric knowledge of the mystic path (ṭarīqah) is given and who possesses the power of miracles (karamāt) and of blessing (barakah). Muslims believe there to be a hierarchy of saints always living in the world and culminating in a principal saint called the Pole (Quṭb).

**Waṣil ibn 'Ata** (*Wāṣil ibn 'Aṭā'*). An early Muslim thinker, commonly said to be the originator of the Mu'tazilī school. He lived between A.D. 699 and 749.

**Wuquf** (*wuqūf*). Lit. "halt," the standing in the presence of God that is part of the pilgrimage. The wuqūf in the plain of 'Arafah is the heart of the pilgrimage, but there are other occasions of wuqūf in the pilgrimage, as well.

**Yathrib.** An oasis city on the Red Sea coastal plain of Arabia to which Muḥammad and his followers emigrated when their situation in Makkah became impossible. It was afterwards known as Madīnat al-Nabī, the City of the Prophet.

**Zabur** (*Zabūr*). The Islamic name for the Psalms of David.

**Zakat** (*zakāt*). The alms "in the way of God" which every believing Muslim is obligated to pay as part of his religious duty.

**Zawiyah** (*zāwiyah*). The name given at present in North Africa to the headquarters of a Ṣūfī brotherhood. In Turkey and Iran the corresponding terms are tekke and khānqāh, respectively.

**Zayd ibn Thabit** (*Zayd ibn Thābit*). One of the Prophet's secretaries who wrote down the revelations and, according to most accounts, was responsible for assembling the extant text of the *Qur'ān* in its present form.

**Zaydi** (*Zaydī*). An adjectival form referring to the Zaydīyah, one of the subgroups of Shī'ī Muslims. The sect recognizes Zayd, the son of Ḥasan, 'Alī's oldest male offspring, as the carrier of the imāmah instead of Ḥusayn, 'Alī's younger son. The sect is found today in Yemen and is noted for its adherence to Mu'tazilī views in theology.

**Zuhada'** (*zāhid*, pl. *zuhadā'*). Ascetics, practitioners of zuhd.

# INDEX

Athenagoras, 58
Augustine, Bishop of Hippo, 84–89
Augustine, Saint, 48, 65, 90, 93, 138
*Augustinus,* 91
Augustus, 45
Aurelius, Marcus, 44, 56
Ave Marias, 116
Awza'i, al-, 189
Awrangzeb, 217
Azariah, Rabbi, 96
Azhar University, 219

Baal Shem Tov, 109–110
Babylonian exile, 14–15, 18–19, 29, 42–43, 72, 74
Babylonian Talmud, 75
Badr, battle at, 167
Bahya Ibn Pakuda, 106, 109
Bani Hawazin, 167
baptism, 60, 85–86
  of Jesus, 34
Baptists, 143
*baqa',* 203
Baqillani, al-, 181–182
Barclay, Robert, 93
Barnabites, 144
Basil, 65, 66, 81
bathing rituals, in Islam, 193
Batiniyah, *see* Isma'ilis
Battle of Balakot, 218
Battle of the Ditch, 167
Battle of Hunayn, 167
Battle of Nihavand, 169
Battle of Uhud, 167
behavior, *see* morality
ben Bag Bag, Rabbi, 77
ben Maimon, Moses, 102
Benedict of Nursia, 65, 66, 70
Benedictine monastery at Cluny, 65, 129
Benedictines, 65
Berdyaev, Nicholas, 119
Berengarius, 113
Bernard, Saint, 90
*Bet Joseph,* 108
Beyond, the, 111–112, 127
Bible
  critical study of, 135
  and Israelis in exile, 16–18
  and Lutheranism, 141
  *See also* New Testament; Old Testament
biblical religion
  contemporary situation of, 150–152
  covenant as foundation of, 3–7
  effects of, 127–128
  *See also* Christianity; Judaism, etc.
bishops of Catholic Church, 61–62
*Bismillah al-Rahman, al-Rahim,* 174–175
blood feuds, of pre-Islamic Arabs, 163
Bolsheviks, 215
Book of Acts, 42, 66
*Book of Beliefs and Opinions, The,* 101
Book of Common Prayer, 115
Book of Daniel, 26, 37
Book of Isaiah, 16
Book of Judges, 7
Book of Leviticus, 19
Book of Psalms, 116, 121
Book of Revelation, 119
*Book of Splendor,* 107
*Book of Sports,* 115
Bossuet, Bishop, 146
Bound, Nicholas, 115
bourgeoisie
  and Calvinism, 141–142
  Jewish, 148
bread and wine, *see* Eucharist
Breviary, 116
British
  and Mughal Empire, 215
  and Mujahidin, 218
  *See also* England
brotherhood, *see tariqah*
Brothers of the Common Life, 136, 144
Brunner, Emil, 119
Bruno, Saint, 129
Bucer, 144, 145
Buddhism, and Islam, 179
Bukhari, al-, 187–188
Byzantium, 82

Caesarea Philippi, 33
Cairo, Fatimis in, 211
calendar, Judaic, 19, 121–122
Calvin, John, 91–93, 114, 141–142, 144
  *See also* Calvinism
Calvinism, 141–145
Canaan, conquest of, 6
Capuchins, 144
Caraffa, Gian Pietro, 144, 145
Carthusians, 129
Cassianus, John, 88
Catellio, Sabastian, 145
Cathari, 130
Catholic Church
  and Counter-Reformation, 144–145
  distinction between clergy and laity in, 66
  emergence of, 61–63
  and Jansenism, 91
  and modern-day problems, 151
  and Montanism, 63
  as "mother," 83
  and purgatory, 89
  revolts against, 62–63
  role of, 127–131
  *See also* Roman Catholic Church
"Catholic consciousness," 60–61
Catholic Counter-Reformation, *see* Counter-Reformation
Celestius, 87
celibacy, and Montanism, 63
cenobitic, 64
Central Asia, 215, 221
Cerdo, 59
charity, *see* almsgiving
Charles Borromeo, Saint, 150
Chiliastic phenomena, 70
Christ, *see* Jesus Christ
Christian Church
  early life in, 59
  and Gnosticism, 59–60
  in second century, 56
  *See also* Christianity
Christian community, ideal, 70
Christianity
  and Apologists, 58–59
  Augustine on, 84–89
  beginnings of, 29–33
  Chiliastic phenomena in, 70
  and Christology, 51–56
  crisis of sixteenth century in, 133–136
  and church-state issue, 131–133
  and Constantine, 80
  and Counter-Reformation, 144–145
  and differentiation of Holy Spirit from Christ, 63
  and early gentile world, 42–45
  and early Jewish sects, 29–31
  and emergence of Catholic Church, 61–63
  in Greece and Rome, 43–45
  and Gnosticism, 50–51, 59–61
  and Greek philosophy, 47–48, 78–79
  and Hebraic law, 32
  and independence from Jewish nation, 40–41
  in institutionalization of Christian Church, 56–63, 127–128
  and interpretations of Christ, 51–56
  and Islam, 179
  and Jesus of Nazareth, 34–42
  Jewish converts to, 32–33
  and Judaism, 31–33, 115, 136–139
  and modern Islam, 219–220
  and monasticism, 63–68
  and Muslim invasions, 170
  and mystery cults, 46–47
  and mysticism, 118–119
  and passion and death of Jesus, 36–39
  post-Apostolic, 56–63
  and resurrection of Jesus, 38–39
  and secularization and science, 145–147
  and Stoicism, 48–49
  theological conflicts in, 78–84
  and this-worldly existence, 151–152
  traditions of, 68–70
  and Western culture, 126–127
  worship and prayer in, 111–118
  *See also* Christians; Catholic Church; Protestantism, Roman Catholic Church
Christians
  attitude toward Jews, 137–139
  and Muhammad, 172
Christmas, 115
Christology, 51–56, 79–83, 136
*Chronicle,* 96
*Church History,* 80
Church of England, 83–84, 114–115, 119, 142
Church-state conflict
  Augustine on, 86
  and Christianity, 131–133
  and crisis of sixteenth century, 133–136
  and *zakat,* 196
Cicero, 48
circumambulation of temple, 196
circumcision, of early Christians, 41–42
Cistercian monks, 116, 129
*City of God,* 86, 93–94, 138
City of the Prophet, *see* Madinat al-Nabi
civilization, and Christianity, 126–127
clan solidarity, *see 'asabiyah*
clans, *see* sects
Clement of Alexandria, 58, 83, 89
"cluniac reformation," 65, 129

Cluny, 65
*Collationes,* 88
Colloquy of Regensburg, 144
Commandments, *see* Ten Commandments
*Commentary to the Mishnah,* 102, 104
*Commonitorium,* 88
communion of bread and wine, 39
confession
in Judaism, 124
origins of, 66
Confession of Augsburg, 144
*Confessions,* 84, 87
Congregationalists, 143
consensus, see ijma', 188
Constantine, decree of, 115
Constantine, Emperor, 80
Constitution of Madinah, 166
constitutions of Muslim states, 191
consubstantiation, 113–114
Contarini, Cardinal, 144
convents, 64
conversion
of Augustine, 85–86
to Christianity, 60, 62
of Christians to Judaism, 138
among diaspora Jews, 44
of al-Ghazali, 204
of Jews to Christianity, 32–33
to Judaism, 22–24
in Judaism and Christianity, 47
Cordovero, Moses, 109
corruption, in Christian Church, 133
Council at Carthage, 87
Council of Chalcedon, 81, 82, 83
Council at Constantinople, 81
Council of Ephesus, 83
Council at Nicea, 80
Council of Trent, 114, 145
Counter-Reformation, 144–145
courts, Islamic, 190
covenant of God with Israel, 3–7
and Christianity, 32–33
"cradle Christians," 62
creation myth, of Lurianic mystics, 98–99
crimes, in Islamic law, 185, 191
crucifixion, 82
Crusades, persecution of Jews during, 96
cults
of Ka'bah, 165
Sufi, *see* Sufism
*See also under individual names of*
culture
of diaspora Jews, 22
Greek, 43
Hellenistic, 48
Jewish assimilation of, 18, 20
secularization of, 146
Cynics, 48–49
Cyprian of Carthage, 61, 87, 113
Cyril of Jerusalem, Saint, 81
Cyrus, King, 19

*dahr,* 162
Damascus, 169
Ummawi rulers of, 177–178
Damasus, Bishop of Rome, 81
Daniel, 26
*darwishes,* 206
"daughters of Allah," 162
David, 96, 172
Davidic line, 34
day of Rejoicing in the Law, 122
Day of Atonement, *see* Yom Kippur
*De incarnatione,* 81
*De Mortibus Persecutorum,* 80
dead, *see* death
Dead Sea, 27
Dead Sea Scrolls, 30, 32
death
of Athanasius, 81
of Jesus, 37
of Muhammad, 167, 168
of Peter and Paul, 56
of *shaykh,* 206
Decius, 56
Defensor Pacis, 132
*Dei Genetrix,* 83
deities
of pre-Islamic Arabs, 162
*See also* gods; goddesses; *and individual names of*
Demeter, 45
demons, Jesus' victory over, 36
Deutero-Isaiah, 16–18, 22–23
Jesus as Servant of, 112
Deuteronomy, 33, 47
*devotio moderno,* 135–136
*dhikr* ritual, 205
*Dialogues,* 89
diaspora Jews, 22
of Babylonia, 72, 74
and hellenistic culture, 42–43
and Mishnah, 75
and rabbinical rule, 72, 74–77
*Didache,* 59
dietary laws, in early Christian era, 41–42
Diggers, 143
Diocletian, 79–80
disciples, 33, 39
as "Christians," 43
divine justice, and Islam theology, 180
Divine Office, 116
divine origin of Jesus, 55
Divine Reality, union with, 203–205
Divine Word, *see* Logos
divinities, *see* deities; gods
divorce, Islamic regulation of, 191
Docetists, 59, 80
Dominic, Saint, 116, 129
Dominican Order, 116, 129
"dominion," concept of, 130
Domitian, 56
Donatism, Augustine and, 85
"Door of Ijtihad," 190, 191
Druze, 211
dualism, Gnostic, 51, 59
*Duties of the Heart,* 106, 109
dynamis, 36

Easter, 39, 115
Easter Sunday, 115
Eastern Europe
and Hasidism, 109–110
and Muslim invasions, 170
Eastern Orthodox Church
definition of Triune God in, 82
Eucharistic service of, 113
liturgical calendar of, 116
and monasticism, 65
on Original Sin, 89
Edict of Toleration, 80
education, and rise of philosophy, 49
Egypt
and Israelites, 3–4, 12
Israeli exodus from, *see* Exodus from Egypt
Jewish community in, 43, 102
monasticism in, 66
election, doctrine of, 136
Eleusinian mysteries, 45
Elijah, 9–10, 34, 58
Elizabeth I, Queen, 142
emancipation, *see* liberation
En Sof, 108
England, Reformation in, 142
Enoch, 27
Epicureanism, 48
Epiphanius of Salamis, 80, 81
*Epistle ad Lucidim,* 89
*Epistle to the Romans,* 84
*Epistle to the Smyrnans,* 113
Erasmus, 136
esoteric teaching of Isma'ilis, 211
Essenes, 27, 30
ethics
of Judaism, 10
*See also* morality
Eucharist, 57, 89, 112–114
eunuchs, 64
Europe
and church-state conflict, 131
and Islamic world, 214–216
and Reformation, 139–143
rise of secular states in, 145–147
*See also* Eastern Europe, Western culture
excommunication
of Luther, 140
of "Spirituals," 129
exile of 1492, 98
Exile of Israelis, 14–19, 95
and Lurianic mysticism, 98–99
second, 71–77
existence, in philosophy, 49–50
Exodus from Egypt, 3–4, 122
Ezekiel, 15
chariot vision of, *see maaseh merkavah*
Ezra, 20, 29

faith, *see imam*
Fall, the, 90, 91
*fana',* 203
faqihs, 185, 191
*fard,* 184
fasting,
and Montanism, 63
in Islamic worship, 195
in month of Ramadan, *see sawm*
father-god, 80
Fatimi dynasty of Egypt, 211
Faustus of Rhegium, 88–89
feast of Deliverance, *see* Passover
feast of the Epiphany, 115
feast of Jesus' circumcision, 115
feast of the Nativity, 115
feast of Pentecost, 115
Feast of Tabernacles, 20
feasts of saints, 115
festival of the breaking of the fast, *see* 'Id al-Fitr
festival of sacrifice, *see* 'Id al-Adha

festival of Weeks, *see* Shavuot
festivals
  in Jewish year, 122
  *See also under specific names of*
*fiqh,* 199, 212
First Baptist Confession of Faith, The, 93
Five Books of the Law, *see* Torah
Five Pillars of Islam, 192–197
flagellation, 210
4 Ezra, 27
Francis of Assisi, Saint, 129
Francis de Sales, Saint, 150
Franciscan Order, 129, 135
free will, 89–92
  Augustine on, 86
  Bernard on, 90
  in Islamic theology, 178

Gabriel, angel, 173
Galatians, 41
Galilee, 33
Galileo, 146
Gallus, 79
Gamaliel II, 72
Gaon, Elijah, 109–110
genealogy, 163
Genesis, *see maaseh bereshit*
gentile religion, *see* Christianity
gentile world, early Christianity in, 43–45
Ghazali, al-, 179, 195
ghetto, Jewish, 138
*gnosis,* 50
Gnosticism, 50, 59, 128
  and Christianity, 59–61, 69, 78
God
  Augustinian concept of, 88
  as center of worship, 112
  in Christian Church, 79
  covenant with Israel of, 3–7
  and Gnosticism, 50–51
  in Islamic theology, 183–184
  and Jesus of Nazareth, 36
  in Jewish prayers, 120
  as Lord of history, 32
  in Lurianic mystical thought, 98
  and mysticism, 118–119
  *Qur'an* as words of, 172–173
  *See also* Godhead; gods
Godbearer, *see theotokos*
goddesses
  of pre-Islamic Arabs, 162
  *See also under individual names of*
Godhead
  and Holy Spirit, 81
  prayer to, 117
gods, Greek, 44–45
Good Mind, *see* Vohu Manah
"good works," 140
Gospel of Thomas, 51
Gospel of Truth, 51
Gospels
  Fourth, 53, 54–56, 57, 119
  on Jesus, 34–42
  of Matthew and Luke, 36
  and monasticism, 64
Gottschalk, 92
government, *see* church-state conflict; religious law
grace, 90, 130, 136
  Augustine on, 86
  Jansen on, 91
Gratianus, 66
Greek language, diaspora Jews and, 43
Greek philosophy, 47–50
  and Christianity, 58–59, 78–79
  and Islam, 180
  *See also* philosophy
Greeks
  influence on Mu'tazilah, 180
  and Judaism, 22
Gregory the Great, Pope, 89
Gregory VII, Pope, 66, 129, 130, 134
Gropper, 144
guerilla warfare of Maccabee, 24–25
guidance, *see hudan*
*Guide for the Perplexed,* 102–103, 104
*Guide for the Perplexed of Our Time, The,* 105

Ha-Meiri, 137–138
Habad movement, 110
*hadith,* 187
Hafiz, 173
Hagar, 136
*Haggadah,* 18
*hajj,* 196
*halakah,* 74, 76, 77
*halal,* 184
Halevi, Judah, 105–106, 125
Hallaj, al-, 204
Hanafi, 189
Hanbali, 189
Hanbali *madhhab,* 190
Hanifs, 162
haqa'iq, 211
*haram,* 184
Hasan al-Basri, al-, 201, 209
Hasidism, 24, 29, 99–100, 109–110
Hasmoneans, 25
Hay, Malcolm, 139
Hebrew Christians, 42
Hebrew Law, *see* Judaic law; Law of Moses
Hebrews, *see* Israelis; Jews
hellenistic period
  Judaism during, 22–100
  philosophical schools of, 48–49
hellenizing decrees of 168, 25
Heracleitus, 58
Hermas, 59, 89
hidden God, *see* En Sof, 108
High Holy Days, *see* Rosh Hashanah
higher religions, *see* historic religions
Hildebrand, 129
Hillel, 75
Hincmar of Reims, Archbishop, 92
Hippolytus, 60
*hirah,* 165
history, and Yahweh, 6–7
Holy Eucharist, 85
  *See also* Eucharist
Holy Spirit, 63
  relationship to Godhead, 81
holy war, and Israelites, 7
*homoousion,* 81
Honorius II, Pope, 67
*Hortensius,* 48
Hosea, 12, 35
Hubal, 162
Hud, 172
*hudan,* 183
Hugh of St. Victor, 66–67
Husayn, 209
Huss, John, 130, 133
Hussites, 130
"Hymnal of the Second Temple," *see* Book of Psalms
hymn(s), of Luther, 91
hypostasis, 82

*'ibadat,* 184
'Id al-Adha, 196–197
'Id al-Fitr, 195
idolatry, of self-assertion, 11
  *See also gods*
Ignatius, 61
*Ihya' 'Ulum al-Din,* 204
*ijtihad,* doctrine of, 190–191, 210
ijma', 188
image worship, *see* idolatry
*imamah,* doctrine of, 603, 606
*imam,* 572, 587, 604–605
Imam Husayn, 198
*Imitation of Christ,* 135–136
Immaculate Conception, 83
Independents, *see* "Left-Protestantism"
India
  incorporation into British Empire, 215
  Muslims in, 169
Indian Mutiny, 215
Indian Wahhabism, 218
individualism
  and Calvinism, 141–142
  and obligations of Islamic law, 185
Indonesia
  Dutch control of, 215
  Muslims in, 169
indulgences, sale of, 89, 134, 140
infallibility, of pope, 135
Inge, Dean, 119
initiation rituals, of Dionysius mystery cults, 45
Innocent X, Pope, 91
Inquisition, 145
*Institutes of the Christian Religion,* 91, 92
institutionalization of Catholic Church, 62–63
intermarriage, Jewish laws on, 19
*Iqra',* 172
Iran, Shi'ah in, 212
Iraq, Shi'ah in, 212
Ireland, monasticism in, 66
Irenaeus, 50–51, 60, 113
Isaac, 96
Isaiah, 11, 35, 95
Isis and Osiris cult, 46
Islam
  description of, 160
  expansion of, 169–170
  and Jews, 22
  and Judaism, 100
  law of, *see* Islamic law
  modern-day, *see* Islamic modernism
  and Muslim modernists, 218–220
  and *Qur'an, see Qur'an*
  and reform movements, 216–217
  religious practices of, *see* Islamic worship

Islam (*continued*)
and rival religious systems, 179
and rule of Rightly Guided Khalifahs, 168–170
sects of, *see* Shi'ah; Sunni Muslims
theology of, *see* Islamic theology
and tribal loyalty, 164
and Waliyullah, 217–218
*See also* Muslims
Islamic law
and 'Abduh, 219
and analogical reasoning, 188–189
classification of actions in, 184
and criticism of *hadith,* 187
development of, 185–186
as divine law, 183–184
and *ijma'* of community, 188
and *ijtihad,* 190–191
modern-day practices in, 190
and modernists, 191
obligations under, 184–185
regional practices of, 190
schools of, 189–191
scope of, 184–185
and Six Sound Books, 187–188
and Sufism, 203–204
and *sunnah* of the Prophet, 186–187
and traditions, 186–188
Islamic modernism, 218–220
characteristics of, 220–221
and Christianity, 219–220
and rise of Western Europe, 214–216
Islamic mysticism, 199–201
Islamic Scripture, *see Qur'an*
Islamic theology, 177–182
Islamic worship
and birthday of Muhammad, 197
and *dhikr* ritual, 205
and Five Pillars of Islam, 192–197
and martyrdom of Imam Husayn, 197–198
Isma'ili school, 204, 211
*isnads* of the *hadith,* 187
Israel
and Babylonia, 14
election of, 100
God's selection of, 124–125
historic role of, 95–96
*See also* Israelites; Judaism
Israelites
and Assyrians, 12
and conflict between religious and secular interests, 7–8
exile of, 14–19
Halevi on, 106
and prophets, 9–14
as sons of God, 124–125
under leadership of Joshua, 7
during Restoration period, 20–25
and Yahweh, 3–7

Jabariyah, 178
Jalal al-Din al-Rumi, 205
Jamal al-Din al-Afghani, 218–219
James, 34, 42
James I, King, 115
Jamnia rabbis, 71–72
Jansen, Cornelius, 91
Jansenism, 91
Jason, 24
Jehoiachin, 14
Jeremiah, 13–14, 35
Jerome, 65, 66
Jerusalem
fall of, 72
Jesus arriving at, 37
*Jerusalem Talmud, see Talmud*
Jesus Christ
Apologists on, 58
ascension of, 40
body and blood of, *see* Eucharist
as Christ, *see* Christology
Christian interpretations of, 51–56
in Christianity and Judaism, 109
and eunuchs, 64
and Gnosticism, 59
and Holy Spirit, 63
humanity of, 80
last supper of, 112
as Logos, 54–55
as Messiah, 33, 52
miracles of, 36
of Nazareth, 29, 34–42, 79
passion and death of, 36–39
quoting from *Shema,* 33
in *Qur'an,* 172
relation to Zealots, 32
resurrection of, 38–39
and resurrection of, 38–39
and resurrection of dead, 31
and salvation, 86–94
as Savior, 79
sayings of, 53–54
second coming of, 56–57
and Teacher of Righteousness, 32
theological disputes about, 80–84
Jesuits, 144
Jewish Council, *see* Sanhedrin
Jewish festivals, decrees against, 24
Jewish law, 76–77
evolution of, 74–76
and Karo, 108
and Maimonides, 102
Jewish life, 75–76
foundation of, 108–110
and *halakah,* 76
and *yeshivah,* 120
Jewish nationalism, 149
Jewish rebellion, 71
Jewish ritual year, 121
Jewish Sabbath, *see* Sabbath, Jewish
Jewish Scriptures, psalter in, 116
Jewish War against the Romans, 30
Jews
conversion to Christianity of, 32–33
diaspora, *see* diaspora Jews
exiled in Babylonia, 18–19
as followers of Muhammad, 165
and foreign cultures, 22
hellenization of, 22–24
and Law of Yahweh, 21
and Maccabees, 24–25
and Muhammad, 166–167
relations with Christians, 137–138
as subjects of Roman Empire, 25
survival of, 14–19
Jezebel, 9
Joachim of Fiore, 130–131
Joachimite movement, 70
John XXII, Pope, 135
Johanan, Rabbi, 123
Johannine Gospel, 53, 81
John, 34, 80
John the Baptist, 33, 34
John of the Cross, Saint, 150
John of Damascus, Saint, 118, 179
Josephus, 29–30
Joshua, 7
Judah, *see* Israel; Israelites; Judaism
Judah ha-Levi, Rabbi, 75, 97
Judaism
and Bahya Ibn Pakuda, 106
and Christian ritual, 47
and Christianity, 29–33, 136–139
Christians as sect of, 56–57
and emergence of apocalyptic spirit, 25–28
and exile and redemption, 95–96
and Halevi, 105–106
Islamic period of, 100–102
and hellenistic culture, 22
after Jewish rebellion of A.D. 70, 71–77
and Kabbalah, 107–108
and Karo, 108–109
legal structure of, 76–77
and Maimonides, 102–105
and messianism, 97–98
in Middle Ages, 106–108
and monasticism, 63–64
and mysticism, 27–28, 118
and pietistic literature, 106
and rabbinical rule, 71–72
during Restoration period, 20–28
and rise of Islam, 100
and secularization, 147–149
separation of Christianity from, 40–41
survival of, 14–19
worship and prayer in, 120–124
*See also* Israel; Israelites
Judas the Galilean, 29, 30
Judas Iscariot, 138
Judas Maccabeus, 24, 25, 29
judge, in Islamic law, *see qadi*
judgment, and Rosh Hashanah, 123
Jupiter, 46
jurisprudence, *see* Islamic law; Jewish law; religious law
justification of man, 52, 91
Justin Martyr, 58

*kaba'ir,* 178
Ka'bah, 162, 167
circumambulation of, 196
Kabbalah, 107–108
*kalam,* science of, 180–181, 184–185, 199
*Kalam Allah,* 173
Karaites, 101
*karamat,* 205
Karbala', battle at, 209
Karo, Rabbi Joseph, 108–109
*kavannah,* 120
Kempis, Thomas à, 135–136
Kerygma, 39, 40
Khadijah, 160
*khalifah,* 169
Khanates, 215
*khanqah,* 206
Khawarij sect, 178, 208
*khutbah,* 193–194
kingship, in Israel, 8
*Kitab al-Muwatta',* 189
*koine,* 43

Kruspedai, Rabbi, 123
Kulayni, al-, 212
*Kuzari*, 97, 105
Kyrios, 52

Lactantius, 80
*laikos*, 61
laity, of Catholic Church, 61–62
language, of early gentile world, 43
Last Supper, 37, 39
Lat, al-, 162
Lateran Council, Fourth, 113
Law of Moses, 20, 25
laws, religious, *see* religious laws
"Left-Protestantism," 143, 145
legend
  of Muhammad's Night Journey from Makkah, 201
  of Rabbi Yohanan ben Zakkai, 71
  *See also* myths; tales
Leibnitz, 146
Lent, 115
Leon, Moses de, 107
"Letter to Arius to Eusibius of Nicodemia," 80
Levellers, 143
Levi, Rabbi, 122
Leviticus, 33, 47
liberation, in Judaism, 28
life after death, *see* afterlife
"Light Verse" of Surah, 200
liturgical calendar, 116
liturgical year, 115
liturgy, 65
Logos, 54–55
Lollards, 130
Lombard, Peter, 113
"Lord's Day," *see* Sabbath; Sunday
Lord's Prayer, 36, 116, 117
love, biblical idea of, 35
Loyola, Ignatius, 144
Luria, Rabbi Isaac, 98, 109
Lurianic mysticism, 98–100
Luther, Martin, 63, 79, 90–91, 134, 135, 136, 140, 144, 146
  on Eucharist, 113–114
  on salvation, 92
Lutheranism, 140–141, 143

*maaseh bereshit*, 27
*maaseh merkavah*, 27
Maccabee, the, *see* Judas Maccabeus
Macedonian Empire, 43
*madhhab*, 189
Madinah
  and Malik ibn Anas, 189
  Muhammad in, 165–167
Madinat al-Nabi, 165
*Maggid Mesharim*, 109
Magi, 115
Maimonides, Moses, 102
Makkah
  in Islamic prayers, 193
  Muhammad's capture of, 162, 167
  in Muhammad's time, 160–161
  pilgrimages to, 162, 196–197, *see also hajj*
Makkans
  description of, 160–161
  opposition to Muhammad, 164–165
  and war with Muslims, 167
*makruh*, 184
Malik ibn Anas, 182, 195
Maliki, 189
man, in Islamic theology, 183–184
Manat, al-, 162
*mandub*, 184
Manichaeans, 84, 85
*maqamat*, 203
Maratha, 215
Marcion, 59, 60
Mark, 34
marriage
  Islamic regulation of, 191
  of Luther, 140
  of Muhammad, 160
Marsiglio of Padua, 132
martyrdom
  of Imam Husayn, 209–210
  of Jews, 96
*Martyrium Polycarpi*, 61
Marwah, hill of, 196
Mary, 83, 115
  Assumption of, 116
  title of *theotokos* for, 83
Mass, 112–114, 115
  prayer giving glory to God in, 117
  and Reformation, 114
  and unity of Catholics and Protestants, 144
Mattathias, 24
Matthew, 36
Matthew's Gospel, 37
Maudgalyayana, *see* Mokuren
Mawlawiyah, 205–206
Mayence, Jews of, 96
meat, abstinence from, 63
Mecca, *see* Makkah
Medina, *see* Madinah
meditation, of Muhammad, 159
Melanchthon, 144
memorization of *Qur'an*, 173
Mendicant Orders, 129
Menelaus, 24
Meng-tzu, *see* Mencius
Mennonites, 143
*merkavah* mystics, 27–28, 107–108
Messiah(s), 26, 150
  false, 99
  Jesus as, 33, 52
messianic age, 97
messianism, 97–98
  and Christianity, 29, 136
  and Judaism, 136
  and Lurianic mysticism, 98–100
Methodists, 93
Michael, 26
*midrash*, 76
*mihrab*, 193
Middle Ages
  Catholic Church in, 83–84
  Christian theology in, 89–90
  Jewish-Christian relations during, 137–139
  Judaism in, 106–108
  monastic orders of, 129
  politics and Catholic Church during, 130
  protest movements in, 128
  status of Jews during, 96–97
militarism, of Israelis, 11, 13
Millenarians, 143
Millerites, 70
Mina, 196
miracles
  of Baal Shem Tov, 109
  of Jesus, 36
  of Yahweh, 9
  *See also karamat*
miraculous powers, *see karamat*
*Mishnah of Avot*, 72, 75, 76, 102, 109
Mishnah-angel, 109
missionaries, Jewish, 23
Mithra, mystery of, 46
Mithraism, 46
monasteries,
  first Christian, 64–65
  of Essenes, 30
  *See also* monastic orders, monasticism
monastic orders, of Middle Ages, 129
monasticism
  rise of, 63–68
  and Sufism, 206
  western, 65
Monophysite churches, 82
monotheism
  and Hanifs, 162
  and Muhammad, 160
Montanism, 63, 64, 70, 128, 135
Montanus, 63
month, sacred, 195
morality
  of Israelites, 5–6
  and monasticism, 64–65
  of mystery cults, 46–47
Morocco, French control of, 215
Moses, 9, 58
  and early Christians, 42
  and Jesus, 34
  in *Qur'an*, 172
  and Yahweh, 3–4
"Mother of the Book," *see Qur'an*
"Mother Church," 83
Mother of God, *see* Dei Genetrix; Mary
Mount Cassino, 65
Mount Hira', 172
*mu'adhdhin*, 194
*mu'amalat*, 184
Mu'awiyah, 169
*mubah*, 84
Mughals
  conquests of, 215–216
  decline of, 215–216
*muhaddithun*, 187–188
Muhammad
  and 'Ali, 209
  background of, 160–161
  birthday of, 197
  called to prophecy, 172–173
  capture of Makkah, 162
  and death of Abu Talib, 164
  departure from Makkah, 165
  early life of, 160
  and *hadith* collections, 187–188
  in Islamic prayers, 192
  and Islamic law, 183
  on Islamic sects, 208
  and Jews and Christians, 172
  and Jews of Madinah, 166–167
  in Madinah, 165–167
  Night Journey from Makkah, 201
  opposition to, 164–165
  and preparation of *Qur'an*, 175
  as prophet, 159

Muhammad (*Continued*)
and Quraysh tribesmen, 165
religious action of, see *sunnah* of the Prophet
as religious leader, 159
successors to, 168–169, 209
and Sufism, 200–201
and war with Makkans, 167
Muhammad 'Abduh, 218, 219–220
Muhammad 'Ali Pasha, 219
Muhammad ibn Isma'il, 211
Muharram, 197–198
Muharram festival, 210
Muhiy al-Din ibn al-'Arabi, 203
Mu'in al-Din Chishti, 205
Mujahidin, 218
*muqallad,* 191
Murji'ah sect, 179, 208
*murshid,* 206
Muslims
and adaptation of Hindu customs, 217
conquests of, 169–170
definition of, 160
and Khawarij uprisings, 178
and Muhammad's death, 168
numbers of, 169
and *Qur'an, see Qur'an*
religious practices of, *see* Islamic worship
and war with Makkans, 167
*See also* Sunni Muslims
Muslim Empire, 214–216
*See also* Muslims
Muslim modernists, 218–220
Mu'tazilah, 101, 179–181, 201, 213, 220
mystery cults
compared with Judaism and Christianity, 47
of Roman Empire, 45–46
*See also under individual names of*
mysticism
in Christianity, 118–119
and Hasidism, 109–110
and Islam, *see* Islamic mysticism
Jewish, *see* Kabbalah
Lurianic, *see* Lurianic mysticism
myth, of Proserpine, 45
*See also* tales

Nahman Krochmai, Rabbi, 105
Najd tribes, 161–162
nationalism
and Hussites, 130
*See also* Jewish nationalism
nativity stories, 34
nature, and mystery cults, 46
Navoth, tale of, 9
Nazzam, al-, 179
Nehemiah, 20, 29
Neoplatonism
and Christian mysticism, 118–119
and Christianity, 126
and Judaism, 105–106
Nero, 56
New Platonic Academy, 84
New Testament, 30, 61–62
Acts of the Apostles, The, 36, 39–42
canon of, 60
and Christian tradition, 68
Gnosticism in, 50
and Jesus of Nazareth, 34–42
on Jesus' resurrection, 39
and mysticism, 119
on Pharisees, 31
New York State, Millerites of, 70
Newton, Isaac, 146
Niceano-Constantinopolitan Creed, *see* Nicene Creed
Nicene Creed, 81–83
Nicene party, 81
Niebuhr, Reinhold, 119
Noahide commandments, 138
Nominalism, 135
Norbert, Saint, 129
Northern Kingdom of Hebrew Tribes, 12
Nusayris, 211

oasis of Yathrib, 165
obligations of Islam, *see* Five Pillars of Islam; *'ibadat; mu'amalat*
observances, *see* prayers
occult, *see* mysticism
Ockham, 135
*Octoechos,* 116
"On Grace and Free Will," 90
oppression, *see* persecution
Oral Law of Judaism, 74, 102
Oratory of Divine Love, 144
orders, *see* monasteries; *and individual names of*
ordination
of priests, 140
*See also* ordination rites
ordination rites, 62
Original Sin, 83, 87, 89–90, 93
Orphic mysteries, 45–46
Orphism, 46, 47
orthodoxy, in Catholic Church, 62
Ottoman Turks, 170
in Vienna, 214
and Wahhabis, 216–217
*ousia,* 82

Pachomius, 64–65
*Paedagogus,* 83
Pakistan, as Muslim state, 221
Palestine, during Restoration period, 20–25
*See also* Israel; Israelites
pantheism, and Sufism, 203
papacy, 68, 134, 144
Paris debate of 1240, 137
Parousia, 56–57, 63, 70
passion motif, 209, 210
Passover, 122
Jesus at, 36–37, 112
Pastoral Epistles, 50
*Pastoral Rule,* 89
Patristic age, protest movements of, 128
Paul, 32, 38–39, 41–42, 52–53, 56, 60, 84, 85, 91, 138
Paul II, Pope, 144
Paul IV, Pope, 144
Pauline Epistles, 57, 119
Pauline tradition, 81, 87
*pax romana,* 44
Peasant Revolt of 1381, 30
Peasant revolts of 1524–1526, 140
Pelagius, 86–87, 88
penance, for Muslims, 195
Pentecost event, 40
*Pentacostarion,* 116
"people of unity and justice," *see* Mu'tazilah
period of grace, 130
persecution
of Christians, 56, 79–80
of Jews, 24, 137
in Middle Ages, 96–97
of Muhammad, 164–165
Persian Empire
fall of, 22
Persian rulers, and Jewish exiles, 19–20
Pesach, *see* Passover
*Pesikta Derekh Kahanna,* 96
*Pesikta Derrabh Kahannah, Bahodesh,* 125
*Pesikta Rabbati,* 125
Peter, 33, 34, 36, 39, 40, 42, 56, 60, 132
Peter, Bishop of Alexandria, 81
Pflug, 144
Pharisaic Judaism, *see* Pharisees
Pharisees, 29–31, 71–72
Philo, 22, 58
philosophy
Jewish, 100–101
as religion, 49–50
rise of, 48–50
Phrygia, 63
pietistic literature, 106
pilgrimages
to Makkah, 196–197
of pre-Islamic Arabs, 162
spiritual, 203
"pious ones," *see* Hasidim
*pir,* 206
Pistorius, 144
Pius IX, Pope, 83
Pius XII, Pope, 83
Plato, 22, 43, 46, 48, 58, 88, 100
Platonism, 48
and Christian theology, 86, 90
Pluto, 45
pogroms, 137
Pole, Cardinal, 144
politics
and Christianity, 80
and early Islam, 177–178
and Israelites, 7–9
and Jews, 96–97
and Muslim rulers, 177–178
and Reformation, 139–140, 142
of Zealots, 30–31
Polycarp, 61
Pompey, 25
Pontius Pilate, 82
pope(s)
infallibility of, 135
and persecution of Jews, 139
rival, 132
*See also under individual names of*
pork, in Islamic law, 184
poverty, and Franciscans, 129
power, *see dynamis*
*Praeveniret,* 89
prayer(s)
in Christianity, 111–119
in early Christian Church, 59
distinction between vocal and mental, 118
Islamic, 192–195

prayers (*Continued*)
  Jesus on, 35–36
  Judaic, 18, 76, 120–125
  to martyrs, 83–84
  to saints, 117
  special days of, 115–116
  of Sufi, 201
  for universal deliverance, 97
  *See also under individual names of*
prayer leader, *see imam; mu'adhdhin*
preaching, *see* Kerygma
predestination, 89, 90, 91–93
  Augustine on, 88
  in Islamic theology, 177, 178, 180, 181
  Wycliffe on, 130
Premonstratentions, 67, 129
Presbyterianism
  credo of, 93
  and Westminster Confession, 114
pride, sin of, 11
processions, of Shi'ah, 209–210
Prophecy, Islamic doctrine of, 171–172
Prophet, the, *see* Muhammad
prophets
  Amos, 10
  Deutero-Isaiah, 16–18, 22–23
  Elijah, 9–10
  emergence in Israel of, 9–14
  Ezekiel, 15
  Hosea, 12
  Isaiah, 11
  Jeremiah, 13–14
  Muhammad, *see* Muhammad
  in *Qur'an,* 171–172
proselytism, of Christians by Jews, 138
Proserpine, 45
protest
  in Christian tradition, 69
  as religious behavior, 128–131
Protestantism
  attempts at unity with Catholics, 144–145
  and definition of role of Church, 142–143
  and Eucharistic worship, 115
  and Mary, 83
  and mysticism, 118–119
  response to secularization, 150
  and this-worldly problems, 151
psalms, 116
  *See also* Zabur
pseudoepigraphical works, 27
Ptolemies, 22
punishments
  of Israelites, 10–14, 95
  *See also* Exile
purgatory, 89
purification, and Islamic worship, 193
Puritan Commonwealth, 115
Puritan Revolution, 142, 143
Puritans, and Sabbath, 115
Pythagoras, 47
Pythagoreans, 46

Qadariyah order, 178, 204
*qadi,* 185
*qiblah,* 193
*qiyas,* 188–189
Quakers, 93, 143
Quirinius, 30
Qumran group, 30, 32
*Qur'an,* 165
  divine origin and character of, 173
  and Islamic theology, 177
  on opposition to Muhammad, 166
  origin of, 171
  and political controversies, 178
  recitation of, 192–193, 195
  structure of, 173–176
  and Sufism, 200–201
  theme of charity in, 195–196
Quraysh, 161, 164
Qusayy, 161
*Qutb,* 205, 210–211

rabbinic school of Karo, 109
rabbis
  emergence of, 72, 74
  Jamnia academy of, 71–72
Rabi'ah al-'Adawiyah, 201
*rahbar,* 206
Ramaden, 195
Rashi, 108
Rashid Rida, 219
Real Presence, doctrine of, 113, 114
Reality, *See haqa'iq*
recitation, of *Qur'an,* 192–193, 195
recite, *see* Iqra'
redemption
  in Christian belief, 136
  in Judaic belief, 95–96, 136
  and Lurianic mysticism, 98–99
  Yahweh's plan for, 16–17
reform
  of Catholic Church, 128–131
  and "cluniac reformation," 65
  and Council of Constance, 132–133
  and Council of Trent, 145
  of Islam, 216–217
  of Judaism, 149
  in sixteenth century, 133–136
  *See also* Reformation
Reformation, 139–143
  and Christian theology, 90–91
  and Eucharist, 113–114
  and failure of Council of Constance, 133
  and Mass as sacrifice, 114
  and mysteries, 116
  and Original Sin doctrine, 87
  origins in Middle Ages, 133–136
  and Sabbath, 115
  and sacraments, 85
Reformed Church at Dort, 93
religion
  definition of, 127
  of Najd tribes, 162
  symbols used by, *see* symbols
  *See also individual names of*
religious festivals, *see* festivals
religious law
  of Christian Church, 133
  and contact between Jews and Christians, 139
  of Israel, 5
  and mixed marriage, 19
  and Mawlawi *dhikr,* 206
  against proselytism of Christians by Jews, 138
  and Sabbath, 115
  *See also* Islamic law; Jewish law; *halakah*
religious reform, *see* reform
religious symbols, *see* symbols
religious wars, 140
Renaissance, 133–134
renunciation, and monasticism, 64
repetition, *see* recitation
repression, *see* persecution
Restoration period, Israeli exiles during, 20–25
resurrection
  of dead, 30, 31
  of Jesus, 38–39
revelation(s)
  and Judaism, 100
  Maimonides on, 103
  Saadia on, 101–102
  of *Qur'an* to Muhammad, 162–164, 171
*Revivification of the Religious Sciences, see Ihya' 'Ulum al-Din*
Rightly Guided Khalifahs, 168–170
*Risalat al-Tawhid,* 220
rites
  Christian, 47
  of passage, *see* initiation rituals
  *See also* rituals
ritual(s)
  of Eucharist, 112–114
  and Judaism, 10
  of last supper, 112
  of mystery cults, 45–46
  during pilgrimages to Makkah, 196–197
  prayer, *see salat*
Riyadh, 217
Robert, Saint, 129
Roman Catholic Church
  and Council of Trent, 145
  Mass in, 115
  and secularization, 150
  *See also* Catholic Church; Christian Church
Roman Empire
  Christianity in, 43–44, 79–80
  in early Christian period, 43–44
  Jewish missionaries in, 23
  Jews as subjects of, 25
Roman law
  and Christianity, 41, 56, 66
  and Stoicism, 48
Rome
  Alaric's invasion of, 93
  fall of, 131
Rosary, 116
Rosh Hashanah, 123–124
rules
  on handling *Qur'an,* 173
  of monasticism, 66
  *See also* religious laws
Russian Revolution, Islamic Central Asia and, 215

Saadia Gaon, Rabbi, 100–102
"sabbatarianism," 115
Sabbath, 18, 24, 77, 120, 122, 124
Sabellius, 80, 81
sacraments
  Augustine on, 85
  challenges to, 134–135

sacrifices
in Islamic tradition, 196–197
and Judaism, 10
Mass as, 114
self, *see* self-slaughter
*See also* animal sacrifice
Sadducees, 30
Safa, hill of, 196
Safawi dynasty, 206, 212, 214–215
Safed mystics, 109
*sagha'ir,* 178
saints, doctrine of the, 204–205
saints
Sufi, 205
*See also under individual names of; silsilah*
*salat,* 192, 194, 195
Salih, 172
Salijuq rulers, 204
Salijuq Turks, 170
salvation
Augustine on, 86
in Christian theology, 58, 90
of Israelis, 16–18
Luther on, 90–91
Paul on, 52
Samuel, 8
Sanhedrin, 125
Jesus before, 37
Sanusiyah order, 206
Sassanian Empire, fall of, 169
Saul, 8
*sawm,* 192
Sayyid Ahmad Khan, 220
Sayyid Amir Ali', 220
scholars, in Jewish life, 108
schools of jurisprudence, *see madhhab*
scientific revolution, Christianity and, 146–147
Scotus, Johan, 92
scriptures
and Christian tradition, 68
and Judaism, 77
Seceders, *see* Khawarij
seclusion of Muhammad, 159
second coming, *see* Parousia
sectarianism, *see* sects
sects
Christian, 61
Islamic, 178, 179, see also Shi'ah; Sunni Muslims
early Jewish, 29–31
Protestant, 143
of Shi'ah, 211
secularization
Christian response to, 150
and Christianity, 145–147
and Judaism, 147–149
Seder, 37
segregation, of Jew from non-Jew, 76, 148
Seleucids, 22, 24–25, 43
self-slaughter, of Jews, 96
"semi-Pelagian" positions, 88–89
Seneca, 50
Septuagint, 43
sermon, *see khutbah*
servant of God, 95
servant of Yahweh, 117
Seveners, 211
sexual intercourse, and transmission of Original Sin, 87
sexuality, and mystery cult rites, 46
Shafi'i, al-, 185–186, 188, 189
*shahadah,* 192
*shari'ah, see* Islamic law
Shavuot, 122–123
*shaykh,* 206
*shekhinah,* 125
*Shepherd of Hermas,* 83
Sheshbazzar, 20
Shi'ah
and 'Ali, 209
compared with Sunni Muslims, 212–213
and *imam,* 210–211
origins of, 208–209
religious elements peculiar to, 209–210
and Seveners and Twelvers, 211
*Shulhan Aruch,* 108
Sibylline Oracles, 27
*sicarii, see* Zealots
"Sick Man of Europe," 215
*suddur,* 120, 121
*sifat,* 181
Sikhs, 215
and Muslims, 218
*silsilah,* 204
Simon bar Yohai, Rabbi, 107
Simon the Just, 108
simony, 129
sin(s)
and exile of Jews, 15
in Islamic theology, 178–179
of Israel, 10–14
*See also* Original Sin
Sinai, revelation at, 6
Six Sound Books, 187–188
Smith, Joseph, 70
social functions
of Sufi *khanqahs,* 206
social order
of Quraysh tribesmen, 161
social problems
and Biblical religions, 150–152
and covenant with Israel, 8
Socrates, 47–48, 58
Sodom and Gomorrah, 11
Solomon bar Isaac, Rabbi, *see* Rashi
Song of Deborah, 37
Spain
Jews in, 98, 138
Ummawi state in, 169
Spirit of Islam, The, 220
"Spirituals," excommunication of, 129
"stabbers," *see* Zealots
state-church conflict, *see* church-state conflict
Stephen, 41, 42
Stoicism, 48
and Christianity, 126
and Paul, 52
Stoics, 48, 49
stone-throwing rituals, 196
students of *hadith, see muhaddithun*
"subsistencies," *see* hypostasis
suffering, and Judaism, 95–96
Sufism, 199–201
and Abd al-Wahhab, 216
and asceticism, 201
definitions of, 200
future of, 206–207
goals of, 203
interpretative differences in, 203–204
opposition to, 204
origins of, 200–201
reconciliation between traditional Islam, 204
and Sufi brotherhoods, 204
and wandering mendicants, 206
Sufficient One, The, *see* al-Kafi
Sufi brotherhoods, 204–205, 206
Sukkot, 123
*Summa Theologica,* 90, 92
Sunday of Advent, 115
*sunnah* of the Prophet, Islamic law and, 186–187
Sunni Muslims, 182, 185
compared with Shi'ah, 212–213
description of, 208
and Islamic law, 189–190
supernatural events
and Jews, 25
*See also* miracles
Surah of the Believers, 174
Surahs, of *Qur'an,* 174–175
Su'ud family of Arabia, 216
Su'udi dynasty, 216–217
Sykes-Picot Agreement, 215
symbol(s)
of Catholic Church, 83
of Israelites, 6
of kabbalists, 108
synagogue, 30
and diaspora Jews, 42–43
early Christian Fathers on, 138
function of, 119
in Jewish life, 18
Synoptic Gospels, 36, 39, 53, 57

*Taanit,* 120
Tabari, al-, 189
taboos, on saying name of God, 52
Taftazani, al-, 179, 181
tales, of Navoth and his vineyard, 9
Talmud, 101
and Jewish-Christian relations, 137
*taqlid,* doctrine of, 191, 219
*tariqah,* 204
*tasawwuf, see* Sufism
Tatian, 58
*tawhid,* 203–204
Teacher of Righteousness, 32
*Teaching of the Twelve Apostles,* 59
*tekke,* 206
Temple of Jerusalem, 24–25
destruction of, 120
temptation narrative, 35
Ten Commandments, 4–7, 119, 123
disobedience to, 7–8
and Jesus, 33
and Lurianic mystics, 99
Teresa of Avila, Saint, 150
terrorism, of Assassins, 211
Tertullian, 58–59, 63, 80, 87
Testaments of the Twelve Patriarchs, 27
Theatines, 144
Theodoret of Cyprus, 80
theotokos, 83
*Thirty-Nine Articles,* 84
this-worldly existence, 150–152
*tigh,* books of, *see* Islamic law
Todi, Jacopone da, 118

tomb(s)
  of Sufi saints, 205
Torah, 20–21, 74, 77, 100, 102, 125, 172
  in Jewish life, 18
  kabbalists on, 108
  and rabbinical rule, 74
  rejection of, 148
  translated into Greek, 22
transfiguration, story of, 34–35
transubstantiation, doctrine of, 113–114, 130
Trinity, theological disputes over, 79–84
*triodion*, 116
*True Doctrine of the Sabbath*, 115
*Tur Orah Hayim*, 120
Twelver Shi'ah, 211–212

'Umar ibn al-Khattab, 168, 175
Ummawis, 169
  controversies surrounding, 177–178
unification with God, *see tawhid*
United Presbyterian Church, 142
unity
  and Christianity, 144–145
  of early Jewish sects, 32
  of Hebrew and Roman Christians, 42
  of Islamic sects, 213
  Jewish, 149
universal cosmic principle, *see halakah*
universal judgment, 97
urban life, in Roman Empire, 44
'Uthman ibn Affan, 168
Uthmanic *Qur'an*, 175
'Uzza, al-, 162

Valerian, Emperor, 79
Victoria, Queen, 215
Vienna, 214
Vilna, as center of talmudic learning, 109
Vilna Gaon, *see* Gaon, Elijah
Vincent of Lerins, 88
violence
  of pre-Islamic Arab society, 164
  of Zealots, 31
virgin birth, 83
Virgin Mary, *see* Mary
Vision of God on the Last Day, Islamic, 181

Wahhabism, 190, 216–217
*wali*, 205
Waliyullah, Shah, 216–218
wanderers, *see darwishes*
war
  between Muslims and Makkans, 167
  and pre-Islamic Arabs, 163
Wasil ibn 'Ata, 179
Western culture, and Christianity, 126–127
Westminster Confession of Faith, 93, 114, 143
Whirling Dervishes, *see* Mawlawiyah
wine, Qur'anic prohibition of, 189
witnessing, *see shahadah*
women, convents for, 64–65
"Word," the, *see* Logos
Word of God, and exiled Israelis, 18–19
world history, periods of, 130–131
world view
  of Islam, 182
  pre-Islamic, 162–163
worship
  in Christianity, 111–119
  definition of, 111
  Judaic, 120–125
  *See also* prayer
Written Law, the, 72
Wycliffe, John, 130

Yahweh, 32
  and Exodus, 122
  as Greek high god, 24
  and prophets, 9
  relationship with Israel, 3ff
*Yebamoth*, 120
Yohanan ben Zakkai, Rabbi, 71
Yom Kippur, 123–124

*Zabur*, 172
*zakat*, 192, 196
*zawiyah*, 206
Zayd ibn Thabit, 175
Zaydi sect of Yemen, 211
Zealots, 30–32
Zechariah, 37
Zerubbabel, 20
Zeus, 25
Zevi, Sabbetai, 99
*Zohar*, 107
Zoroastrians, and Islam, 179
Zosimus, Pope, 87
*zuhada'*, 201
Zurich, 141
Zwingli, Ulrich, 114, 141
Zwinglian Reformation, 141

Printer and Binder: The Murray Printing Company

78 10 9 8 7 6